HOME ECONOMICS: NATIONALISM AND THE MAKING OF 'MIGRANT WORKERS' IN CANADA

D1528668

A massive shift has taken place in Canadian immigration since the 1970s: the majority of migrants no longer enter as permanent residents but as temporary migrant workers. In *Home Economics*, Nandita Sharma shows how Canadian policies on citizenship and immigration contribute to the entrenchment of a system of apartheid where those categorized as 'migrant workers' live, work, pay taxes, and sometimes die in Canada, but are subjected to a legal regime that renders them perennial outsiders in relation to Canadian society.

Sharma argues that it is the acceptance of nationalist formulations of 'home' – informed by racialized and gendered social relations – that contribute to the neoliberal restructuring of the labour market in Canada. She exposes the ideological character of Canadian border control practices that work not to prevent people from getting in but rather to restrict their rights within Canada. *Home Economics* is an urgent and much-needed reminder that in today's world of growing displacement and unprecedented levels of international migration, society must pay careful attention to how nationalist ideologies construct 'homelands' that essentially leave the vast majority of the world's migrant peoples homeless.

NANDITA SHARMA is an assistant professor in the School of Social Sciences at Atkinson College, York University.

NANDITA SHARMA

Home Economics

Nationalism and the Making of 'Migrant Workers' in Canada

UNIVERSITY OF TORONTO PRESS
Toronto Buffalo London

ISBN 13: 978-8020-3840-1 (cloth)
ISBN 10: 8020-3840-9 (cloth)

ISBN 13: 978-0-8020-4883-7 (paper)
ISBN 10: 0-8020-4883-8 (paper)

Printed on acid-free paper

Library and Archives Canada Cataloguing in Publication

Sharma, Nandita Rani, 1964–
    Home economics : nationalism and the making of 'migrant
workers' in Canada / Nandita Sharma.

    ISBN 0-8020-3840-9 (bound)
    ISBN 0-8020-4883-8 (pbk.)

    1. Alien labor – Canada – Social conditions.   2. Canada –
Emigration and immigration – Government policy.   I. Title.

HD8108.5.A2S528 2005   331.6′2′0971   C2005-904971-5

This book has been published with the help of a grant from the Canadian
Federation for the Humanities and Social Sciences, through the Aid to
Scholarly Publications Programme, using funds provided by the Social
Sciences and Humanities Research Council of Canada.

University of Toronto Press acknowledges the financial assistance to its
publishing program of the Canada Council and the Ontario Arts Council.

University of Toronto Press acknowledges the financial support for its
publishing activities of the Government of Canada through the Book
Publishing Industry Development Program (BPIDP).

For Gaye Chan

Contents

Tables and Figures

Figure

Acknowledgments

This study would not have been possible to carry out without the assistance of a very large group of people. This project began as a PhD dissertation and, as such, I would like to thank the members of my supervisory committee, Roxana Ng, Kari Dehli, Sedef Arat-Koc, Kirin Mirchandani, and Robert Miles, for the tremendous help they provided me. I would also like to acknowledge Dorothy E. Smith, whose body of work is a major influence on my own. Courses taken with her during my time at the Ontario Institute for Studies in Education helped me to rethink the importance of asking *how* the world is actually organized. A doctoral fellowship and a post-doctoral fellowship granted by the Social Sciences and Humanities Research Council of Canada were crucial supports for this project and I would like to thank them as well.

I also am indebted to Allison Campbell, John Henry Moss, Fiona Jeffries, Cynthia Wright, Adele Perry, José Palafox, Becki Ross, Deborah Brock, Gary Kinsman, and Bridget Anderson who provided me with a transnational activist space in which to develop my thoughts and reformulate strategies for what needs to be *done* to make home much more than a memory for all people displaced by the practices of ruling groups.

I also want to thank my family who have made me want to 'write back' to Empire: Gaye Chan, Santosh Sharma, Kesho Sharma, Paul Sharma, Jean Chan, and Eric Chan, whose diverse experiences with cross-border migration have made it apparent just how important it is to demand a home in a hostile world.

Last but certainly not least, the editorial team at the University of Toronto Press with whom I had the pleasure to work, Virgil Duff,

xii   Acknowledgments

Anne Laughlin and Ani Deyirmenjian, have my deepest gratitude for their ongoing support during all stages of this project. I would also like to thank Kate Baltais and Mary Newberry for respectively doing a wonderful job with the copy edits and with the preparation of the index.

Foreword

While studies of immigration and immigrants have enjoyed a long and rich history in the Canadian scholarly landscape, the same is not true for inquiries into migrant and undocumented workers. Nandita Sharma began investigating the emergence and proliferation of the use of migrant workers in the early 1990s, when she was a Master's student at Simon Fraser University. As such, she is one of the pathbreakers in this emergent scholarship, which has gained national and international attention with the intensification of globalization.

This book, based on her doctoral research, continues the inquiry she began over ten years ago. It traces the development of the increased use of migrant workers in Canada by analysing parliamentary debates between 1969 and 1973, which led to the development of the Non-Immigrant Employment Authorization Program (NIEAP) – this is the same period in which Canada ostensibly shifted from an Anglo-conformity model of immigrant settlement to a policy of multiculturalism. Sharma's analysis, based on the theoretical formulation of ideology as practice, developed by eminent sociologist Dorothy Smith, and utilizing Smith's method of textual analysis, does not only reveal the hypocrisy of Canadian state policies. More profoundly, it pinpoints the modus operandi of liberal democracy vis-à-vis the advancement of corporate capitalism as it moved into the current era of globalization.

This period is characterized by a central paradox: while nation-states and international bodies such as the World Trade Organization are pushing for the elimination of national borders to facilitate the movement of capital, the same entities are restricting the movement of workers across the same borders through subtle and overt instruments of governance. NIEAP embodies this paradox: its institution both enables employers' ability to recruit workers from around the world without regard to their citizenship and restricts workers' free movement within Canada through a work permit system that ties them to specific employers and hence locality. Furthermore, because NIEAP is not a program for recruiting immigrants, the number of workers recruited does not enter immigration statistics, thereby concealing its double-edged character. When the statistics are deconstructed, we see that the majority of workers so recruited through NIEAP are predominantly from the economic South. This pattern reproduces existing racial inequality, not only within Canada, but worldwide. Sharma argues that it is precisely through programs such as NIEAP that white hegemony is produced and maintained through a global capitalist system. These programs and systems cannot be put in place and made actionable without the active participation of nation-states.

Underpinning such systems of governance is the construction of a set of thinking – an ideology – which delineates citizens from foreigners: those who belong and those who don't. The examination of parliamentary debates analysed by Sharma indicates the discursive shift during the period from 1969 to 1973 with regard to who was and was not a member of the Canadian national community. She argues that current processes of globalization began during this period. Globalization was accomplished, 'not only through a restructuring of the global political economy but also through the legitimization of a different rationality of national state power – one that worked to restructure the criteria of national member' (p. 75).

Historical and contemporary reality indicate that, in spite of measures put in place for border control, the movement of people around the globe, legally or otherwise, has always taken place. Indeed, it has intensified in recent decades due to the militarization and economic devastation of parts of the world, partly as a result of economic globalization accompanied by wars and military conquests. Thus, it is reasonable to assume that the notion of citizenship based on nationality, of who belongs where and who does not, is merely a myth – an ideology, as indicated by Sharma. However, we should not underestimate the power of such an ideology. We see that after 11 September 2001, the U.S. administration, followed too willingly by the Canadian government, has tightened its physical borders through various kinds of measures such as customs and immigration regulations. Meanwhile, it has also extended its borders through invasion and investments in other parts of the world in the name of antiterrorism. The coercive power of the state, in this case exemplified by the United States, is obvious. What is less obvious is the way in which this ideology has seeped into current academic thinking around issues of citizenship. Instead of breaking new conceptual grounds, current debates around nationalism and citizenship reify, rather than challenge, the idea of citizenship on the basis of nationality. In this way, the notion of the existence and preservation of nation-states – a central feature of capitalist social formations – remains intact.

In the last chapter of her book, Sharma poses a controversial and provocative challenge to current academic debates on citizenship and nation-states: what if we abolish the social construction of difference on the basis of nationality? What would a world look like if we imagine it without national borders? How may we rearrange social relations in order to create this world?

By posing these questions, Sharma does more than provide us with a solid and convincing analysis of ideology and how modern nation-states operate through analysing the historical texts of parliamentary debates. This is undoubtedly her substantive contribution to scholarship. More importantly, she inspires us to think beyond existing conceptual boundaries to create a world free of racism embodied in ideological formulations of nationalism. Nandita Sharma urges all progressive scholars to bring their theory in line with their practice to develop a transformative praxis for a free and just society.

Roxana Ng
University of Toronto
September 2005

HOME ECONOMICS

1 Home(lessness) and the Naturalization of 'Difference'

The overweening, defining event of the modern world is the mass movement of raced populations, beginning with the largest forced transfer of people in the history of the world: slavery. The consequences of which transfer have determined all the wars following it as well as the current ones being waged on every continent. The contemporary world's work has become policing, halting, forming policy regarding and trying to administer the movement of people. Nationhood – the very definition of citizenship – is constantly being demarcated and redemarcated in response to exiles, refugees, Gastarbeiter, immigrants, migrations, the displaced, the fleeing, and the besieged. The anxiety of belonging is entombed within the central metaphors in the discourse on globalism, transnationalism, nationalism, the break-up of federations, the rescheduling of alliances, and the fictions of sovereignty. Yet these figurations of nationhood and identity are frequently as raced themselves as the originating racial house that defined them. When they are not raced, they are ... imaginary landscape, never inscape; Utopia, never home.

Toni Morrison, Home

The process of making and maintaining national borders is integral to the material, existential, and ideological practices that organize the contemporary exercise of power. National borders are a set of institutional relationships based on the law, the market, and extant social relations within and across particular spaces. While most people experience national borders as fixed, in reality they constantly shift and move in accordance with changing social relations. Ever since the emergence of the global system of national states only a few hundred years ago, new national states have been carved out of previously existing ones as a prelude to or an outcome of confrontations between the more and the less powerful. Thus, there are constant reorganizations of the 'national community' at ever smaller and higher levels of geographical scale.[1]

Within the global system of national states, borders do not affect everyone similarly. For a small, select group they are mere formalities. Business people, government officials, certain states' armed forces, tourists, and the personnel of legitimated international governmental and non-governmental organizations, for instance, traverse them practically at will and with very little thought. On the other hand, borders never leave others alone. In particular, for people assigned a 'migrant worker' or 'illegal' status in the countries in which they live, work, and sometimes die, borders follow them to school, to work; indeed they encounter borders in every aspect of their lives. Moreover, when James Clifford (1998:367) notes that 'at least since 1492, the outside world is guaranteed to find you,' he draws our attention to the fact that in the global economy the simultaneous existence of national borders and borderless worlds confronts even those who stay put.

National borders and their relationship to ideas of *home*, and in particular, how borders make many people *homeless* in the very places where their lives are lived is the topic of this book. By examining the social organization of one Canadian state category of entry, residency, and work, that of migrant workers, I discuss how it is the very construction of an always-limited sense of homeyness in the Canadian 'nation,' what Benedict Anderson (1991) calls 'nation-ness,' that makes migrant workers non-members of Canadianized society. A type of *home economics* is at play in this process of hierarchically organizing various groups of people through differential state categories of belonging. There is a materiality to the 'differences' between 'citizens,' 'immigrants' (i.e., permanent residents), and migrant workers; this materiality is based in the relationship between ideas of *nation* and those of *race*, *gender*, and *class*.

In this introductory chapter I discuss how the idea of home has been both occupied by nationalist practices and colonized by nationalized imaginations. Within such conceptualizations of home, those with national subject identities come to participate in what Dorothy E. Smith (1990) calls 'relations of ruling.' By making themselves at home in the nation, the national state relies on the complicity of those with national subjectivities to make common sense of the highly differential treatment accorded those classified as the nation's Others, particularly those placed in legal state categories, like migrant worker, that organize their foreign-ness within Canadian space.

In the following chapter, 'Globalization and the Story of National Sovereignty,' the making of migrant workers is situated within the neoliberal turn in Canadian public policy in the late 1960s and early 1970s. The knowledge that we have of this period, however, is not unproblematic, and I examine the dominant discourses of this latest period of capitalist globalization among progressive and even left intellectuals in Canada to understand how their conceptualizations are informed by – and significantly entrench – nationalized forms of consciousness and practices. I show that the characterization of this latest period of capitalist globalization, as one when national state sovereignty was lost, works to centre the *foreignness* of certain capital investments and certain workers as the key problem of neoliberalism.

Within this framework, not only is the relationship between national states and capitalists obfuscated but the fortification of national state boundaries come to be seen as necessary for the protection of 'society.' Such thinking has particularly profound effects in relation to the organization of national labour markets. Acceptance that the national state *ought* to be sovereign legitimates practices that differentiate between citizens and those categorized as 'foreigners' not only across national borders but also within the labour market in Canada. The result is the subordination of all those who can be rendered 'foreign' and an intensification of competition between workers, both globally and within nationalized spaces.

In chapter 3, 'Imagined States: The Ideology of "National Society,"' I extend this discussion to more deeply analyse how liberal styles of governance shape our consciousness about the nature of human society itself. Within liberal democratic forms of ruling, society is made coterminous with the national state through ideas of the existence of the Public or civil society. I examine how ideas of *freedom*, and their manifestation in the identities and material realities of free or unfree workers, rely on national state practices for determining the scope of belonging to this Public.

By problematizing ideas of civil society, through which national subjects come to believe that the state rules *for* them against Others, I show how freedom, and its corollary of unfreedom, have been made 'unpolitical.' Its depoliticization has led to an increase and entrenchment of migrant workers within unfree employment relations in Canada over the last thirty-odd years. The expansion of unfreedom, thus, calls into question classical theories of capitalist political economy that fail to account for the significance of unfree employment relationships within capitalist social relations. By centring the analysis of capitalism on the experiences of free workers, the lived experiences of those rendered unfree through practices of nationalism, racism, and sexism are made invisible, and this leads to fatal flaws in our analysis of how capitalist social relations are actually accomplished.

In chapter 4, 'Canadian Parliamentary Discourse and the Making of "Migrant Workers,"' five years of parliamentary debates on immigration, international trade, and finance within the House of Commons are analysed. A textual analysis of the discursive practices of Ottawa's parliamentarians and their construction of 'national problems' and their 'solutions' makes evident how intertwining ideas of nation, race, and freedom are brought together to organize state practices in ways that facilitate the restructuring of global capitalist social relations and the labour market in Canada. In making migrant workers, the Canadian state made fully realizable the category of 'foreign worker.'

In chapter 5, 'Canada's Non-Immigrant Employment Authorization Program (NIEAP): The Social Organization of Unfreedom for "Migrant Workers,"' I provide a detailed account of how the NIEAP relies on the legal differences organized between citizens, immigrants (i.e., permanent residents), and non-immigrants (or migrant workers) to ensure employers access to a 'just-in-time,' unfree, migrant workforce that conforms to employers' demands for more flexible, cheaper, and more vulnerable workers. By comparing the numbers of people admitted to Canada over the years as either permanent residents or migrant workers, I document an alarming shift in the (im)migration status of those entering Canada to work – a shift that results in the denial of permanent resident status to the vast majority of (im)migrants and their relegation to the ranks of a temporary, unfree labour force. By legalizing the highly subordinated status of migrant workers, the NIEAP is shown to be a vehicle through which the social category of foreigner is *realized*.

In concluding my study of the making of migrant workers for the Canadian labour market, with chapter 6, 'Rejecting Global Apartheid: An Essay on the Refusal of "Difference,"' I challenge the nationalization of space and identity that legitimates the subordinated status of those made into non-members of Canadian national society. As becomes clear with an examination of the NIEAP and its 'differential inclusion' of 'foreign workers' as unfree temporary labour within Canadianized space, I show that the discursive practices of border control are thoroughly ideological. Ever-increasing restrictions on international migration work not to restrict the entry of migrants into Canada but to restrict their mobility, rights, and entitlements within this nationalized space.

Contemporary border control practices, therefore, are products of and produce a global regime of apartheid in which at least two different legal systems operate within the space of any given national state – one that regulates national subjects and another that regulates foreign objects. In this, the imposition of identities, be they state categorical identities or identities imposed by ideas of race, nation, and gender, is crucial. In calling for an end to nationalized imaginations and the practices organized – and made common sense of – through them, I distinguish between social practices of difference-making and those based on diversity – the simultaneous respect for individual singularities and shared commonalities based on practice rather than identity. I end by adding my voice to the growing social movement for a world without borders, a world where people have the ability both to 'stay' and to 'move' according to their own self-determined needs and desires, a world where no one is made homeless.

Occupied Homes and the Making of National Subjectivities

Home, and the ways it helps to organize ideas of family, household, ethnic community, and nation, is one of the most naturalized of concepts and therefore one of the most dangerous. Modernist ideas of home, in particular, help to organize and legitimate the differential treatment of those living within the same space. Differences between diverse indigenous people, citizens, immigrants, and migrant workers are organized through ideas of Canada being the home of some but not Others. With the overlaying of the idea of *home* onto that of *nation*, migrant workers are easily understood as foreigners labouring within a 'foreign labour market' instead of being an integral component of Canadian society.

Home acts as a conceptual bridge between modern notions of family and nation, so much so that, as Anders Johansen (1997:171) notes, the nation is understood to be a 'magnified version of the family and the circle of close friends.' This is well captured by former British prime minister Margaret Thatcher, who characteristically proclaimed that 'the family and its maintenance really is the most important thing, not only in your personal life, but in the life of any community, because this is the unit on which the whole nation is built' (in Rutherford, 1990:12).

Such a link between family and home is not accidental. Luce Irigaray (1993) points out that modernist ideas of family and home are inseparable from patriarchal social relations, observing that the feminization of the family home does not elevate the status of women but that of men, who feel entitled to depend on the housewife's homemaking practices. Doreen Massey points out that the understanding of the separated private sphere of the family home is extended to society which is considered a public or collective home. As the father has authority over 'his' family, the state is seen as the political and geographical expression of the authority of the nation. Massey argues that the primoridialization of homeland security is itself gendered and states (1994:71) that the 'need for the security of boundaries, the requirement for such a defensive and counterpositional definition of identity,' rather than being some universal truth, is in fact a specific and '"culturally masculine" tendency.' Moreover, with the modern family's emphasis on biological connection, hegemonic conceptions of home are based on the idea that there exist communities of similarity. In this, 'the National family [becomes] a symbolic home' (Morley, 2000:104). Thus, while society, as Eric Hobsbawm (1991:67-8) notes, 'cannot belong to us as individuals' we are encouraged to imagine that it can still belong to Us as a People.

As Philip Tabor (1998:218) puts it, 'house identified with the self is called a home, a country identified with the self is called a "homeland."' 'Its territory is our home; its people is marked by a common "character," much like the members of a family; its past is a "heritage" passed down from our 'forefathers' (Johansen, 1997:171). The ties between family, nation, and state are elaborated by Anne McLintock (1995:357), who observes that 'the term nation derives from natio: to be born – we speak of nations as "motherlands" and "fatherlands." Foreigners "adopt" countries that are not their native homes and are nationalized in the "national family." We talk of the "family of nations" of "homelands" and "native" lands. In Britain, immigration matters are dealt with at the Home Office; in the United States the president and his wife are called the First family.'

Home, then, is an idea that masquerades as a place. Having a home within a nation, in particular, is not a geographical signpost but an ideological signifier. Yet, as David Morley (2000:8) notes, 'if home is not necessarily a spatial concept, it is nonetheless often lived out as if it were such.' Because of this, it profoundly shapes our consciousness of the relationship between place and 'belonging.' Its power rests in its ability to project modernist formulations of home back through human history so that our contemporary understandings of homelands come to be seen as merely the outcomes of some supposedly primordial need for rootedness.

Ironically, it was after the onset of European capitalist colonization, with its practices of mass displacement, that processes of constructing boundaries between homes and societies were intensified. Stronger Insides and Outsides were constructed as colonizers made contact with those they colonized and as profits were accrued from differentiating between the two. This, in turn, strengthened the association between family and nation. Krishan Kumar (1994) points out that in the early seventeenth century, separate houses and households came to be more clearly demarcated from each other. Concomitantly, a greater division of labour was implemented within the family home, and the boundaries between members and non-members of the family household became starker.

Eventually, the household in Europe came to be imagined as consisting of only the nuclear, patriarchal family with its fatherly head. Just as the capitalist reorganization of productive activity as either work or non-work according to its value (or valuelessness) in the marketplace helped to create the idea of different gendered spheres of existence (the public–private divide being perhaps the central one), European colonization gave shape to notions of discrete, ethnically bounded homelands. Indeed, a number of domestic metaphors and tropes of privacy have helped to organize the legitimacy for the exclusion of people said to not belong within the 'national home' (Cohen, 1996:68). In this, it is not simply the boundaries of national homelands that are said to be in need of protection but also the boundaries between members and non-members of the national family. Looking at how European colonizers made themselves at home in particular colonies is instructive. The doctrine of *Terra Nullius* that allowed the Americas and the South Pacific to be viewed as empty lands awaiting European civilization and cultivation was, of course, very useful in the 'founding' of 'White settler societies,' such as Canada. The notion that indigenous peoples were never at home on these lands worked to depoliticize their homelessness after the advent of colonialism and the official redistribution of land to White settlers.

Representing indigenous peoples as strangers and European colonial settlers as at home helped to close the conceptual gap between the newness of the New World and nationalist references to antiquity for their exclusive claims to territory. This was further strengthened throughout the eighteenth and nineteenth centuries as elites within the Americas mobilized ideas of the bounded national family to mark the territories they sought to secure 'independence' for – the new national states of which they would be the heads.

The continuous displacement and forced assimilation of diverse people to make new homelands, not only in White settler colonies but also within each and every national state, has not disrupted the notion that national communities are formed through shared, common characteristics. The nation continues to be seen as historically rooted in blood and soil. The concept of *ethnicity*, reliant as it is on the idea that there exist a People that 'naturally' belongs to a given place, figures prominently in this.

Ethnicizing is a process that roots culture to a particular place, one that has greatly informed our ideas of the nation as a homey space – as a primordial homeland (Morley, 2000:212). Imagining the modern nation has entailed the dividing of humanity along lines of ethnicized groups and positing that each human being belongs to only one – such group. Massey (in Mackay, 1997:204) argues that 'in that process the boundaries of the place, and the imagination and building of its 'character' [become] part and parcel of the definition of who is an insider and who is not; of who is a 'local' and what that term should mean, and who is to be excluded.' This works to delimit home as that which stands in contrast to all things defined as foreign or 'unfamiliar.' In other words, the nation occupies not only a territorial space but also an ideological space of belonging.

Being at home in the land – just as *not* being at home – is based both on what Anjelika Bammer (1992: ix–x) calls 'mythic narratives, stories the telling of which has the power to create the 'we' who are engaged in telling them' as well as constructing 'the discursive right to a space (a country, a neighbourhood, a place to live) that is due us ... in the name of the 'we-ness' we have just constructed.' Morley (2000:217) argues that such a discourse 'allows us to imagine that we do not have to share our space with anyone else unless they are of exactly our own kind by virtue of consanguinity.' What such a conflation allows is the identification of family cum nation as race. This has had a particularly damaging effect on migrants.

Historically, as ideologies of highly racialized nations as natural homelands became hegemonic, people's understanding of geographical movements profoundly shifted. Indeed, as borders became more fixed, migrants increasingly were portrayed as trespassers. In other words, as the nation became more homey to those seen as its members, migrants were made even more homeless. To be a migrant became tantamount to being a vagrant. Moreover the imposition of the idea that homelessness is akin to godlessness allowed vagrancy to be understood as a moral (and often a criminal) offence to the community of 'honest residents.' Migrants were thus strongly associated not only with losing their homes but also their moral standing.

This attitude was strengthened as the national state system expanded. Saskia Sassen (1999:78) argues, with regard to events in Europe in the mid-1800s, that 'the coupling of state sovereignty and nationalism with border control made the "foreigner" an outsider.' Within this 'metaphysics of sedantarism,' to use Lisa Malkki's term (quoted in Hebdige, 1995:100), domestic and foreign spaces were related through ideas of purity and contamination. Over time, the naturalization of xenophobia mobilized the idea that nations have some sort of right to preserve their 'purity.'

Anti-miscegenation discourses have become the basis of asserting ethnic identities, and this has often led to virulent forms of homey racism. Michael Keith and Steven Pile (1993:20) have identified such discourses as 'a reactionary vocabulary of the identity politics of place and a spatialised politics of identity grounded in the rhetoric of origins, of exclusion, of boundary-making, of invasion and succession, of purity and contamination ... [in short,] the glossary of ethnic cleansing.'

Increasingly, goals of maintaining a supposed homogeneity are fought for not just in the name of race purity but of preserving 'cultural integrity.' Indeed, postmodern practices of racism and nationalism rely less on ideologies of race separation and more and more on ideas sanctifying culture. An impoverished view of 'culture' has come to overlie notions of biological race so that what connects identity to place is now said to be the historical existence of certain 'traditions.' In this, 'tradition [becomes] the cultural equivalent of the process of biological reproduction' (Morley, 2000:65). Étienne Balibar refers to this kind of racism as a 'differentialist racism' (in Hardt and Negri, 2000:192). This form of racism is heavily reliant on nationalist practices and is evidenced in some of the earliest attempts to debunk psuedoscientific rationales for racism. The United Nations Educational, Scientific, and Cultural Organization (UNESCO), in its 1951 'Statement on the Nature of Race and Race Differences' illustrates this well when it states that 'Americans are not a race, nor are Frenchmen, nor Germans; nor ipso facto is any other national group' (as cited in Guillaumin, 1995:104). In the process of trying to delegitimize some (and only some) commonsensical ideas of the existence of separate and discrete races of humans, such statements further naturalized the existence of 'different nations.' This is not simply a shift in the meaning of race, so that nation becomes race just as in earlier analyses where class came to be conflated with ideas of race (see Goldberg, 1992:564). Rather, it signals the growing importance of nationalism and the maintenance of nationalized borders in the ongoing reconfiguration of racialized identities.

In such 'cultural fundamentalisms' (Stolcke, 1995:5), the difference between nationals and immigrants is the most naturalized. Thus, 'instead of ordering different cultures hierarchically, cultural fundamentalism segregates them spatially, each culture in its place ... [and] the 'problem' of immigration is constructed as a political threat to national identity and integrity on account of immigrants' cultural diversity' (ibid.:8). According to Malkki (1997:42, 62) the assumption that any given culture is rooted in a particular geographical place and is best kept homogeneous 'actively territorializes our identities, whether cultural or national ... [and] directly enables a vision of territorial displacement as pathological.' This leads to a suspicion of migration so that mobility is seen only as crisis-producing (Sutcliffe, 2001). Consequently, as John Bird (1995:119) notes, 'the common experience of the homeless and the migrant is to be made to feel out of place.'

While such practices are often thought as being best understood to be *racist* forms of discrimination, Ghassan Hage (2000:38) usefully points out that racist ideologies that mark people for exclusion because of their foreign standing, rely on *nationalist* practices with their 'categories of spatial management.' Hage therefore, cautions us to pay attention to the significance not only of racist practices but of *nationalist* ones, as well, for this will help us to uncover the *territorial* dimension of contemporary moral panics concerning (im)migration. Indeed, *not* paying attention to the spatial character of how certain (im)migrants face oppression and exploitation – seeing these as only a result of processes of negative racialization – has led to the serious absence of studies to investigate homey forms of racism. In this sense, nationalism both organizes and helps to mask racialized forms of difference that organize inequalities.

Since 'concepts of nation, people, and race are never very far apart,' as Hardt and Negri note (2000:103), an examination of nationalist practices helps to explain why within the homeland 'not all strangers are equally strange' (Peter Fitzpatrick, cited in Morley, 2000:249). Nationalist practices are concerned with issues of spatial allocations of people and the supposedly 'rightful' position of various differentiated people within national states in ways that racist practices are not always. In this regard, Hage (2000:28) maintains that nationalist practices are those that 'assume, first, an image of a national space; secondly, an image of the nationalist himself or herself as master of this national space and, thirdly, an image of the "ethnic/racial other" as a mere object within this space.' Members of the nation have a sense of 'empowered spatiality' in relation to Others who do not, so that 'in every [epithet of you] "go home," there is an "I want to and am entitled to feel at home in my nation"' (ibid.:40).

There is, therefore, a particular kind of national subject that is important to construct and to maintain for power to be wielded within modern national states. Michel Foucault's (1991) discussion of self-regulation helps us to understand the crucial importance of the creation of a particular subjectivity to the realization of national state power. Thus, historically in Canada, 'the entities being regulated were in the first instance the characters of individuals ... but the nation was also seen as held together by a common subjectivity, whose constant re-creation at the individual level ensured the continued survival of the collectivity. The collectivity thus organized had very specific class, gender and racial/ethnic characteristics' (Valverde, 1991:33).

National Self-regulation, then, is not only about constructing and regulating a proper national subject. Instead, having the nation stand in for various levels of homeyness – family, household, ethnic community, all of which are seen as discrete and secure sociogeographical environments – also requires the existence of a 'threat' to create a secure sense of Self. In this regard, Hage (2000:37), using insights from Lacanian psychoanalysis of 'fantasy spaces,' maintains that nationalist discourses would fall apart if there were not Others against whom the nation could be defined. In the never-ending struggle to realize the nation, Hage (1993:99–100) notes that 'in fact, the other is what allows the nationalist to believe in the possibility of that goal. It spares him the anxiety of having to face the fact that such a goal is impossible ... by the very fact of being posited as that which threatens it.' Opposition to foreigners, thus, becomes a way for those Self-defined as being at home to argue for their own fuller integration into the nation.

Hence, Hage argues that nationalist practices are based on discourses of undesirability rather than on discourses of inferiority that underscore racism (2000:37). While discourses of inferiority do not necessarily necessitate Self-defence, discourses of undesirability motivate *action* towards the neutralization of whomever is presented as threatening the security of the homeland. Because the nation is presented as a community of similarity, threats always come to be defined as foreign, regardless of the actual location of the people so identified.

In this the sharp distinction between what Henry Mayhew (in Stallybrass and White, 1986:128–9) calls the 'wanderers' and the 'civilized tribes' produces the image of migrants as polluting the home society. Excluding those who are deemed to be filthy and undesirable, as Anne Michaels shows in her novel *Fugitive Pieces* (1996), comes to be seen as a national *obligation*. About the Nazi policy of exterminating those always constructed as ever-outsiders to the German nation, Michaels writes: 'Nazi policy was beyond racism, it was anti-matter, for Jews were not considered human. An old trick of language, used often in the course of history. Non-Aryans were never to be referred to as human, but as "figuren," "stücke" – "dolls," "wood," "merchandise," "rags." Humans were not being gassed, only "figuren," so ethics weren't being violated. No one could be faulted for burning debris, for burning rags and clutter in the dirty basement of society. In fact, they're a fire hazard! What choice but to burn them before they harm you?'

Foreigners are perceived as weakening the bonds of community said to hold the national family together. Migrants, especially those arriving from places deemed as far (not necessarily only geographically but culturally) from the Self-identity of those claiming home-ownership rights, challenge the very idea of the existence of national homelands. Phil Cohen (1996:75) puts it this way: 'If immigrants put down roots, if ethnic minorities make a home from home, then they are perceived to threaten the privileged link between habit and habitat upon which the myth of indigenous origins rests.'

The very mobility of those particular migrants deemed as 'too strange to be Us' calls into question the segmentation of the world into discrete, demarcated zones of natural belonging. In this regard, Nora Rathzel (1994:91) notes that such migrants are threatening because they 'make our taken-for-granted identities visible as specific identities and deprive them of their assumed naturalness,' hence, 'once we start thinking about them, becoming aware of them, we cannot feel 'at home' any more.' For this reason, the mobility of Others 'becomes a basic form of disorder and chaos – constantly defined as transgression and trespass' (Cresswell, 1996:87). A comment by a Cambodian woman refugee living in Paris puts it succinctly: 'We are a disturbance ... Because we show you in a terrible way how fragile the world we live in is' (in Morely, 2000:152).

The strong association between migration and chaos is borne of colonial flows. The 'similarity' of some and the extraordinary 'strangeness' of Others is one consequence of the global mobility of capital, goods, and people. Many supposedly natural homelands exist only because of the forcible dispossession, displacement, violent assimilation, and sometimes extermination of those who previously built their lives and livelihoods in these places. This is most obvious in the case of the 'New World' where indigenous populations were severely reduced, at times entirely wiped out, through war, forced labour, and disease in order to pave the way for the world's first nation-states (see Anderson, 1991). But it is also the case in the so-called Old World where European national states were built on the ashes of many diverse pre-existing societies. This is also true in Asia and Africa, where explicit colonial divide-and-rule policies translated into ongoing processes of neocolonialism after the emergence of independent national states ruled by a new set of elites (see Miles, 1993; Anderson, 1991). National liberation movements did not liberate people but placed them under the rule of new 'leaders' – this time often of the same 'ethnic type' as the (re)colonized.

Within this complexity of migration, displacement, and the simultaneous experiences of homelessness and claims of homeyness, it is important that we not confuse the problem of colonization with migration per se. Colonization is, first and foremost, a relationship of exploitation and oppression. Colonization can be experienced both as conquest *and* as scattered crossings. The problem with colonization is not the 'strangeness' of the colonizers but their rapacious greed. Indeed, many past colonizers (the 'French' and 'Indian Aryans,' to note two such groups) are now imagined as 'related' to, or the same People as, those whom they colonized.

The migrations of people – be they displaced peasants or jobless urban dwellers, kidnapped Africans, Asian coolie labourers, or, more recently, the supposedly voluntary movements of professionals, the undocumented migrations of the poor, or people fleeing political persecution – are not equivalent to the migrations of colonizers. In fact, it is the mobilities of the former, diverse as they are, that led to the conflation of migration with misanthropy, especially in relation to migration into places that colonizing groups have claimed as their own homelands.

The association between migration and madness has become even more pronounced with the expansion and further development of the apparatus of the national state. There has been a further conflation between concepts of home and ideas of nations resulting in the almost complete collapse of the space between civil society and the national state (see Urry, 2000). Difference-making devices have been focused within national states so that in the twentieth century progressively greater distinctions were made between various kinds of migrants, so that, as Sassen (1999:78) notes, 'the state now [has] the power and the institutional legitimacy to exclude refugees from civil society.'

(To more fully understand the relationships between state practices and forms of social relations based on ideas of a homey racism that allows some to claim exclusive homelands while leaving Others homeless, we therefore need to rethink the separation of state from society that ideas of civil society put into place (see Marx and Engels, 1969). The ideology that something called *civil society* exists organizes the myth that those with a strong sense of homey entitlement – what Hage (2000) calls 'governmental belonging' – in the nation create 'the state' which is supposed to govern *for them* as an objective and autonomous (even if this is 'relative') force (see Poulantzas, 1973).

In fact, Adam Ashforth (1990:15, emphasis added) points out that the claim that the state 'exists to further the welfare of *all* subject to it, that is – the Common Good' is key to its legitimacy. However, in the construction of this Common Good, Ashforth's argument needs to be extended to account for the centrality of separating and identifying those national subjects *for* whom the state rules and those foreign objects whom the state rules *over*. Constructing the national state – the community of the nation with its governing state – requires the formation of a nationalist model of imagination, or what Michael Hardt and Antonio Negri (2000:113) call a 'totalitarian democracy.'

The ideology of the state acting in the 'Common Good,' often formulated as 'democracy,' shapes the legitimacy for the exclusion of Others not only from the space of the nation but from claims to the entitlements associated with membership in it. As Phil Cole (1998:137) notes, the 'existence of a liberal polity made up of free and equal citizens rests upon the existence of outsiders who are refused a share of ... [its] goods' This is not coincidental. Throughout the history of national states, the purported enemy or foreigner has never been limited to those *outside* of national space. In fact, the targeting of people represented as foreigners *within* the nation has often been more of a spur to nationalist activity than outside threats have been (see Hyslop, 1999:405).

Nancy Fraser (1993:8), in rejecting classical theories of national citizenship with their ideas of progressive inclusion of all in the nation, points out that the organization of civil society, or what has been called the public sphere of capitalist liberal democracies, is premised on many layers of separations and exclusions. There is both the separation of state from (civil) society and the existence of separate spaces of belonging for various types of people classified according to deeply entrenched ideologies of separate races and gender roles and, perhaps most legitimately, by the belief that there are different territorial spaces for differently nationalized people. Full inclusion is not a possibility within the logic of national citizenship.

The notion of the nation as a homey place for all who live there (even as a potentiality), then, is ideological. It conceals the fact that the exclusions organized through it are integral – not tangential or merely contingent on historical – processes. In this respect, Avner Offer's (1989:235) argument that racist practices are *part of* the liberal 'virtues of democracy, civic equality and solidarity' takes on greater relevance. So, too, does John Holloway's (1994:32) argument that, because the state is formed through assertions of national sovereignty that are constructed through the organization of racialized differences between Us and Them, 'the very existence of the state is racist.'

The existence of a group of people considering themSelves to be part of the nation (or civil society) and therefore regarding themSelves not as ruled over but as ruled *for* helps to secure ruling relations and the continued existence of the national state. In other words, the construction of a civil or social sphere becomes a way to naturalize the power of the state to rule. It is therefore 'misleading to envisage the dimension of the *social* as the state's antagonist or its prey. In modern liberal societies the social is, characteristically, the field of governmental security considered in its widest sense' (Gordon, 1991:35). By claiming to represent the national family, the state secures its power over both its members and those positioned as their negative reference point.

With regard to national styles of ruling, then, we need to pay more careful attention to Kobena Mercer's (1994) question: 'Why the need for the nation?' Examining '*who* needs it, *who* manufactures the 'need' for it, and *whose* interests it serves' may be an even more urgent task (Burton, 1997:234). The state is one of the main beneficiaries of the existence of the nation. Nation-building practices constitute an important and *con-*

tinuous aspect of state practices and contribute to ongoing processes of state formation. However, the state, like the nation, is *imagined*. As with the imagined character of nations, this does not mean that the state does not exist. It does mean, however, that the state, like the nation, is a form of social relations, an always-incomplete form that requires the continual reproduction of civil society for its own rationalization. The legitimacy and therefore the power of the state relies upon the existence of the imagined community of the nation for whom it is said to operate. Concepts of citizenship are the ideological glue that bonds the nation to the state. Citizenship provides the legal framework through which the state performs its role as ruler *for* the nation. Together they legitimate the power of the state to subordinate foreigners. Denying the rights, entitlements, and protections that citizens have to those positioned as non-citizens is a crucial feature of how hegemonic conceptualizations of nations as homes operate within today's global capitalist economy. In this, citizenship and immigration policies are the key avenue through which nationalism is performed.

Immigration policies have historically played a significant part in organizing, materializing, and then regulating national differences. This is why it continues to be onto the bodies of (im)migrants that a foreign identity can most easily be grafted. In this period of increased mobility (of capital, goods, and people), it is the process of *differential inclusion* – not simply exclusion – that works to facilitate how people are seen – and see themselves – as being at home or not in the spaces in which they find themselves.

National Homelessness: The Making of Non-Immigrant 'Migrant Workers' in Canada

Being homeless in Canada is of particular significance for those categorized as temporary, foreign, migrant workers. The making of migrant workers allows us to clearly recognize how nationality operates as a legitimate mode of discrimination. For the last twenty-five or so years, most people (im)migrating to Canada arrive not as immigrants (those with 'landed' or permanent resident status) but as foreign migrant workers. The state category of *foreign worker* is a clear demonstration of how (im)migration controls are inextricably linked with the regulation of citizenship. Together they define who can be a member of the Canadian nation *and* who can legally make claims for protection or benefits from the Canadian national state. With the categorization of people as migrant workers, the state quietly borrows from the exclusionary practices organized through concepts of citizenship and its ideas of the fictive national society, in order to reposition migrant workers as part of a foreign workforce in Canada.)

The categorization of certain (im)migrants as migrant workers is authorized through the regulatory framework of the Non-Immigrant Employment Authorization Program (NIEAP) introduced on 1 January 1973. Its broad parameters are entrenched within successive Canadian Immigration Acts. By law, a migrant worker is the 'foreign worker' who upon arrival must have with her or him an official temporary employment authorization from the Canadian state. This foreign work visa, as it is commonly known, assigns her or him to a specified employer and stipulates her or his occupation, residence, length and terms of employment in Canada (Citizenship and Immigration Canada (CIC), 1994a:1). Migrant workers must exit the country immediately after their labour contract expires. Written permission from immigration officials is required to alter any of the conditions of work. If the terms are changed without official permission, migrant workers are subject to immediate deportation.

As a result of these conditions, people admitted through the NIEAP are denied the freedoms of labour market and spatial mobility available to those existing within the legal designation of citizen or permanent resident. In fact, the NIEAP exists because it is unconstitutional for the state to restrict the mobility of citizens or immigrants. Such restrictions apply *only* for non-immigrants or 'foreign visitors' who can *legally* be indentured to employers in Canada. The non-immigrant, or migrant worker, category, therefore, allows the social category of foreigner to be fully realized in Canadian law. Through it, the social organization of nationalized difference is materialized within the Canadian labour market and within Canadian society at large.

The NIEAP makes migrant workers available to employers concerned with securing a post-Fordist labour force: efficient, flexible, and globally competitive. Part of the flexibility and competitiveness of migrant workers is that they do not have access to many of the things that capitalist lobby groups complain make Canadian workers 'too expensive': collective bargaining rights and access to social programs and protections (Swanson, 2001). Those categorized as migrant workers have little, or no, de facto claims to the minimum wage and labour standards and protections available to the citizenry (including, for the most part, permanent residents). Migrant workers are also usually made ineligible for certain social benefits, such as unemployment insurance or welfare payments even while they do pay taxes in the country.

Employers benefit in numerous ways as a result. Migrant workers can be paid much less than citizens or permanent residents and be made to work and live under conditions seen as 'unattractive' to Canadians (Bolaria, 1992; Wall, 1992). Moreover, migrant workers are highly circumscribed from collectively organizing to realize the limited rights they do have access to or to agitate for more. This is mainly for two reasons. First, some migrant workers face severe isolation from other workers. For example, migrant domestic workers must live in the residence of their employer(s) as a condition of their temporary employment authorization. Second, because employers can end the labour contract at any time they are dissatisfied, and since such a termination often results in deportation, migrant workers are severely constrained by the system of patronage that develops (Wall, 1992). Such practices embolden employers and contribute to the substandard conditions found in jobs performed by migrant workers.

Unsurprisingly, then, since the introduction of the NIEAP in 1973, the Canadian state has successfully shifted immigration policy away from a policy of permanent immigrant settlement towards an increasing reliance upon unfree, temporary migrant workers. Such a shift is part of the overall neoliberal turn in state policy. For the majority of the years following its introduction, the number of people admitted to work in the labour market in Canada as immigrants (i.e., permanent residents) has declined both in proportion and in number relative to those recruited as migrant workers. From making up 57 per cent of the total number of those recruited for the Canadian labour market in 1973, only 30 per cent of the (im)migrant workforce received permanent resident status by 1993 (Sharma, 1995a:122). By 2004 the proportion of (im)migrants admitted with permanent resident status was 35 per cent (see table 5.5). By looking only at the numbers of people admitted as part of the independent class,[2] the shift is even greater: by 2004 only 22 per cent of all (im)migrants recruited for the Canadian labour market were given permanent resident status and rights while 76 per cent were recruited as migrant workers (see table 5.6).

Yet, despite such dramatic changes in (im)migrants' status, there has been very little attention and even less outcry about the NIEAP. This is because the NIEAP does not work against but *through* hegemonic notions of Canadian nationness. The commonsensical understanding of migrant workers is that they are non-Whites from the global South who are lucky to work legally in Canada. The act of allowing Them into the country with a temporary employment authorization is seen as an act of charity extended by Canadians to foreign Others (Arat-Koc, 1992).

In conjunction with bounded ideas of national homes, creating conditions of work that are unacceptable, even illegal, for Canadians is easier to impose on those non-citizens who are also seen as racialized and/or cultural outsiders.[3] Hence, because migrant workers are not entering a 'neutral ideological context' (Miles, 1982:165) when coming to Canada, the NIEAP needs to be located within the ideological organization of the Otherness of non-Whites both historically and during the time of its introduction. A look at Canadian parliamentary debates in the five years prior to 1973 is illuminating in this regard.

As official discourses are an integral part of how the state constructs national society and its members, these debates not only articulate the agenda for specific state policy directions and provide a blueprint for policy implementation, they also shape the discursive framework of state practices. That is, they actively reshape, recreate, and redefine the 'issues of the day' and, as such, constitute a site where a certain kind of discursive practice is put together around the framework of problems and their solutions. In doing so, such official discourses, because they are infused with societal norms and values help to construct subject – and object – identities (Doty, 1996). Part of the work done by such discourses, then, is to provide a particular frame for reading (and hearing) the debates whereby a certain kind of knowledge helpful to the accomplishment of ruling is produced (Smith, 1990).

Kari Dehli (1993:87) notes that such discursive state practices have 'consequences beyond the contexts in which they are written and read.' Parliamentary debates get entered into the work process of state apparatuses and by doing so help to construct categories of legally differentiated membership. These categories become what Lim Pui Huen and Diana Wong (2000) have called 'discursive facts' that shape how people both know and interact with one another. State categories, thus, become cultural forms (Corrigan and Sayer, 1985:3).

Since parliamentary debates take place for the expressed purpose of governing society, they have great power not only in constructing but also legitimizing state categories. Parliamentary debates, in this sense, can be seen as a *technology* of liberal democratic forms of ruling that normalizes both the exercise of state power and the boundaries of those who belong – as well as those that do not – within national society (Foucault, 1991). A textual analysis of these debates, then, provides more than an interpretation of the utterances of parliamentarians. Rather, an analysis of them helps to uncover the social relations and social practices that allow these utterances to make common sense. This method of inquiry reveals that parliamentary debates, though not synonymous with ruling relations or state power, are a *form* of constructing knowledge through state practices, a form particularly attentive to the performance aspects of state authority and power.

In the context of Canada's liberal democracy the performance of parliamentary rituals is especially productive of notions of nationhood that legitimate the wielding of state power. This is most clearly evident in the daily Question Period where questions and answers between members of Parliament of different political parties are publicly conducted.[4] Adam Ashforth (1990:11) rightly points out that it would be more useful for us to interpret public performances of this type 'less as instruments of "policy" and "intelligence" and more as symbolic rituals aiding in establishing and reproducing the power of modern states.' Hage adds that debates on immigration in particular ought to be seen 'in a more anthropological spirit, as rituals of *White empowerment* – seasonal festivals where White[s] ... renew the belief in their possession of the power to talk and make decisions about Third World–looking people' (2000:241).

Significantly, the problem that the NIEAP is said to have solved is the problem of the *permanence* of non-Whites within Canadian society. Following the liberalization of Canadian immigration policy in 1967, non-Whites admitted as immigrants, that is, permanent residents, came to have (virtually) the same rights as White Canadians. Moreover, after 1967, a growing proportion of immigrants came from the global South, eventually becoming the majority of new permanent residents by 1974. In the five-year period surrounding the introduction of the NIEAP, a common conceptual practice within Parliament was to organize the discursive problem of there being 'too many' non-Whites in the country and the resulting irreparable damage that was being done to the 'character of Canadian society.'

The NIEAP was one parliamentary solution to this problem. It legalized the resubordination of many non-Whites entering Canada by recategorizing them as temporary and foreign workers. Following the reversal of the liberal policies of the mid to late 1960s, then, the racialized criteria of admittance in Canadian immigration policy was shifted from the pre-1967 categories of 'preferred races and nationalities' onto 'globalization'

the new category of non-immigrant (or migrant) worker. One trend towards the liberalization of racism was met by a counter-trend towards the greater restriction of the rights and entitlements of non-Whites.

Parliamentary discursive practices and the legislative changes they legitimate have, in this, the early part of the latest period of capitalist globalization, worked to reconstruct the idea of nations as homes for some but not Others. One result has been greater competition within the labour market in Canada. This has worked to reorganize national labour markets to become more competitive within global markets for both capital and labour. Parliamentarians, therefore, have contributed both materially and ideologically to processes of globalization. The construction of the NIEAP is, of course, an extension of past global practices that saw non-Whites brought to Canada as indentured workers while Whites were positioned as permanent settlers. Indeed, Hyslop (1999:405) shows that, historically, an imperial White working class made itself through a common ideology of homey racism that was, in part, designed to secure them access to key and relatively privileged parts of nationalized labour markets.

A significant aspect of White, male privilege was the claim to freedom from constraints on their mobility in the labour market. In making their claims to national subjecthood, it was the continuing unfreedom of negatively racialized and gendered Others that consolidated the view among White men that contractual servitude was involuntary labour. Consequently, those made to labour in unfree employment relationships, although integral to the production and reproduction of Canadian society, were constituted (in varying degrees) as foreigners to it. Such arguments came to form an integral part of nationalist practices of Othering. It can be said, therefore, that the freeing of White male workers *strengthened* racialized and gendered understandings of who could be a member of the nation.

Being rendered a foreign Other within Canadian society and working in unfree conditions within its nationalized labour market have, thus, often been historically coterminous. Organizing unfreedom for Others has operated as a technology of keeping these Others in their place, both spatially as well as keeping them as subordinated people within Canadian society. The contemporary practice of organizing a migrant labour force in Canada, many from the global South, demonstrates how racism and sexism continue to operate *through* nationalist practices. Because such practices are seen not only as legitimate but as *necessary* for the defence of the home(land), nationalist practices are

able to accomplish racist and sexist aims in a social and policy environment where explicit racialized criteria in immigration selection have
been mostly removed.

In this latest period of globalization, *nationalist* practices that produce feelings of both homeyness and of foreignness have become even
more important. Because the state is widely seen to be legitimate in
using its power against foreigners, the existence of people as migrant
workers in Canada is predicated on naming those 'embraced' by this
category as *not* being at home. As in the past, the construction of subordinate categories of entry and work (slave or coolie labour and now
migrant worker) shapes the competitiveness and profitability of contained and therefore competitive labour markets.

Thus, in contrast to John Holloway (1994:30) who argues that 'the
destruction of personal bondage was also the destruction of geographical constraint,' it is clear that the existence of unfree labour is not predicated on people's spatial *immobility* but on exactly the opposite.
Oftentimes (though not always) it is people's dependence on migration across nationalized boundaries that places them in situations
where, having been categorized as foreigners, they are denied the
same rights that citizens lay exclusive claim to. Immigration policies
become the vehicle through which their unfreedom is organized precisely because they allow the national state to utilize its internationally
recognized power to determine membership in the nation.

A critical examination of the migrant worker category, thus, reveals
that border controls and immigration restrictions are thoroughly ideological. This is for two reasons. First, they do very little to actually control people's mobility across borders. Second, because they are
imagined as natural, and as crucial manifestations of state sovereignty,
their operation as an integral feature of the global expansion of capitalism is concealed. Thus, whether we talk about such border control spectacle, as the more than 2,000-mile long steel fence erected, patrolled, and
armed by the U.S. Immigration and Naturalization Service across the
border separating Mexico from the United States, or the spectacle of
'Europe's new Berlin Wall': the eight-kilometre fence between the Span-
ish-claimed enclave of Melilla and the rest of Africa or the ever more
restrictive immigration policies of virtually every national state in the
global North, restrictions on who is legally able to enter with full status
do very little to actually restrict migration itself. Nor would I argue are
they intended to.

Restricting *immigration* is not tantamount to restricting people's

'restrictions on freedoms'
a tool used by gov t
Home(lessness) and the Naturalization of Difference   25

mobility. In Canada, where there has been a steady closing down of avenues to obtain immigrant (or permanent resident) status over the last thirty years, there has been an increase in the numbers of people legally admitted to work in the country. The categorization of the majority of (im)migrants admitted to the country as migrant workers has meant that they encounter a differential regulation of their labour power and a differentiated position once within Canada than do immigrants. In short, constructing people as foreigners has not resulted in their exclusion from Canadian society. Limits to immigration, then, lay not so much in the ability of states to restrict people's geographical mobility but to restrict their freedom once they are *within* nationalized labour markets.

The greater policing of the purified boundaries of nationalized identities have therefore been beneficial to employers trying to gain advantages from the dramatic increase in people's displacement and subsequent migrations. The simultaneous presence of anti-immigration discourses evident in Canadian parliamentary debates and increases in the number of people entering Canada as non-citizens without permanent, full status are, therefore, not at all contradictory but are instead complementary processes. As Hage (2000:135) comments, 'anti-immigration discourse, by continually constructing the immigrants as unwanted, works precisely at maintaining [their] economic viability to ... employers. They are best wanted as "unwanted."'

Greater competition within national labour markets relies on the social organization of difference and the regulation of this differentiated inclusion through the disciplinary model of nationalism with its exclusionary inclusivity. In this regard, the rhetoric of border controls with its accompanying moral panics against those identified as (im)migrants helps to further the project of capitalist globalization. By first creating a group of foreigners and then presenting Them as the problem facing Us, the reality that the NIEAP, with its institutionalization of differentials in wages and standards, actually works against the interests of *all* workers becomes difficult to see.

Border controls enable national states to reorganize their nationalized labour markets to *include* a group of migrant workers who are made vulnerable to employers' demands through their lack of status. In the current historical juncture where both people's displacement and subsequent migration are occurring at a historically unprecedented level – the United Nations (2003) estimates that every year more than 175 million people migrate across national borders – nationalism, with its legit-

def of belonging

imization of differential treatment for foreigners and citizens, has become a motor force of capitalist globalization. It is the social organization of difference that regulates the space between national homes and global capitalist economics.

To better understand the significance of difference to such ruling projects, we need to problematize the existence of differences by clearly distinguishing between difference and diversity. Diversity is the tangible existence of heterogeneity and mutual reciprocity within nature and within that part of nature that is humanity. Differences, on the other hand, are socially organized inequalities between human beings and between humans and the rest of the planet. The social organization of difference is the effect of practices and beliefs founded upon hierarchies of differential value and worth.

When we say someone is different, we are not recognizing that person's singularity. Instead, we are setting her or him aside as a member of a group that does not meet normative or hegemonic standards for subjecthood, agency, and belonging. Difference, then, is mutually constitutive. It is relational. As Brah (1996:124) points out, 'the proclamation of a specific collective identity is a political process [whereby] the commonality that is evoked can be rendered meaningful only in articulation with a discourse of difference.' It is to this relational aspect of difference that Gregory Bateson (1979:78) refers when he says that 'it takes at least two somethings to create difference ... Clearly each alone is – for the mind and perception – a non-entity, a non-being ... An unknowable, a *Ding an sich*, a sound from one hand clapping.'

In the making of difference, however, the 'two somethings' are quite unequal in their respective ability to affect both the relationship and the representation of themselves. The norms which are constructed through such binary oppositions always pivot on the experiences, desires, and power held by those in the dominant half of Self/Other codes. Frantz Fanon (1965:32) understands this well when he states, 'it is the [colonial] settler who has brought the native into existence and who perpetuates his existence.' Sardar et al. (1993:89) add that within such binaries, even the 'the distinctiveness of a particular Other ... [is] lost in the generality shared with all Others, that of being different ... from the West,' so that one overarching category of Other is created as the definitive opposite of the Self.

The politics of constructing and maintaining negative dualities of worth in which one half of the binary equation is privileged both symbolically and materially is what constitutes the identity politics of rulers (see Bannerji, 1995). This is evident in everyday understandings of difference. People who are different are so identified because of the ways they are seen as standing apart from those with the power to define them. Their difference is organized by the ways they have been negatively racialized, gendered, sexualized, classed, and so on. The lines of difference drawn between Self and Other are related to narratives of belonging.

In this, history and context matter. In Canada it has been the many-centuries' process of colonization that has prepared the groundwork for the contemporary organization of difference. It has been the world view of colonists, informed through the linear ideals and dualistic practices of Western Enlightenment philosophy that has shaped the range and intersectionality of social relations in Canada. The domination of Man over women and all of nature; the violence done to Muslims, Jews, Queers, and other Others; the enclosure of common properties; the construction of 'imagined' nations and races; and the creation of Europe and the colonization of its Others: the relationships structured through these practices have come to shape the everyday understanding of what it means to 'be Canadian' and therefore what it means to be not-Canadian (Sharma, 2001).

The racialization and regulation of diverse indigenous peoples into 'Indians'; the changing hierarchical organization of various racialized populations over time: 'Blacks,' 'Asians,' 'Whites,' 'Irish,' 'southern,' and 'eastern' 'Europeans,' 'Latinos' – all these have been at various times organized in opposition to 'Canadianness.' In short, it is through people's relationship to the Canadian Self-identity of being White, heterosexual, and male that difference has been structured.

The central distinction between difference and diversity, then, is that unlike diversity, difference, perhaps ironically, has *homogeneity* as its architectural frame. The organization of difference is about ensuring conformity to hegemonic beliefs and practices in an attempt to shape the world in the image of dominant groups. Difference, then, is about universalizing a *particular* parochial interest. Vandana Shiva (1997:93) sees the process of taking diversity and filtering out of it any divergence from the norm the creation of a 'monoculture of the mind.'

What, then, are we to make of current attempts to validate and valorize *difference* within postmodern and post-structuralist theory with its rightful attention to the politics of representation and identity (Young, 1989:261)? I will elaborate on this in the concluding chapter of this book. For now, it is important to note only that such celebrations of difference have often conflated difference with diversity, and this leads to a serious lack of attention to how the organization of differences is a strategy of ruling.

The attempt to end oppressive and exploitative social relations, particularly those of racism, through an acknowledgment of *differences* has led to political solutions such as the official promotion of 'tolerance' for different people. This kind of political practice has come to be called demonstrating a 'respect for diversity.' Of course, the stated aim of this respect is to secure the proper functioning of society as a singular body, again, in the image of Self-defined rulers. In such rhetoric, the nation is thought to be able to simply transcend conflict through a respect and celebration of difference without the eradication of any differentials in power and wealth and with no transformation at a systemic level.

This is, of course, the kind of diversity embraced by the state. It is one that enables those in positions of power over Others to tolerate people who have been differentiated. Yet, as Hage (2000) well notes, when those in positions of power are asked to be tolerant, their power to be intolerant is not taken away from them. It is, in fact, reasserted by the very request to have them not exercise it. In this regard, respect for diversity does not eclipse the social organization of difference but becomes a contemporary form of reproducing hierarchal social relations and recentring the White national subject. It legitimates the continued organization of difference in order to both organize and legitimate the subordination that the differentiated experience.

This kind of *official diversity* needs to distinguished from the kind of diversity I have discussed earlier. Perhaps we need to rename that kind of diversity, *radical diversity* since the former has been co-opted and has come to connote its exact opposite: the power of One (one law, one society, one People) over the Many, or what Deleuze and Guattari (1987) call the 'multiplicity,' and what Hardt and Negri (2000; 2004) refer to as the 'multitude.' Social systems based on radical diversity, unlike those founded on differences, are wholly dependent on maintaining heterogeneity while recognizing commonalities based on shared practice or experience for their continued survival and pleasure.

The social organization of difference is, therefore, a highly ideological practice and one linked to the material production of unjust social relations. In this regard, it is crucial to recognize that difference has its own materiality. Indeed, the entire history of the capitalist mode of production and its ever-expanding global reach has been organized through the structuring of difference. How one is identified shapes how one is positioned within global capitalism. The accumulation of capital continues to take place through the social and legal differentiation of labour (Lowe, 1996:159).

Within the conceptual carving out of differentiated zones of belonging lie concealed the interconnected relations and mutual constitutiveness between so-called local and global spaces, between the inside and the outside of nations. Indeed, the idea that there exist two supposedly discrete spaces – the national one in which Canadians exist and a global or foreign one that contains Others – has structured the sense of Canadian homeyness that legitimates the subordination of migrant workers within the space occupied by Canada.

The social organization of difference, therefore, always works to create forms of separation, whereby discrimination is organized through exclusionary inclusion. Nationalized differences, in particular, are consequential to the emergence and further entrenchment of what Anthony Richmond (1994) has aptly identified as 'global apartheid.' He refers to the organization of an ever-widening differentiation between people in wealthy and impoverished national states through restrictive immigration policies that imprison impoverished people within zones of poverty. This book continues this work by turning our attention to what happens when foreign-Others *are* allowed into wealthier national states but who, through the exclusionary notion of homelands, remain impoverished and are rendered homeless once there.

This project asks us to politicize the process of identification, particularly state identification schemes. Identifications are always about positioning people within a grid of power in which ideas of belonging mark not where one is located geographically but where one is positioned within the global political economy of home. Differentiated identities are part of a kind of *home economics* whereby people are separated from one another not by space or place but by being 'embraced' by the nation and the state in highly differential ways. Thus, this book asks that we be able to distinguish between diverse self-determined identities and the process of differentiation used to mark Others as subordinated beings.

This book therefore makes the case for nationalism to be seen as a practice that organizes discrimination within a globalized system of national states. Despite or rather *because of* its almost complete hegemonic character – Benedict Anderson (1991:3) notes that 'nation-ness is the most universally legitimate value in the political life of our time' – and because of the enormous consequence nationalism has for the organization of inequalities, we need to regard nationalism as being one of the key methods by which people are differentiated in order to be ruled over.

This book, then, is about how the nation-state system has limited our sense of Self and belonging and left bankrupt our ability to empathize and connect to people beyond national borders and identities. Our understanding of nationalism needs to look beyond the artificial homeyness of belonging to the nation to include the oppressive practices that purposefully create and maintain national borders between and *within* national states. We must understand that the very practices that purportedly affirm Our belonging in the nation are the same ones that allow the Canadian national state to legitimately mark some Others who live there to be socially and legally inscribed as foreign bodies.

Without challenging nationalist thought and practice, justice for (im)migrants left displaced through the operations of capitalist globalization becomes unthinkable. In today's world, where there is a growing level of displacement and international migration, we desperately need to trouble and unsettle nationalized imaginations. As Michael Hardt and Antonio Negri (2000), point out, this calls for new social bodies that are not founded on any of the prevailing myths that sustain the current World Order: social bodies that can create and carry out a real alternative to the way social relations among us are currently arranged. Such bodies would be based not on imposed identities organized through the binaries embedded within ideas of nation, race, gender, and sexuality, but upon radically diverse ways of organizing life across this planet.

Lest this call is heard as wholly utopian, it is worth noting that many in the world today who, while not able to stand *outside* of capitalist power relations in the sense meant by Deleuze and Guattari (1987), are nonetheless fighting to retain ways of being that are antithetical to the values inscribed by the nexus of capitalism–nationalism. Although not all migrants can be attributed with such aspirations, their acts of spatial mobility across borders do assert a will not contained by hegemonic ideas of home, nationhood, and belonging. They harbour a possibility that human beings can recognize their own value and their own autonomy outside of ruling relations. It is within this possibility that hopes for liberation live. It is for the nurturing of this possibility that this book is written.

2 Globalization and the Story of National Sovereignty

Trying to unravel the various ways in which legitimacy is organized for an immigration and labour market program that recruits the majority of (im)migrants entering Canada as unfree, temporary migrant workers begins with an examination of Canadian state practices in this period of neoliberal restructuring. The formulation of Canada's Non-Immigrant Employment Authorization Program (NIEAP) in 1973, through which the legal category of migrant workers is made, took place during a period widely regarded as the starting point of this, the most recent period of capitalist globalization. Since this time, profound changes have taken place in how social relations of ruling are organized in Canada and throughout the world. The further liberalization of global flows of capital, the retrenchment of key aspects of state welfare policies that helped workers decommodify themselves, the deregulation of the conduct of capitalists, and the expansion of capitalist social relations through intensifying processes of proletarianization and privatization have been examined by a growing body of work investigating changes in the relationships between capital, the state, and citizens.

In this chapter, I examine whether the construction of the migrant worker category can be accounted for by prevalent theories that propose that the further globalization of capital has put an end to the sovereignty of the Canadian national state and an erosion of the duties it has to 'its citizens.' As this question defines the debate between those who are ostensibly concerned with the effects of globalization on workers' rights, I further investigate the link between the assumptions embedded within this key debate to see how it helps to frame the problem of globalization in such a way that legitimizes the conditions of unfreedom 'foreign migrant workers' are made to work in, conditions considered unacceptable for Canadian workers. The differences and similarities within the arguments held by those taking either of the two major positions in this debate reveal how the reproduction of the centrality of Canadian national subjects is an effect of both sets of arguments. My hope is that such an examination will tell us how the organization of the category of migrant workers makes sense to many because it is constructed out of the nexus of ideologies of nationalism and capitalist state power that define contemporary ideas of Canada as a national community within its home(land).

The State of Globalization

On one side of the (decidedly masculinized) debate on the Canadian state and globalization, national states are seen as neutered, even hapless, bystanders of 'globalizing forces.' Responding to the 'laws of capitalism,' capitalist globalization is seen to represent the 'triumph' of transnational corporations (TNCs) over the national state and 'the close of the national history of capital' (Teeple, 2000:9-10). Those taking this approach generally see state policies as having been rendered 'meaningless' (ibid.). On the other side of the debate, national state power is seen as more muscular, indeed as the site *through* which globalization has been organized. According to this view, 'nation states are not the victims of globalization, they are the authors of globalization. States are not displaced by globalized capital, they represent globalized capital, above all financial capital' (Panitch, 2000:7).

Those holding the position that national states have been fundamentally, even fatally, weakened with the advent of globalization hold what Evans et al. (1998:9) have termed a 'strong globalization' thesis; *strong* because processes of globalization are thought to have overpowered national state structures. Their shared belief in the structural inevitability of the ascendancy of TNCs over state power is said to result from the formation of a transnational capital class with no 'loyalty' to any national state (Teeple, 2000:10).

Undoubtedly from the 1960s to the mid-1990s there was an acceleration in the globalized character of capitalist enterprises: a fifteen-fold increase of cross-border trade has taken place since this time, and from the mid-1980s to the mid-1990s, alone there was a 500 per cent increase in foreign direct investment (Ruggiero, 1996:2). By 2000 the international trade in goods and services had a combined value of approximately six trillion dollars (U.S.), and TNCs controlled over 70 per cent of global trade (Shiva, 1997:113). One result is that a growing proportion of the world's labour force now produces for globally dispersed markets rather than for 'national' ones (ILO, 1997:3–4). Strong globalization theorists conclude that *because* of these developments, the nation-state is doomed to disappear as an economic unit and a political entity.

Bob Jessop (1993), for instance, argues that in Canada the requirements of a restructured global capitalism have brought about shifts in public policy. To be globally competitive within a field where production has been increasingly internationalized, he argues, the state has shifted its support for a Keynesian-type welfare state to a 'Schumpeterian' workfare state.[1] Such shifts lead Jessop to conclude that a 'hollowed-out state apparatus' emphasizing labour market flexibility and structural competitiveness, provides the best mode of regulation for a post-Fordist regime of accumulation and form of work organization (1993:7, 9; also see Aglietta, 1979, and Lipietz, 1987).

Although Jessop insists that his argument concerning the 'hollow' nature of national states does not mean that they have had their power taken from them by transnational actors, his argument does direct us to such a conclusion. Because of globalizing forces, Jessop (1993:10) contends, power has shifted away from the nation-state in the last decades of the twentieth century towards the private holders of capital. While he says that the state 'remains crucial as an institutional site and discursive framework for political struggles,' Jessop goes on to say that this is 'primarily as a juridical *fiction* reproduced through mutual recognition in the international political community' (ibid., emphasis added). In his view, the post-Fordist state is simply a political tool that serves as a legitimization device for the operation of capitalist power (1993:7, 22). Ultimately, his argument portrays the nation-state as a victim to an increasingly global capitalist class.

Within this approach to what Tanya Basok (1996) calls the 'destatization' of public policy, Stephen Hymer (1979) concludes that the increasing bargaining power of TNCs threatens all states' autonomy but asymmetrically so that the so-called weak states of the 'less developed countries' are more negatively affected than the 'strong' states of the 'developed countries' (Frank, 1967; Amin, 1974). Borrowing concepts from classical Marxist theories of imperialism, as well as from more recent world systems approaches, this variant of the strong globalization thesis presupposes at least a partial conflation between TNCs and the national states of developed countries. This is not surprising given that 70 per cent of all TNCs have their global headquarters in the North, mostly in the United States and Japan (Shiva, 1997). Yet, while it is assumed that the more powerful national states are better able to resist the incursions of TNCs into their spheres of influence, it is maintained that even much of their sovereign power to set national policies has been lost (Hymer, 1979).

While there are numerous and troubling assumptions with the assertion that the recent activities of the owners of TNCs have resulted in their 'disloyalty' and unaccountability to any one national state, I shall focus on one of the more serious problems of the strong globalization thesis: the idea that *prior* to this period of globalization, capitalists were positioned within 'national capitalist' formations and had roots in and loyalty to 'their' national state and, by extension, to the nation of Canada (Teeple, 1995:9). This is an ahistorical understanding of the relationship between national states, capital, and citizens that strengthens ideas of a unified, discrete Canadian society in ways that naturalize ideas of national homelands, even as this nationalized society undergoes neoliberal restructuring. Arguments advancing the supposedly beneficial aspects of national capital romanticize the history of the formation of the Canadian state, the construction of a Canadian nation (with its 'founding races,' later to be called the 'founding nations,' of France and England) and the organization of colonial capitalism within Canadianized territory. In such a view, the social relations of capitalism are depoliticized as the interests of capital are conflated with the multiple and conflicting interests of the population in Canada.

Consequently, this population is imagined as a singular and bounded community, one sharing a national interest in preserving its home in Canada. By redefining the TNCs of another era, such as the Hudson's Bay Company, as 'national capitalists,' there is an erasure of the roots of corporate ventures in the processes of capitalist globalization and nation building of a previous era. The political, financial, and military support given to securing the operations and profits of such TNCs by the British Empire and later the Canadian national state is thus obscured. By naturalizing the symbiotic relationship between some segment of the bourgeoisie and national states, the assistance and protection that these capitalists receive from the state is represented as a legitimate support that the nation extends to a member of its family.

What positioning these capitalists as 'one of our own' does, then, is to screen from view the *global* character of their operations and source of profits. Moreover, since having had one's own national capitalist class is said to have resulted in citizens having greater leverage over their own governance and realizing tangible benefits as a result, such an ideological rendering of the past contributes to the homogenizing tendencies of all nationalist practices, namely, to naturalize the organization of diverse populations as nations and misrepresent them as labouring together for a common purpose. The result is the depoliticization of the exploitations that occur within the global mode of capitalist production and the gendered racialization of class (see Teeple, 1995:15–16).

That Canada was forged out of the desires of relocated elites from 'France' and 'Great Britain' to become heads of their own state is completely elided in accounts of natural national homes. Through such renderings, the Canadian nation becomes a home for Canadian capitalists, with the state acting as the head of the Canadian household. This leaves us with a homey picture of the nation as a *domestic* space, with its own domestic economy wherein the benefits of membership in the dominant group are mistaken as the universal reality for all who find themselves within that national space. In Canada the group whose experiences are made most invisible by such an ideological portrayal of past state and capitalist practices is undoubtedly diverse indigenous people. In the formation and reproduction of the Canadian national state as the homeland for those signified as White, western, and civilized, their economic, social, legal, scientific, and political formations were destroyed (or at least seriously misshapen) (Ward, 1978; Bourgeault, 1989). However, all those constructed as the Canadian nation's racialized, gendered, and sexualized Others have been negatively affected by the Canadianization of space, place, and identity.

In contrast to those advancing a strong globalization perspective, there are theorists who argue that decisions made by those working *within* national states, especially at the executive level, have been integral to the organization of recent processes of globalization. From this perspective it is the political decisions made in various departments of the state – particularly the growing power of departments handling finance, international trade, and foreign affairs – and *not* the structural imperatives of an ever more global capitalist market – that have caused shifts in national state practices.

Evans et al. (1998) call this the 'national voluntarism' thesis because it is thought that over the last three decades the national state has *voluntarily* relinquished its power to international institutions, such as the World Trade Organization, the International Monetary Fund, and the

World Bank to ensure the further globalization of capitalism. Thus, it is argued that the shift from Fordist to post-Fordist forms of production from the late 1960s to the early 1970s took place with much assistance from the Canadian state. William Carroll (1989:87) maintains that

> the Trudeau era of Liberal dominance in federal politics (1968–1984) began at the climax of Fordist regulation, embodied in Keynesian economic policies and the social-democratic rhetoric of the 'Just Society.' But as the Bank of Canada adopted monetarist policies in the 1970s and the federal government introduced deflationary wage controls, tentatively in 1975 and more comprehensively in the '6 and 5' program of 1982–84, a drift toward neoliberalism set in ...
>
> As elsewhere, these moves comprised a macroeconomic *volte face*, from state-supported valorization of productive capital around the mass worker-consumer, to a policy perspective that prioritized the restoration of 'sound money' so as to force 'sound micro-economic reasoning upon the state and society as a whole.'

Within the national voluntarism paradigm, then, the dismantling of the welfare state that began in the late 1960s and early 1970s (with varying intensity and effect) throughout the global North is not equated with the loss of state power but rather as an exercise of its power. Actions taken to bypass the post–Second World War tripartite compromise between state, capital, and labour unions are viewed as evidence of *active* state involvement in facilitating the further globalization of capitalist social relations (Standing, 1989; Brodie, 1996; McBride, 2001).[2]

The national voluntarism perspective places much more of an emphasis on analysing the social relations of capitalism than does the more economistic and reductionist strong globalization school. Neoliberal state practices are seen as driven by the desire to reconfigure the social relations of capitalism to the greater benefit of capitalists, particularly those operating within global markets (Radice, 1984:120). The reorganization of global relations of ruling within a neoliberal framework has been negotiated, it is argued, between various powerful groups of 'employers, bureaucrats and politicians' in and across nationalized societies (Panitch, 2000:5).

The significant difference in opinion between these two schools concerning the scope of state power within processes of globalization leads to disagreement over the future democratic potential of national states. For those who see national states as inherently weakened and always in a position of reacting (usually ineffectually) to the structural ascendancy of globalizing processes, it is no longer considered a viable political site. Thus, for theorists of the strong globalization school, the level of political manoeuvring is said to have moved from a national to a global realm. As the state is enfeebled, so are its citizens. The result is the creation of a 'democratic deficit' and the emergence of ever more powerful 'global' elites with no allegiance to any citizenry.

For those utilizing a national voluntarism perspective who see states as 'acting as the midwives of globalization' (Brodie, 1996:386); however, there remains an attachment to national states as the *only* possible site for the exercise of people's democratic control. Thus, despite the recognition of state participation in the very processes of neoliberal restructuring, the site of politics and therefore of 'society' is said to remain national. Stephen McBride (2001:154) encapsulates this view well in arguing that 'any loss of power by the state is ... a lost opportunity for democratic decision-making.' Once reined back under the control of its citizens, it is argued, the national state can regain its role as the key site of 'local' resistance to powerful globalizing forces (Helleiner, 1994; Evans et al., 1998; Panitch, 2000:12; McBride, 2001; Laxer, 2002).

The debate between these different perspectives continues unabated, while the *similarities* between these two dominant positions have been left unexamined (see Evans et al., 1998). Although those arguing one or the other perspective clearly hold quite divergent views regarding the role of the state, processes of globalization, and the possibility of citizens regaining state power to reverse neoliberal policies, there are two startling convergences in the main conclusions reached by both sets of theorists. These similarities are based in certain shared assumptions regarding the essential character of national state power – at least when it is acting properly – and of nationalized spaces and identities.

First, for both, globalization is theorized as resulting in the *loss* of national sovereignty with the resultant destruction of democratic forms of governance: only in an analysis of *how* national state sovereignty has been lost and whether national democracy can be regained does any disagreement occur. Thus, while national voluntarism theorists see the state as being the author of globalizing process, like those working within the strong globalization perspective, they too view the 'sovereignty' of the nation, including its capitalists, as the ontological subject of their study. Both conclude that, willingly or not, the ability of the Canadian state to set a national economic agenda has been severely diminished.

Such state-centric approaches tend to leave intact the idea that the nation is the 'right and proper subject of history' (Burton, 1997:231). Great emphasis is placed on how processes of globalization in Canada have led to the extension of:

> national treatment for foreign firms which prohibits any kind of industrial or employment strategy based on favouring domestic firms, and opens new fields, such as services, to American corporations; prohibitions on use of the price system in energy to favour domestic interests over exports; inability to discriminate against American banks; recognition of the U.S.'s right to take 'measures of equivalent effect' to compensate for losses caused by Canadian cultural policy; protection of 'intellectual property rights'; weakening the state's ability to set high health, safety, environmental and labour standards; and limits to the state's ability to regulate foreign investment or establish public corporations. (Evans et al., 1998:16)

Globalization, therefore, comes to mean the denationalization and dedemocratization of public policy for both schools of thought. While in the above quote the authors speak specifically about the binding effects of the 1994 North American Free Trade Agreement (NAFTA) between Canada, the United States, and Mexico, generally the problem of globalization for both those working in either the strong globalization or the national voluntarism perspectives is the triumph of the foreign over not only the state but also the imagined community of the nation. This is the second major convergence between theorists using either a strong globalization or a national voluntarism approach.

If the golden days prior to globalization consisted of a time when the triumvirate of national capitalists, the state, and the nation all worked within a single society which they shared and collectively tried to improve, then globalization is seen as the imposition of outside forces into the home space. State practices that limit public policies that are (sometimes) beneficial to (some) citizens are, therefore, regarded as 'internal threats' that along with 'global threats' (i.e., TNCs) have destroyed 'Canadian sovereignty' (Clarke and Barlow, 1998). A globalizing state, then, is a *traitorous* state – betraying the nation by freeing capital from its rightful national moorings.

For both sets of theorists, the rise of global mobilities against the supposedly local, unified, and fixed space occupied by the nation and its state is thought to be symptomatic of the weakening of society itself and even to what Alain Touraine (1997) refers to as 'demodernisation.' Processes associated with globalization, such as the extension of 'national treatment' rights in Canada to capitalists, are therefore portrayed as being 'about restricting or eliminating choice at the *societal level*' (Evans et al., 1998:17, emphasis added). National voluntarism theorists therefore help to extend the argument of the strong globalization theorists that prior to globalization the national state was the singular unit shaping society (Billig, 1995:53; also see Holloway, 1994).

It is accepted that only within nationalized spaces can people be *at home* in society. As such, when the supposedly symbiotic relationship between nation and state is said to break down, society itself is believed to be under attack. While strong globalization theorists generally laud the era when capitalists and economies supposedly met on the terrain of the national state but are pessimistic about the return of this golden era, national voluntarism theorists long for its return and urge people to struggle for a reinvigorated sovereign state. Consequently, both see state support for 'domestic capital' as key to citizens' power and to the realization of democratic principles.

This produces the idea that the Canadian state finds itself constrained or restricted in its own sovereignty *because of* its treatment of foreign capital as if it were Canadian. The logic inherent in this argument presupposes that democracy is having one's home in the nation, that is, democracy consists of the People governed by a strong sovereign state, one, of course, that favours its own capitalists. Democracy therefore means the nation having the instruments of national economic policy, such as tariffs, exchange controls, and direct interventions in industry and finance in the hands of national state actors (Clarke and Barlow, 1997; Cohen, 1994; Dillon, 1991:17).

Together, the two assumptions held in common by those working in the two dominant paradigms – that processes of globalization are a form of 'foreign domination' and that these have resulted in the loss of national sovereignty cum democracy – help to concretize the notion that citizens, including 'corporate citizens,' naturally exist in discrete and autonomous nations made internally cohesive through governance by the nation's state. Such a nationalist approach presumes that some capitalists (those controlling TNCs) operate in a separate field of power from the national state and national capitalists, thereby organizing a tension between those said to inhabit national spaces and those who are global. As in all binaries, national states and TNCs are constructed as *mutually antagonistic*; each holding separate and conflicting sets of interests. The problem of globalization for the Canadian People becomes a problem of *foreigners* usurping national sovereignty.

Such nationalized readings of space are highly exclusionary and limit homelands to some gendered and racialized group of national subjects. In this regard, Akhil Gupta and James Ferguson (1997:7) point out that 'the local is often associated with femininity and seen as the natural basis of home and community, into which an implicitly masculine global realm intrudes.' This hostile global force with its aggressive mobility is also conceived of as a racialized threat since in dominant versions of antiglobalization, production sites in the global South with their 'cheap workers,' often women, are portrayed as the main competition for Our jobs and security. By naturalizing national labour markets and homeland security, the construction of separate national and global spaces reinvigorates the negative duality of a racialized and gendered Us and Them, as such ideological renderings of space and belonging (including who jobs belong to) always exist in the context of a global concentration of power and wealth in the global North.

Through the mobilization of nationalist discourses in the attempt to understand globalizing processes, people come to see themselves as living and working within a national space that is in conflict with a negatively racialized and gendered foreign one. Within this trope of threatened national homelands, it becomes natural that the state discriminate against foreigners, ostensibly foreign capitalists but also foreign workers, thereby naturalizing the discrimination faced not only by those denied entry into Canada but also by those who, like migrant workers, live and work in Canadian society as its non-members.

The contemporary reconceptualization of space as either national or global in this era of neoliberalism is based in the 'conceptual practices of power' organized during the post–Second World War period through Keynesian macro-economic theories (see Smith, 1990). The extension of the Canadian state into ever-more arenas of life through the greater regulation of labour unions and the workplace as well as the extension of provisions to decommodify workers, however stingy, in the immediate postwar era constructed a form of knowledge that naturalized the existence of national economies and strengthened notions of national subjectivities. Hugo Radice (1984:121) argues that this is because Keynesianism operated, in the first instance, as 'an economic theory of the national economy' and that 'the national economy is privileged in Keynesian theory for the purely practical reason that the nation-state system defines geopolitical space with the necessary features convenient for the theory: a common currency, common laws, and shared institutions, both private and public, which provide the common sense to justify the attribution of homogeneity to 'consumers,' 'investors,' the 'public sector,' etc.' (ibid.:122).

Keynesianism thus provided a conceptual framework for the state's favouring of a set of capitalists defined as 'national' and this came to be understood as pursuing the 'interests' of the nation. In this regard, Nigel Harris argues that 'The ideology of the managed economy ... gave labour in the industrialized countries the illusion of control. It seemed that the national patch in principle could be controlled – full employment, rising real incomes and expanding welfare systems could all be attained by skillful direction of the State' (1983:237).[3] By redistributing some of the benefits of the capital's global hegemony to the working class in Canada, such nationalist practices were conceptualized as a paramount objective as well as something that was progressive.

It comes as little surprise, then, that the strongest evidence offered for either the state's current 'meaninglessness' or its 'traitorous' actions in the face of globalizing processes is the dismantling of Keynesian macroeconomic national social welfare policies (Bakker, 1996; Teeple; 1995, Watkins, 1992; Drache and Gertler, 1991). The dismantling of the welfare state therefore has not lessened the appeal of notions of national economies, even in the face of evidence showing how such policies have been highly racialized and gendered, both in their application and in their retrenchment (Fraser and Gordon, 1992; Baines, 2002).

Indeed, for nationalist critics of globalization in Canada, defence of the national economy or the national interest has come to be seen as the main alternative to processes of globalization. In particular, defense of the welfare state in Canada is associated with defence of the nation-as-community (ACN, 1997; Brodie, 1996; Cohen, 1994; ECEJ, 1993; Watkins, 1992). Since 'democratic governance' is defined as being 'tied to communities (nation-states) which are capable of controlling policy decisions and political leaders' (Evans et al., 1998:19), the political goal of many, if not most, antiglobalization actors in Canada (and the world over) has been the call for a restrengthened (arguably remasculinized) national state. This nationalist response to globalization is a predictable outcome of the naturalized nationalism of the Keynesian era, for as Jane Jenson (1989:84) notes, 'The paradigm which helped to stabilize the Fordist mode of regulation in Canada after World War II was organized around national identities ... The social compromises and institutionalized relationships of the welfare state were rationalized in terms of the needs of the whole nation and of the federal system. Therefore, when the Fordist paradigm began to dissolve, it would do so around the issues of national existence and proper state forms.'

Racialized identities of who belonged in the Canadian nation were crucial to the acceptance of growing state power in the post–Second World War period. As Jonathan Hyslop (1999:403) argues, 'the idea of the welfare state as belonging to a 'white' nation was there at the start.' He (ibid.:401) adds, 'welfarism enabled the formation of a ... "national community" which attached the working class to national racial symbols and state institutions.' White women, while excluded from many welfare entitlements through the state's privileging of White male workplace experiences, were nonetheless regarded as 'mothers of the White race' and, as such, as members of national society (Valverde, 1992).

Key to the organization of the current sense of nationalist entitlement, then, is the hegemonic idea that the formation of the welfare state in Canada was a national affair, that is, the welfare state is seen to have come about through the Self-contained work (and struggle) of the White Canadian nation, particularly since in the period of its expansion, non-Whites were still constrained by the 'preferred races and nations' criteria of immigrant (i.e., permanent resident) selection (in place until 1967). Consequently, decreases in the welfare state since the late 1960s in Canada have been predominately represented (in Parliament, for instance) as a result of the permanent settlement of those who are foreign to the nation. Non-Whites have been particularly singled out, as have diverse indigenous people. The dominant presentation of both is that they unfairly 'live off of the system' rather than contribute to it.

This allows us to ignore that the original and continued rationality for the welfare state *as a national* project was organized through the racialization and gendering of the nation for whom social compromises were supposedly negotiated (Fraser and Gordon, 1992). This is not coincidental. As Phillip Cohen (1996:15–18) points out, 'the myth of a golden age ... before the Others came, when the world was a safe and friendly place' has been what organizes the 'rationale for social closure around a racialized model of community.'

In this regard, what many theorists of globalization fail to consider is the fact that national state power and nationalized identities have never existed outside or in opposition to larger spatial relationships but have been constituted *through* racialized, gendered, and classed relations that have always been global in scope. The formation of gendered, racialized national identities through the implementation of welfare reform embody 'a set of *world historical relations* (including a continuing supply of cheap raw materials, especially oil, as well as the existence of labour reserves contiguous to metropolitan regions)' (McMichael and Myhre, 1991:86).

The post–Second World War period therefore has not signified the formation of an entirely new relationship between national and global forces. Instead, it has been characterized by an increasing fetishization of the nation-state. By further entrenching notions of the national economy and national capitalist class, the national state has come to be imbued with the power to protect the nation from outside incursions against its sovereignty – if only it had the temerity to do so. With continued adherence to such notions in this latest period of capitalist globalization, the nation, perhaps even more powerfully than ever, continues to serve as 'the ideological alibi of the territorial state' (Boyce Davies, 1994). Today, declarations of sovereignty continue to allow national states, and those espousing nationalist aims, to conceal the global character of capitalist social relations and, often, their privileged place within them.

The welfare states of the North have been and continue to be funded, in part, from the enormous transfer of wealth from global South to the North. According to the United Nations Development Program (UNDP), approximately U.S. $500 billion is transferred from the South annually in the form of interest payments on debts and the results of unequal terms of trade (in Shiva, 1997:11). Only about one-tenth of that, approximately U.S. $50 billion, flows back to the South in terms of highly condition-laden aid from the North (ibid.). These enormous shifts in wealth take place through the interwoven practices of both private (corporate) and public (national states and international bodies, such as the United Nations, International Monetary Fund, and World Bank) actors.

The Global Arena of Capitalist and Nation-State Practices

This leads me to discuss the most significant point of contention I have with the idea that globalization has led to a loss of national sovereignty or that globalization refers to the dominance of foreign powers in the national homeland. My point is not that the Canadian national state actually *has* sovereignty or that capitalists do not indeed operate within a transnational environment. Clearly, both the national state and capitalists operate in a global field of power and under a global set of constraints. The problem with nationalist approaches to understanding issues of state sovereignty and capitalist power lies in the assumption that sometime before this period of globalization national states were actually sovereign. After all, to have the state's sovereignty either taken by TNCs or to have voluntarily given it up to them, the Canadian state must have once held it.

In such assumptions there is little or no recognition of how the practices of either the national state or capitalists have *historically* been part of the process of capitalist globalization. Instead it is argued that the ascendancy of global processes and with it the destruction of national sovereignty is a relatively recent phenomenon. The term *globalization*, then, is not used historically but is meant to signify that only recently have people's lives been organized through coordinated global activities.

The idea that globalization is primarily characterized by the process of denationalizing helps to conceal the reality that the notion of 'a self-contained ... national capitalism which only later became international, is a mere fiction' (Ruccio et al., 1991:35). Regarding national states as having once been sovereign simply belies the historical record of how state practices have been *a part of*, and not a populist response against, global capitalist social relations. Historically, the nation-state system has not been predicated upon sovereignty, but upon its linkage to a global capitalist system and the structural interdependence that national states – and the people living within their boundaries – have with each other (Wallerstein, 1979). Practices of capitalists (be they mercantalist, industrial, and/or financial) have historically been fundamental to the formation of the global system of national states and what Benedict Anderson (1991) calls a national 'style' of ruling.

Within the formative period for the national state form in the seventeenth and eighteenth centuries, many capitalists were already operating within a transnational space and doing so as *sovereign* entities unto themselves. For example, the Virginia Company established plantations in Virginia, the British Empire's first colony in the Americas, and was empowered to act as police, judge, and executioner of those made to work for it (Linebaugh and Rediker, 2000:29–30). Likewise, the Hudson's Bay Company, given a charter by the British Empire, not only profited from but also administered vast tracts of land in what is now Canada (Backhouse, 1999:53). Diverse indigenous peoples living on these lands were subject to the rule of these companies.

As competition among capitalists grew, previously localized leaderships consolidated their power, and their combined territories were formed into nationalized economies that were artificially enclosed in some ways so as to promote certain patterns of production, exchange, and military action. Significantly, many key aspects of these new *nationalizing* economies and states, of both the most and least powerful, were not contained solely within national boundaries. Markets for capital, raw materials, manufactured products, and, notably, labour, always overreached the scope of the national state. Indeed, so-called national economies historically relied on their continued access to such global markets, be they for gold, rubber, unfree (slave or indentured) labour, or (im)migrant workers' remittances. It was national states that helped to coordinate and administer these global market exchanges. Indeed, I argue that national states ought to be recognized as one of the first regulatory institutions of capitalist globalization.

That national states have always existed as part of a global system is evident in how processes external to the territory have always shaped the social practices that organize so-called domestic life. This is most obviously true for colonized people and lands but it is also the case for colonizing groups. Each 'national society' can only be fully comprehended *in relation* to others: they are integrally linked to each other, culturally, politically, and economically. For this reason, John Holloway (1994:32) argues that national states are a 'territorial fragmentation of a society which extends throughout the world.'

In this regard, it can be said that the entirety of the capitalist era has been concerned with the making of a global space (Habib, 1995; Said, 1993). The making of this global space, moreover, was very much hinged on the formation of national states. The modern Westphalian system of 'sovereign' national states therefore arose in the seventeenth century out of a context of global capitalist colonization with its origins in the sixteenth century and remains wedded to it. From an examination of the existing literature on the creation of the nation-state system, Elizabeth Petras (1980:159) notes that 'prior to the 17th c., fixed borders between political communities did not exist.' Passports and other forms of nationalized identification regimes that gave the national state what John Torpey (2000) calls a 'monopoly of the legitimate means of movement' came even later in the late nineteenth century, and were only fully enforceable on a global scale after the Second World War.

Joseph Nevins (2002:156) notes that 'out of this complex web of rapidly evolving social relations emerged new social identities, most notably those of the national and the alien.' In this regard, Benedict Anderson's (1991:77) observation that 'in world-historical terms the bourgeoisie were the first class to achieve solidarities on an essentially imagined basis' is highly revealing. The development of nationalized spaces was a part of the bourgeois revolution. Indeed, as Michael Hardt and Antonio Negri (2000:76–7) well note, the existence of national space is one of the victories of the capitalist class. Their victory was secured through the formation of identities that were *governable* within their 'new world order.' Instead of the freedom-seeking identities held by the multitude: displaced peasants, the newly formed urban poor, and colonized peoples, the newly formed identity of the national subject allowed for both the weakening of liberation projects and the growing attachment of legitimacy to the national state and its monopoly on lawful violence.

The result, then and now, is the naturalization of global inequalities through violence. As Nevins (2002:154) points out, national 'boundaries are normally not the result of consensual processes. Rather, they typically grow out of violence or the threat of force.' The reliance of transnational companies today on national state militaries to secure the terms, conditions, and potential of their investments is not so dissimilar to the transnational companies of the past that were also global in their operations and relied upon national states for their continued success. The Dutch and British East India Companies, the Virginia Company, and the Hudson's Bay Company are only a few of the more notorious past examples of the close relationship between what musician Gil Scott Heron has aptly called 'the military and the monetary.' The oil companies operating in Iraq today provide more contemporary evidence of this.

Contemporary processes of globalization, then, should not be understood as *jeopardizing* national state power. Rather, as Bina and Yaghmaian (1991:125) note, the intrusion of global capitalist social relations into the lives of more and more diverse communities of people has resulted in an increase in the coordinating and organizing work done by various national states. In this sense, rather than a successive *decline* in national state powers, there has actually been a 'consolidation and extension of the national state' (Picciotto, 1991:53).

It would, of course, be incorrect to argue that no new and significant policy changes have taken place over the last thirty years. However, the current historical shortsightedness of the dominant paradigms used to understand processes of globalization fundamentally delink its latest manifestation from prior processes that can also be seen as globalizing, namely, colonialism and imperialism, the very systems through which nation-states emerged as the dominant global style of governance.

It is an adherence to nationalist forms of consciousness that enables these theorists to leave the historically global nature of the nation-state system unexamined, even when it is the authors' main intent to examine state practices within the context of globalization. Within such perspectives, the previous 500 years of global human history is written out of the story of globalization altogether. For many, globalization can reasonably be seen to be a relatively new phenomenon only because prior to this time, non-White people living in the South were defined as standing outside the centre of world activities. In the last thirty years, the importance of peoples in the South simply cannot be as easily dismissed as peripheral or marginal to the operation of global ruling relations or seen as disconnected from the activities of people in the North. This is because the global South has become a major site of production, and this challenges the supposed centrality of the White male workforce to global capitalism.

The presentation of globalization as heralding a new epoch is, I argue, a White nationalist representation of world events. The lack of historical accuracy regarding processes of globalization in the national voluntarism and strong globalization theses is, I argue, a result of a shared commitment to such a White nationalist project. Within both paradigmatic frameworks, the People whose sovereignty has been eroded by processes of globalization are clearly not Indigenous peoples or other non-White people but White Canadians, again most often White men – the main beneficiaries of the approximate quarter century golden age of nationalist development in Canada. The losses (of land, self-determination, identity, wealth, security, and life) associated with previous periods of globalization, *because* they are overwhelmingly the losses of indigenous peoples and other non-Whites, are rendered unimportant. Not only is this racist, it is also nationalist: it is a White nationalist response.

Such a serious disregard for non-White people is not accidental but *essential* to the perpetuation of the White nationalist view that the Canadian national state is the primary site of democracy and the proper home of the Canadian nation. Maintaining the centrality of Whites as quintessential citizens is crucial to the maintenance of Canadian national state power and the existence of a Canadian society.

This has become increasingly clear to me as, over the years, in one public forum after another, when indigenous or other non-White people are asked to speak about globalization, many do so from the standpoint that what is being termed 'globalization' is, in fact, 'nothing new' but is a process of recolonization (see Shiva, 1997). This is often puzzling, even frustrating, to many Whites in attendance as *their* major concern seems to rest precisely on the events of the last thirty or so odd years. However, the *newness* of endemic job insecurity, ever-declining wages, working, and living standards, the degradation of the environment, the realization that the national state is not working in one's best interests, and so on is experienced as new not by *all* people in Canada but by Whites, and especially White men, in the post–Second World War era. All of these realities have long shaped the experiences of non-Whites in Canada. Of course, these realities have shaped the lives of the working class of those people now signified as White but the ideology of racism has obscured this and given Whites a sense of natural (national) entitlement that such things should not be happening to them but to Others.

As such, to say that Canadians are experiencing insecurity and that these experiences constitute a radical break from the past only makes sense from a White nationalist standpoint trying to rationalize the diminishing power of the White, male working class within both the Canadian nation and global society. Since they are no longer as well represented by the state as during the historic post–Second World War compromise, a call for a reinvigorated Canadian nationalism with its favouring of members of the National Family seems like the only plausible response (Laxer, 2002).

A nationalist response to capitalist globalization has done nothing to diminish the process of capitalist globalization. Its main effect has been to deflect attention away from the causes of the growing violence against non-White people. This is harmful not only to those foreigners said to reside outside of particular national territories, as is brutally evident in the execution of imperialist wars, but also to those rendered as Others *within* the nationalized territory occupied by the nation. Nowhere is this more evident than in the figure of the migrant worker within nationalized labour markets.

National Borders and the Regulation of Labour

It is important to recall von Braunmuhl's (1978:176) argument that constructing the apparatus by which to territorially delimit labour power is one of the two basic principles of national state practices (the other being the regulation and guarantee of the conditions required to reproduce capitalist social relations). The continual assertion of discrete national identities aids greatly in the realization of both these principles, for it gives commonsensical validation to a nationalized labour-regulatory regime.

While capital has historically been able to operate, relatively more or less unfettered, both within and outside of the restrictions of a nationalized space, most aspects of the sale of people's labour power have been regulated by national states. Nationalist ideological practices contribute greatly to the creation and restructuring of national labour markets and the differential categorization of various groups of workers within it by the state. The notion that there *ought* to be separated spaces for differentiated peoples is, in part, what allows for the structuring of competition within what has always been and remains a global market for labour. The reproduction of labour markets *as national* is an important part of nation-building exercises that assist in the reproduction of not only the state but also of global capitalism.

Nationalized labour markets, then, are as much *ideological* boundaries between different 'imagined communities' of people as they are *material* boundaries between different physical spaces controlled by national states. The fact that people's lives are always experienced in *locally* grounded spaces is manipulated through nationalist ideologies that present the nation as some sort of local space and all else as that which is outside of this as foreign to people's experience and exercise of community. Through nationalist claims on jobs in their Canadian home, White workers continue to have more power than those cast as foreigners within nationalized labour markets. What they gain through this is the existential power of being seen to be Canadian and the material affects such an identity organizes. Therefore, privilege and a certain kind and amount of power lies in the hands of those who are seen to be the ones *for* whom national spaces are organized. Establishing mechanisms to regulate people's movement both across and within national borders is a key aspect of producing the nationalist imagination essential to depoliticizing this privilege.

The Canadian state's regulation of people's mobility across its borders through the formulation of immigration policies is what allows it to decompose global labour markets into national units. Immigration policies, because they help to shape the characteristics of the sale and regulation of people's labour power, also assist national states in organizing the circumstances through which capital can be accumulated within the territories they control (Sassen, 1993; 1988). The ways that people's (im)migration is regulated affects the price as well as the strength of those categorized as citizens, permanent residents, or as migrant workers. Indeed, the work that these policies do in the accumulation process helps to explain the tenor of most immigration policy changes in Canada during the late 1960s and early 1970s. These policies have mainly been about shaping the supply of labour in Canada to be more competitive with nationalized labour markets elsewhere.

My argument, therefore, stands in contrast to Evans et al. (1998:17) who argue that 'so far, the most dramatic *withdrawal* of the federal government has been in the labour market policy area' (emphasis added). Their argument presupposes that the state is no longer engaged in regulating the availability of workers in Canada. Ironically, even though they fall squarely in the national voluntarism camp of theorists on the role of the state within processes of globalization, they assume that *only* those labour market policies that are beneficial to Canadian workers constitute state activity.

These two misconceptions contribute to the ideological notion that those categorized as migrant workers are part of a foreign labour force in Canada. However, once we recognize that the Canadian state continues to be active in the arena of labour market policy and that immigration policies are a significant part of this activity, it is evident that Canadian state practices shaping the labour market have not been abandoned but, rather, have changed. One of the main reasons for the shift in policy, argue Storper and Walker, is that 'labour is, on average, the greatest variable cost of production ... [and because of this] firms are becoming more, not less, exacting in their location decisions' (1983:3–4). While their emphasis is on the relocation of sites of production, the relocation of cheapened and weakened supplies of workers is just as important in decisions about where to invest.

Indeed, because of the existence of competition organized through globally differentiated wage scales, most national states have given greater – not less – emphasis to the procurement of whole new labour forces of migrant workers in order to enforce greater restrictive conditions of employment within nationalized labour markets. National state immigration policies, now as in the past, have played a crucial part in this procurement.

Conclusion

The Canadian national state is both powerful *and* lacking in sovereignty. Canadian state practices are part of the globalizing forces that have reorganized social relations over the last thirty years. Indeed, processes of globalization have not taken place in a space existing somewhere outside of Canada but through almost every aspect of state activities. Rather than illuminating or challenging the global character of power, however, the debate taking place between those critically examining the state and processes of globalization have actually helped to abstract it further. Continual reference to the democratic necessity of the state fulfilling its rightful role as the protector of national society has contributed to the naturalization of binaries of national versus global space.

By discursively constructing the global space as a relatively recent phenomenon, a space in which Canada does not exist, the national space has easily been reframed as a place (and a time) when the national family was secure and sovereign, that is, Self-sufficient. By concealing the violent, conflict-ridden history of ongoing nation-building practices of securing the homeland, Canadian state practices have been ideologically reframed as representing the desires of the People. Concomitantly, global space has been conceptualized as foreign and threatening to Canadian society and Canadians. As a result, capitalist globalization has been represented as a foreign problem instead of a problem of globalized exploitative relationships – the same set of relationships that have existed *within* Canada since its formation.

Prevalent theories of the state have further aided in the territorialization of people's consciousness. Such theories have lent progressive legitimacy to practices that discriminate against people on the basis of their categorization as foreigners. In doing so, they have both ideologically and materially helped in the restructuring of global ruling relations. The fact that nationalist practices, instead of working for the benefit of all workers living within the national state, have led to the creation of conditions of *apartheid* within national boundaries and, consequently, to considerably greater competition within nationalized labour markets has been roundly ignored. This is ironic for a group of theorists who for all intents and purposes are most interested in how processes of globalization have reshaped workers' experiences.

The state's power to categorize some workers as foreign migrant workers in order to restructure nationalized labour markets has been overlooked due to the continued nationalization of imagination. The national state is simply not a problem for theorists considering themselves national subjects. This allows most state theorists to continue to be able to ignore the very real, and very negative, results of nationalist practices by redefining them as essential to the protection of the nation.

What is challenged are a particular set of leaders and policies rather than how the national state is a major conduit through which global capitalist power flows.

In this period of globalization, then, nationalism and the practices organized through it are as important as ever in creating ideological unity of a population around the legitimacy of ruling relations, even when such practices work against the interests of the majority of this same population. It is important, then, that we see the continued, even increased, assertion of the need for national state sovereignty as part of how ruling relations that are truly global in reach have been objectified over time.

Having considered how theories of globalization contribute to the reconstitution of a national space and the reconstruction of national subjects who have the only legitimate claims to being at home in Canada, it is time to examine how the ideology of civil society further contributes to the legal categorization of some people who live and work as migrant workers within conditions of unfreedom in Canada.

3 Imagined States: The Ideology of 'National Society'

Nation-building projects, by constructing certain spaces as the homeland of some and not others, act as technologies of making and regulating differences under capitalist globalization. It is through the material force of ideologies of nationalism, and its related ideas of race and gender, that certain people living *within* nationalized societies are represented as existing outside of the boundaries of both the nation and the state, as are migrant workers in Canada. Not only are migrant workers denied the legal entitlements and protections of being classified as citizen or permanent residents but by being seen as *foreign* workers, they are also seen as the legitimate objects of the national state's coercive powers.

In this chapter, I build on my previous argument that seeing national states as whole, discrete societies helps to solidify the national state system for the supposed benefit of those who are seen as its members. By further examining the organization of a consciousness and practice of belonging in the national home, I move to a discussion of how the social regulation of belonging (and, therefore, of *not* belonging) is an essential component of organizing material realities in Canada, including those that organize both a free and an unfree labour force.

Notions of belonging help to legitimize the very existence of the national state and its wielding of power against its foreign objects. State practices work in dialectic fashion to continuously (re)construct national subjects who, in turn, grant legitimacy to national state forms of governance *because* they see the state as an essential component of their own power. This points to the importance of recognizing that the construction and continual reproduction of the nation is essential for the realization of state power.

Such a recognition requires a shift in the focus of analysis from an investigation centred on the 'state' (its structure, policies, and so on) as a discrete entity within national society to one looking at the social practices of *governing* or *ruling*. Antonio Gramsci's (1971) concept of hegemony, Michel Foucault's (1991) discussion of governmentality (or governmental rationality), and Dorothy E. Smith's (1990) concept of relations of ruling all encourage such a shift. Each emphasizes governance as a *practice*. Each pays attention to the *social* organization of a certain way of thinking and acting directed at variously making, regulating, or concealing the rule of some over others. In all of their work, there is an acknowledgment of the importance of abstracting lived experience in order to exercise power.

While Foucault does not use the concept of ideology in describing this process he, like Gramsci and Smith, is interested in how at the heart of techniques of maintaining power lie practices that take out of the realm of the contestable the everyday political, economic, social, and cultural practices of governing. This process of 'normalizing' is similar to the Marxist understanding of the concept of ideology used by Gramsci and Smith. Ideologies are thus understood not simply as a set of certain thoughts or phrases but as a *method* of organizing the material world (Marx and Engels, 1969:18–19).

In this, Smith (1990:35, emphasis added) advances Marx's work by arguing that 'ideology names a kind of *practice* in thinking about society' whereby primacy is given to *concepts* over the social relations that arise in and from people's activities. In particular, ruling is organized in such a way that power is abstracted and categories come to stand in for the actual people whose lives are ordered by them. For instance, in nationalist ideological practice, the everyday lived experiences of people are transformed into objectified forms of knowledge where categories, such as citizen or migrant worker, come to substitute for lived actualities. Naming someone a migrant worker is no longer seen as a *social* process but as an embodiment of what that person actually is. In this, the differences organized between those categorized as migrant workers, citizens, or permanent residents is naturalized. Such an abstracted view of everyday life obscures the connectivity that exists between differently categorized people and how these categories occupy the same social field – that of the national state.

Foucault's discussion of self-regulation within practices of power – that there is a particular kind of Self that is important to construct and to maintain if power is to be reproduced – is also of use in accounting

Journal

for the construction of people as migrant workers. This is because such an understanding of power no longer sees government as simply a part (or even the sum) of the state apparatus(es). Instead, governing occurs through the organization of certain kinds of identifications and the subsequent material relationships between people that these engender. However, Foucault's insight into the importance of self-regulation needs to be reworked so that we not only pay attention to the kind of Self that is organized by the architectural frame of binary codes but also examine the organization of particular kinds of requisite Others. This is because when investigating the making of some people into migrant workers, it is important not only that a particular kind of Self (the citizen) is necessary but also a particular kind of Other (the foreign worker). Disciplinary modes of power, therefore, not only create docile bodies that can be governed but also bodies that even the docile can imagine themselves as ruling over. Within the national state form of power, national subject-Selves are disciplined into ruling over, through state practices, those seen as foreigners in their home.

In making the shift from studying state power to studying practices of governance, it therefore becomes important to radically deconstruct the liberal rhetoric that defines the state as being of 'all and each.' Instead of simply asserting that not all are equally served by state practices (i.e., that the state is discriminatory), we need to recognize that processes of Self-regulation are also about how those represented as Canadians regulate the existence of people rendered as Others. This sheds further light on how in Canada White nationalist ideologies ensure the power of national state practices and secure the legitimacy of state controls on immigration and citizenship. It also demonstrates how the simultaneous existence of both a Canadian-Self and a foreign-Other in both the legal-juridical space as well as the ideological space of Canada is vital to the ability of rulers to rule.

In Canada, only those representing themSelves as White have been able to unproblematically assert their membership in the Canadian collective. Nationalism in Canada has worked, in large part, to construct a racialized sense of home. Whether in the form of special head taxes for people (im)migrating from China (1886–1924), restrictions on the number of people, particularly women, from India (1908–45), China (1886–1945), and Japan (1908–45), the Chinese Immigration Act that banned the entry of people from China (1923–47), to the setting up of dichotomies between preferred and non-preferred races and nations until 1967, racialized membership in the Canadian nation has been rein-

I do not agree

forced so that people from the global South are seen as a particular danger to the 'character' of the nation (see chapter 6).[1]

Analysing relationships among differentiated groups in Canada as only a racist form of practice, however, is insufficient. Such practices of Othering are better understood as *nationalist* practices that are most concerned with the proper spatial allocation of differentiated people across the globe. As Ghassan Hage (2000:28) points out, nationalist practices 'assume, first, an image of a national space; secondly, an image of the nationalist himself or herself as master of this national space and, thirdly, an image of the 'ethnic/racial other' as a mere object within this space.' Studying the racialization of people within nationalized space as nationalist practices, therefore, allows us to discuss the spatial character of power in the practices of Othering and the territorialization of subject – and object – identity.

Within such a discussion, it is important to remember that not all those currently signified as White have always been welcome members of the nation. Whiteness, because it is a social identity that is relative to one's relationship to power, shifts along with shifts in power. Yet, it is equally important to understand that the construction of an overarching White identity has been crucial to rulers' attempts to impose unity on the very disparate groups included in the category of Canadian. Indeed, it is a strategy that has worked all too well to ignore. Whiteness works as a ruling identity precisely because it is *relational*. Whiteness becomes a privilege because it is positioned higher on the value scale of racialization than is non-Whiteness. Thus, while most of those who participate in the process of Othering non-Whites in (and outside of) Canada are also ruled over in a myriad of ways, it is important that we not discount the important part played by practices of racialized, in this case White, nationalism in realizing exploitative practices – against both non-White and White workers.

In other words, an examination of how White Nationalism helps to organize and legitimize the state category of migrant worker is important not because the state is a discrete entity or an instrument of one particular group's (e.g., Whites) interests but because state practices are a *form* of social relations in which certain people have been rendered as part of the National Family and others as outsiders to this. In this chapter, then, I try to uncover some of the methods of governance that make it possible to have certain, identified groups of people live and work in conditions that are seen as antithetical to the very character of Canadian society. Such a disjuncture between lived experience and ideological concepts are perhaps nowhere more evident than in the construction of citizens (and permanent residents) as free members of national civil society while migrant workers are unfree foreigners in the same society that many of them call home.

'Civil Society'

Liberal styles of governance, unlike previous historical domains of ruling, are particularly concerned with the ideological construction of a civil society *for* whom the state is said to rule (Marx and Engels, 1969; Foucault, 1991). Civil society is the 'imagined community' of the nation and as such is said to have *made* the state, which then governs on the nation's behalf as an autonomous and objective force for the 'common good.' The concept of civil society thus presupposes that the state, in upholding the rights of citizens *represents* the nation. With the general acceptance of such assumptions, 'the transcendence of the law, of which the state is cast as the revocable custodian, is dissolved; law now becomes the historically relative emanation and expression of society' (Gordon, 1991:32). And since the nation appears to its members as an accomplished fact, it ex post facto justifies state practices done in its name (Bamyeh, 2002:3).

The legitimacy of modern state power within liberal democracies is therefore rooted in it being widely regarded as flowing from popular public consent. Concomitantly, the People are touted as holding the power to revoke this legitimacy. Not only do these related ideas conflate the existence of the national state with the political rulers of the moment, it also obfuscates how the history of national state formation was born of struggles over land, labour, and life, struggles lost by those who fought against processes of colonialism and proletarianization and for common, rather than private or public (i.e., state) property.

Ideological notions of civil society that legitimate state practices have historically been constructed through the architecture of nationalism and, as such, help to concretize the commonsensical notion that there is one group (national subjects) *for* whom the state rules and another group (foreign objects) that it rules *over*. Michael Hardt and Antonio Negri (2000) show that notions of the state ruling *for* the nation have always been instrumental in upholding the legitimacy of the state. In the initial period of national state formations, the idea of the state ruling for the civil society of the nation worked to counteract the revolutionary potential of the project of modernity, namely, that power was not transcendent (located in divinely ordained rulers) but imminent and located within social relations. Within challenges to the fixed, hierarchical organization of life was the demand that the resources of material life be equally redistributed.

Such radical thoughts, and the actions mobilized through them, were countered by bourgeois contentions that it was not they who were the new rulers but that it was instead a unified group of the People who came together as a nation (Hardt and Negri, 2004). The idea that the power held by the People was to be wielded by their representatives located in newly formed proto-national state institutions was advanced. The liberal democratic national state, therefore, was camouflaged as an institution, indeed the *one* institution, designed specifically to *serve* the new social entity of the nation. The discourse of the national state existing to service the common good, rather than as an apparatus of *ruling*, was therefore a key accomplishment of liberal democratic forms of governance. It embraced the People into the everyday operation of power and in so doing ensured the twinning of nation with state that is unique to modern forms of governance. With the consolidation of the national state form in the late eighteenth century, the focal point of most debate has been on the proper definition of the common good rather than uncovering the locus of usurped power.

Central to the establishment of what this common good entails is what Benedict Anderson (1991) refers to as the 'limiting' of the nation or identifying *who* constitutes the People. This has never been a straightforward geographical calculation since the criteria of establishing who the People are and who are the foreigners are not ones concerned with the physical insides and outsides of national states alone. Instead, both are wholly existential and ideological categories that are mobilized to name entire populations as either being at home or not at home within national space. Thus, though it is often assumed that members of the nation live within the spaces claimed by it (or ought to) while foreigners live outside of them, history shows us that constructing and taking action against people represented as foreigners *within* the national homeland have more often been a spur to nationalist activity than socalled external threats have been (see Hyslop, 1999:405).

The process of making some people foreigners within nationalized spaces is more than a social process, however. It is given material force through state practices of assigning legal categories of membership and non-membership. The distribution of rights within national states falls along these lines of status with national citizens being granted the greatest privilege and the lack of rights of those classified as *non-members* is seen as legitimate. While this is true to a certain extent with regard to those who have been given de jure citizenship status but are not seen as rightful members of the Canadian nation, such as non-Whites in Canada, it is most pertinent for those who the state officially classifies as foreigners – the non-immigrants, the non-members within Canadian society. It is this category of people, the one where we find people classified as migrant workers, who are seen as the most legitimate objects of the coercive powers of the state.

State actions against foreigners are among the easiest to legitimate to the members of national society. The existence of foreigners, especially within, can even be said to be *necessary* for the reproduction of nationalized forms of consciousness and therefore of the existence of national state forms of ruling: as the foreigner is made, so too is the national subject. In this way, the power mobilized through nationalism is not centralized within state apparatuses but is diffused to some extent throughout the population rendered as being at home in Canada.

Thus, the state has not been the only active participant in the Canadian nation-building project. Rather, those who have what Hage (2000) calls a 'managerial' sense of being at home in the Canadian nation have contributed in ruling over foreigners within Canadian national territory. In Canada, as in other White settler societies, Whiteness, as a positively racialized national identity has been crucial in who comes to have a sense of managerial entitlement. A 'fictive community based on Whiteness,' Peter Linebaugh and Marcus Rediker (2000:209) point out, has, since at least the eighteenth century, been essential to the exercise of liberal democratic power. This is because the formation of a White identity helped to construct differences – and put a halt to disruptive solidarities – between the many people exploited in the process of consolidating European colonization and expanding the social relations of capitalism (Linebaugh and Rediker, 2000). In place of solidarities based on lived experiences of a common exploitation, Whiteness, as a shared identity helped in the formation of subjectivities and solidarities on the basis of racialized categories.

The process of racializing certain groups of workers as Whites and Others as non-Whites worked rather well. As Hyslop (1999:405) shows, throughout the nineteenth century a shared ideology of racism among the ruling and working classes came to be hegemonic. Racism ensured access for a now *White* working class to key and relatively privileged parts of nationalized labour markets throughout the British Empire. In this respect, the formation of a White (and masculinized) working-class consciousness took place in a global space beyond that existing within the newly constructed boundaries of national state. However, it was through national state intervention that such a consciousness was materialized in the capitalist mode of production. The development of racialized labour markets, in particular, those labour markets designated as belonging to Whites, was absolutely bound to ideologies of a shared White national subjectivity. Thus, as Hyslop (1999:414) argues 'the pressure for a stronger boundary to "Whiteness" also came from below, and was not merely imposed by upper class advocates of "national community."'

During this period in Canada, state practices relied upon White men and women within non-state organizations, such as Christian churches, organized labour, and collectives of emergent feminists to secure governance in a newly articulated Canadian society. These social–political–cultural–economic formations were a significant part of the establishment and concretization of the ruling relations embedded within practices of White nationalism. For example, years of pressure from organized labour led to state practices that differentiated between Whites and non-Whites (im)migrating to Canada (Ward, 1978). Capitalists' specific opposition to restrictive immigration policies, based on their collective realization that these would deny them unrestricted access to cheapened supplies of negatively racialized workers, enabled White workers in Canada to see their anti–non-White immigrant practices as both a sign of their membership in the nation and as anticapitalist. Likewise, White suffragettes argued for the benefits of civil citizenship rights based on their being the 'mothers of the White race.'

Whites, thus, made their claims on the Canadian national state on the basis that they were 'racial partners in empire' (Hyslop, 1999:405). White workers demanded that the state represent them as Canadians in order to protect their relatively privileged position within global capitalism. The fact that state practices did distinguish between Whites and non-Whites in every field of public policy helped to make sense of the idea that the Canadian state ruled *for* Whites as a distinct group *over* Others. Such White nationalist practices helped secure for the Canadian state an almost complete sense of legitimacy in the eyes of those signified as Whites and in so doing ensured the reproduction of global capitalist social relations (Valverde, 1991:26).

Citizenship and Freedom: The National Formation of Free and Unfree Labour

Nowhere was this more evident than in the set of relationships marked by the related concepts of freedom and unfreedom. Historically, the 'free-born,' with their ambitions of achieving a broader franchise and greater rights, took on the identity of the respectable 'citizen-worker' to advance their claims. As is evident in the term, 'free-born English-man,' the very first assertions of a free legal and personal identity were simultaneously racialized, ethnicized, gendered, and, importantly, nationalized. Since freedom as a concept only emerged as a negation of conditions of unfreedom (namely, slavery and indentureship), the assertion of being free was always made in relation to those Others who remained unfree (Patterson, 1982:95).

In the process, those left to labour under conditions of unfreedom were also rendered as foreigners within the spaces that the free claimed as their home. Thus, the process of existentially and materially locating some workers as free occurred through the project of national-izing identity. It was through the ability to legitimately claim (and be granted) membership in national civil society that certain people were freed. Indeed, being free and being White together helped to define emergent nationalized subjectivities within a global system of capital-ism. Together, these discrete and exclusive identities worked to nullify any solidarities born of the shared lived experience of the emerging global proletariat.

In the initial period of capitalist development, conditions of unfree-dom were the typical conditions of work for most agricultural work-ers, plantation workers, sailors, and those in the handicrafts, whether they were from what came to be known as Europe, Africa, Asia, the Pacific Islands, or the Americas. Until the eighteenth century, most workers laboured under conditions of servitude as service meant being bound to one's master (Linebaugh and Rediker, 2000:76). Servants and slaves found themselves sharing much of the same material reality: exploitation, terror, brutal labour conditions, and an early, often vio-lent, death. In this context, 'the distinction, often made, between selling [one's] labor as opposed to selling their persons [made] no sense what-soever in real human terms' (Patterson, 1982:97). Both servants and slaves considered themselves to be defined by the constraints imposed against them: they were unfree.

Initially, the struggle against slavery and for freedom was often a common one. Distinctions between those suffering from the enclosures of common property, indentured servitude, forced plantation labour, and the slavery imposed upon those pressed into military or commercial service were not generally made. Quite the opposite: solidarities were explicitly expressed. For example, Gerard Winstanley, in struggling against the various Acts of Enclosure in what was quickly becoming defined as 'England,' 'saw that justice could not be a national project, nor could the commons exist in one country only' (Linebaugh and Rediker, 2000:141). Likewise, for the Levellers, in their *Agreement of the People*, neither the citizen nor the nation was the subject of struggle against the enclosure of the commons (ibid.:235). Rather, theirs was an undifferentiated demand that truly 'one and all' be delivered from slavery.

It was only later, as the revolutionary hopes of the 'motley crew' gave way to those, like Oliver Cromwell, who agitated for a British parliament that ideological practices of nationalism destroyed the solidarities wrought of shared lived experiences. The 1659 English parliamentary debate on slavery and the free-born Englishman, held just prior to the restoration of Charles II and the Stuart monarchy, was a serious setback for struggles born of radical cosmopolitanism and workers' solidarity (ibid.:132). It was therefore in the context of *counter-*revolution, the early formation of the national state system, the emergence of doctrines of liberal democracy, and the further entrenchment of the African slave trade that the trope of the free-born Englishman became part of the expanding vocabulary of White supremacy. Indeed, it was during the counter-revolution in England and the period following it that a consciousness of race, gender, and nation grew and flourished throughout the various parts of the British Empire.

The nationalist impulse dictating the shift was clearly part of a ruling strategy to offset the threat of those demanding a common freedom and a future without rulers. In the period when the trade in African slaves was becoming more integral to the profits of investors in incipient transnational corporations, as Hilary Beckles points out, 'what planters feared most of all was a rebellious alliance between slaves and servants' (in Linebaugh and Rediker, 2000:126). These fears were real, as there were countless examples throughout the Americas, Africa, and Europe itself of groups of self-organized workers joining in collective, non-racialized, and non-nationalized struggles against capitalist exploitation.

The ruling strategy to destroy such organized attempts at self-rule entailed codifying tenets of White supremacy into the new laws being put into place to regulate an ever-growing number of European colonies. Much of this centred on racializing and later nationalizing the relationship between freedom and unfreedom. Legal distinctions between Whites and non-Whites were put into place through the comprehensive British Slave and Servant Code of 1661. Through it, White servants were legally differentiated from Indigenous and Black slaves. Those classified as servants were offered some benefits and protections made unavailable to slaves (ibid.:127). Servants were ultimately remade into a sort of a labour aristocracy of artisans, overseers, and members of the militia. The ability for White workers to gain their freedom, along with the steady decline in the practice of White servitude, led to a growing chasm between newly formed Black and White subject identities (Fredrickson, 1988).

The result of these kinds of legislative measures was the coming together of the emergent concepts of race and freedom with those of gender and nation (or citizenship). Freedom, therefore, was a key organizing concept that allowed working men to imagine themselves as White, particularly in White settler colonies, such as the United States and Canada where they were part of the large non-slaveholding White populations and therefore closer to power than were the now non-White and unfree labourers (Frederickson, 1988). Of course, Whiteness was not simply left to their imaginations to conjure up. Their White identities were actively constructed and institutionalized through national state citizenship laws, such as that of the United States which in 1790 restricted citizenship to 'free white persons' (Nevins, 2002:102).

In the nineteenth century the ascendant social and legal identity of the newly free-born Canadian man borrowed heavily from such ideas and such practices. The freedom of Canadian men was organized in stark contrast to the continuing unfreedom of Indigenous men and women, Blacks, Asians, and at times immigrant White women (Bourgeault, 1989; Parr, 1990).[2] In claiming their freedom White, Canadian men often made the argument that *they* should not have to work under the same conditions that the negatively gendered, racialized, and nationalized Others did (see Li, 1988; Chan, 1983; Warburton, 1981). From their Self-identification as Canadians, they argued, should flow certain rights that Others *should not* enjoy.

Significantly, in the interplay of racism, sexism, and nationalism, people made to work within unfree employment relationships were reconstituted (in varying degrees) as *foreigners*. Indeed, it can be said that the freeing of White male workers, but not their Others, contributed to the further *strengthening* of racialized and gendered understandings of membership in the Canadian nation. One would not be recognized as a full-fledged member of Canadian civil society, or fully enjoy its entitlements, unless one was a free White male. Consequently, instead of being recognized as part of the national community of civil society, Indigenous people, other non-Whites and, at times, White women, were increasingly considered as *rightfully* governed *over* not only by employers but also by those workers now designated as free and *their* representative state. Thus, not only the existential but also the legal and material privileges that White men enjoyed vis-à-vis the Other were increased through the 'invention of free labour' (Steinfeld, 1991). The most lucrative parts of the labour market in Canada were secured for free Canadians, that is, White men.

Consequently, the existence of conditions of unfreedom did not stem exclusively from state practices designed to assure capitalists a supply of labour, as historian H. Claire Pentland has supposed (1981), or to assist in the cheapening and weakening of that supply. Neither did they arise solely out of state practices that attempted to handle the class conflict between capitalists and workers (Poulantzas, 1978). Instead, notions of freedom and unfreedom were integrally related to the interplay of relations of nationalized, racialized, classed, and gendered domination and subordination in Canada. As Roxanne Doty (1996:185) notes, the practices of freed worker-citizens to differentiate themselves from Others can be seen as 'a kind of statecraft from below wherein 'authentic' citizens [were] motivated to engage in governmental practices that reproduce[d] territorially bounded identities as natural and given.'

Indeed, it was the social acceptance of legally differentiating and ranking people through hierarchical categories of nation, race, and gender that led to the development of Canada's famed 'high wage proletariat' (see Panitch, 1981). That only a small subset of White, male workers in Canada could hope to be included within its ranks was clouded by scholars (and critics) of capitalism who took too literally the notion that free wage workers alone constituted the capitalist labour force. Their insistence on centring the experiences of this 'labour aristocracy' as typical of the position of all workers within capitalist social relations resulted in a serious error in conceptualizing both the historical and continuing significance of unfree employment relations to capitalism.

For instance, writing at a time when many indigenous people and Blacks throughout the Americas were enslaved and the trade in Asian peoples as coolie labour (i.e., indentured workers) was growing,[3] Karl Marx (1977:274), advanced the argument that capital could 'arise only when the owner of the means of production and subsistence finds the free worker available, on the market, as the seller of his [sic] own labour-power.' Marx went on to say that 'this one historical pre-condition comprises a world's history. Capital, therefore, announces from the outset a new epoch in the process of social production' (ibid.). However, capitalism clearly did not wait for freedom, although the rapid globalization of the labour market that it spurred on certainly led eventually to distinctions being made between freed and unfreed workers by the national states that regulated this and other markets.

Marx's misformulation of free employment relationships as necessary for the emergence (and reproduction) of capitalist social relations continues to inform many contemporary studies of unfree labour (Sharma, 1997b). Despite the historical and contemporary reality that unfree employment relations are as global as capital, they continue to be regarded as peripheral to the capitalist world economy. Indeed, the exploitation of people's labour power under unfree conditions is seen by some as a 'relic' of feudalism (Ruccio et al., 1991; Meillassoux, 1981:46; Pentland, 1981) or as a 'necessary anomaly' within otherwise free capitalist social formations (Miles, 1987; see also Luxemburg, 1951). This has contributed to concealing the social struggles and processes that have made workers either free or unfree.

For the most part, this is done through the failure by most scholars to include the experiences of those working in unfree employment relationships within the political economy of capitalist labour markets or within analyses of immigration policies. However, even when such employment relationships are explicitly addressed, some continue to argue that any relationship that does not involve the direct selling and buying of free wage labour is non-capitalist even when unfree workers are working within capitalist labour markets (Ruccio et al., 1991). Thus, people forced to work under unfree conditions are seen as not only marginal to the societies where they work, but the imposition of conditions of unfreedom upon them is interpreted by some as an indication of the 'backwardness' of the very people made unfree.

Claude Meillassoux (1981) has been the most forthright in arguing that the people whose labour power is bought under unfree conditions are *themselves* part of precapitalist social relations (also see Pentland, 1981). Adapting (perhaps overly stretching) the conceptual framework of 'articulated modes of production' developed by Rosa Luxemburg

(1951),[4] Meillassoux argues that migrant workers working in the capitalist economies of the North ought to be considered a part of a *precapitalist* mode of production. In making this argument, he implies that individual migrant workers actually *embody* an entire mode of production that, with them, migrates to the countries in the North. Thus, Meillassoux (1981) advances the idea that wherever unfree migrant workers may work and whatever they may do, they are repositories of a precapitalist social formation by virtue of the fact that they are not free.

Rather than examine the ways in which socially differentiated groups of workers face differential state regulations governing their employment relationships, Meillassoux thus categorizes unfree workers themselves as precapitalist.[5] Unfreedom becomes part of the baggage a migrant brings with him or her. Thus, the responsibility for their unfreedom seems to rest with them. Such notions help to secure the process of rendering as wholly Other those who are made unfree in the same society in which citizens are able to live and work as free labour. However, people themselves cannot *embody* an entire mode of production, be it precapitalist or capitalist. No single worker, or even group of workers, can transport with them an entire mode of production.[6] Instead, a mode of production is defined by the ways in which surplus is produced and controlled, or in Marx's words, 'the direct relationship of the owners of the conditions of production to the direct producers' (as cited in Bottomore et al., 1983:337).

David Goldberg uncovers some of the ideological practices at work in conceptualizing unfree migrant labour as distinctly precapitalist by linking it discursively to notions of certain racialized people as being premodern. He also notes the significance of liberal democratic ideologies of civil society within the binary of free and unfree when he states that 'the self-conception of "modern man" as free, productive, acquisitive, and literate is not delimiting of racism's expressions but a framework for them. It forms the measure by which racialized groups are modern and deserving of incorporation, or premodern and to be excluded from the body politic' (1993:108-9). Goldberg is rare in his ability to connect the imposition of conditions of unfreedom with ideological practices of racism and nationalism. Most other scholars of freedom and its binary opposite remain entrenched in the type of political economy approach that does not pay sufficient attention to the material force of ideologies. Two of the more influential ones are Philip Corrigan and Tom Brass.

Philip Corrigan (1977) maintains that the organization of people's labour power through unfree employment relationships is a part of the most recent phase of capitalist reorganization. Corrigan (1977:441) argues that the exploitation of unfree labour power cannot simply be seen as a feature of an early stage of capitalism or a feudal relic appended onto capitalist economies when there are shortages of free wage labour. Instead, it is a pervasive and integral part of capitalist expansion itself. Thus, Corrigan (ibid.) contends that 'the expansion of capitalism, in fact, hinges on the introduction on a very large scale of unfree forms of labour.'

In this, Tom Brass (1988) concurs. He shows that, oftentimes, it is the *surplus* of workers that sets the parameters of state practices that help to organize unfree employment relationships. This is not to say that unfree labour is not used during times of labour shortages, but like Saskia Sassen (1988:87), he points to the double meaning of the notion of shortages. Shortages do not always refer to a *quantitative* or actual lack of workers but the shortage of a particular *kind* of work force, that is, cheap, politically repressed, and so on. Robert Miles expands on this insight by arguing that 'the precondition for labour migration was a shortage of labour within the capitalist economies of Western Europe which could only be "solved" by recruitment within the various social formations by increasing wages to attract workers from other economic sectors. Such a solution would have obstructed the capital accumulation process, and so another source of labour power from outside these social formations was sought' (1987:167).

For Brass, these kinds of capitalist restructurings of national labour markets helps to successively weaken the working class within the global North and expand the use of unfree labour:

> It is precisely in the combined circumstances of anti-union legislation, compulsory 'training'/'retraining' schemes for youth and the long-term unemployed, the replacement of welfare provision with workfare, cutbacks in the social wage, declining real wage levels, and the rising unemployment now occurring in the [Northern countries] that the linkage between an oversupply of workers and unfree relations becomes important. In short, this development challenges the assumption that the expansion and operation of the industrial reserve army necessarily leads to and takes the form of an extension of free wage labour. (1988:186)

Brass argues that the reimposition (or the continuation) of unfree forms of labour power should be seen within the context of the attempt by employers to secure (or increase) their profits and to further weaken the strength of workers:

> The advantage of work force restructuring ... where *externally* recruited labour is involved – permits them [employers] first to lower the cost of the *local* work force by *importing* unfree, more easily regulated, and thus cheaper *foreign* labour, and then in turn to lower the cost of the latter when the original *foreign/local* wage differential has been eliminated. In this way, conditions and payment of both components of the work force can be decreased continuously, and the level of productivity/profitability (or rate of exploitation) correspondingly maintained or increased. (1988:188, emphasis added)

In talking about 'importing' workers and regulating their unfreedom and cheapness, there is clear recognition of the importance of state practices to the existence of unfree employment relations. Corrigan goes even further and argues that the imposition of conditions of unfreedom, in fact, make 'state control visible' (1977:444). However, because of the tendency of both Brass and Corrigan to pay insufficient attention to the work of state practices in organizing differences between so-called local and external workers, they take for granted that there naturally exists a group of people known as foreigner workers. This is due, in large part, to the lack of attention paid to the interlocking ideological processes of racism and nationalism in securing the unfreedom of some workers (and the freedom of others). This results in a failure to investigate the social relations and practices of White nationalism in the national states of the global North that organize the foreignness *and* consequent unfreedom of certain *migrating* people within a labour market naturalized as free. Such a gap results from the tendency to see the creation of conditions of unfreedom as resulting solely from the common economic strategies of the bourgeoisie and the state apparatus. This is evident in Brass's assertion that it is the class struggle between labour and capital that shapes the use and scope of unfree labour (1988:186). While this is certainly true, it is only true in the very broadest sense.

Such an argument neglects to examine the set of social relations that makes it possible to have some workers be free(d) while Others are made unfree. The approach taken by Corrigan and Brass leads them to focus on how unfree foreign workers are used by capital and the state to negatively affect local workers who are free. The assumption is that the free(d) do not have any effect on the unfree or that concepts of freedom themselves do not provoke such a situation. This is apparent in Corrigan's (1977:448) assertion that 'migrants also serve political ends; lacking the most elementary 'civil rights,' denied membership of a trade union – what better vanguard against the organized labour movement could be found?' While focusing on how the state is able to utilize practices of unfreedom to restructure labour market protections for free workers, he fails to question either the effect of legalized unfreedom on migrant workers or how the practices of free workers may contribute to their unfreedom.

While Corrigan is able to recognize that the vulnerability of migrant workers is caused by how they are denied membership in the state, he ignores the importance of White nationalist practice to the existence of conditions of unfreedom. Consequently, he does not question the social process through which migrant workers are made ineligible for most, if not all, of the rights associated with national membership *and how this is widely legitimate*. This is because, in his work, there is a tendency to naturalize the process of differentiating between citizens and migrant workers and to take for granted that conditions of unfreedom are first imposed upon certain (im)migrants.

Thus, there is ultimately a failure to connect the formation of restrictive (im)migration policies with broader social relations within receiving countries. This leads to a more serious flaw in both Corrigan's and Brass' work: the failure to understand that freedom and its antithesis are both legal-juridical *and* social and ideological categories, categories fundamentally informed through ideologies of nationalism, racism, and sexism. It is these everyday or 'banal' forms of discrimination that organizes the legitimacy for their legal-coercive consequences.

It is precisely *because* unfree employment relations in Canada are currently organized exclusively through immigration policy that it becomes even more important to uncover those ideological practices that distinguish between Canadian and foreign workers. To do so the binary concepts of freedom and unfreedom need to be unpacked and the social relationships informing them exposed. After all, there exists only *one* labour market in Canada, a labour market in which differences of nationality and immigration status – each reliant on ideologies of proper homelands for discrete, unified populations – organize the legitimacy for highly varied wage levels and access to protections.

The work of Immanuel Wallerstein is of some help in this regard. He argues that slavery, debt bondage, and other forms of unfree labour under capitalism can be viewed as 'modes of labour control' (Wallerstein, 1979:33). He asks whether capitalism should not be seen 'as a system that combines within its economic arena some firms largely based on contractual wage-labour and some (even most) firms based on one variant or another of coerced or semi-coerced semi-wage labour?' (1976:1212). However, as is clear from the previous quote, within Wallerstein's work there is a tendency to see contractual wage-labour as non-coercive.

Here, the work of Orlando Patterson is of more use, for he sees all forms of exploiting another's labour power as entailing the use of force. He maintains that 'in the course of human history there have been two polar extremes in the idiomatic handling of the coercive aspect of power. One has been the tendency to acknowledge human force openly, then to humanize it by the use of various social strategies such as fictive kinship, [and] clientship ... The other extreme has been the method of concealment, in which coercion is almost completely hidden or thoroughly denied. Indeed, it is even presented as the direct opposite of what it is, being interpreted as a kind of freedom' (1982:39).

These insights extend the work of Marx – at least in his discussion of the fetishism of commodities. Marx provides us with the insight that in the capitalist mode of production the fetishism of commodities is a social process that acts as a 'fantastic form' to conceal the *social relational* aspects of power and exploitation. These are hidden from view through the idea that relationships between people are merely relationships between the inanimate objects that workers make and capitalists sell (1977:163–77). Indeed, Marx sees the concealment of the social relations that organize capitalist production as going some long way in explaining how it is continuously reproduced.

Regrettably, Marx failed to expand his critique of bourgeois economists who make a fetish of the *products* of labour to his understanding of the commodification of labour power itself (1977:164).[7] Instead, in making strict distinctions between free and unfree labour and associating only the former with the capitalist mode of production, Marx argues that *only* free labour is commodified: only the relationship between free waged workers and their bosses are *abstracted* (also see Miles, 1987[8]). Of course, the corollary to this is the notion that the use of force in compelling people to work as unfree labour is not abstracted and is fully visible to all.

Marx, and those who follow his lead in this area, do not address the fact that in those capitalist societies where labour market freedom is said to be the normative employment relationship, it *has* been – and widely remains – legitimate to have *certain* people work as unfree labour. While the exploitation of free labour power may very well be concealed through the operation of the ideology surrounding the concept of freedom (although this is not always the case), the exploitation of unfree labour *also* remains concealed in Canada (and elsewhere) through the operation of various ideological practices.[9]

Robert Steinfeld's work (1991) addresses the fact that freedom has comfortably existed alongside unfree employment relationships and helps us understand how freedom has come to be distributed within the capitalist labour market.[10] Through a historical examination of employment relationships in both England and the United States between 1350 and 1870 Steinfeld helps to blur the sharp distinctions made between free and unfree labour not only by challenging the notion that only free labour is abstracted but also by troubling the widely held assumption that free wage labour constitutes the natural employment relationship within capitalism. Instead, Steinfeld investigates how the modern *conception* of free labour emerged. In doing so, he exposes the tautological nature of the argument that free labour is more economical and efficient than the exploitation of unfree labour power, as Marx and others have maintained:[11] 'for centuries, all forms of labor operated under legal duties that obligated them to complete their contractual undertakings. In those circumstances, it is difficult to imagine what the proposition that free labor was more efficient than unfree labour could have meant. Only after the possibility of free labor in the modern sense had begun to emerge could that argument begin to be put forward' (1991:112). This insight is substantiated through an examination of the period of laissez-faire capitalism in England. During this time, any supposed logic said to exist in the emergence and consolidation of the capitalist system was not incompatible with the continuation of unfree forms of labour power in England. Indeed, Steinfeld writes that in eighteenth-century England, 'not only did the old Tudor contract clauses continue to be enforced but the new market spirit moved Parliament to supplement the old clauses with new statutes aimed at stopping contract breaking in certain *increasingly commercialized* sectors of the economy' (ibid.:113, emphasis added). Furthermore, 'far from being inconsistent with the logic of contractarian market individualism ... indentured servitude actually represented an expression of that logic: a private bargain between autonomous individuals in which one sold the legal right to his [sic] capacities for another for a term in exchange for a valuable consideration' (ibid.:90–1).[12]

In other words, unfree labour power was no less essential to capitalist societies than was free labour. It was not freedom that defined the emergence and entrenchment of the capitalist mode of production but the creation of a labour force through the destruction of the commons and the freeing of people from their own means of production. In fact, as noted earlier, not only was there an ongoing use of people as unfree workers, these types of employment relationships actually *expanded* and *intensified* in the shift to capitalist social relations (Linebaugh and Rediker, 2000).

Statutes legislating unfreedom in England remained in effect until 1875, when criminal sanctions for premature departure from a contracted place of employment were eliminated (Steinfeld, 1991:115, 160). Consequently, in England and in North America free labour emerged as a supposed voluntary form of working. This, too, was more an ideological rethinking of capitalist employment relationships than an indication of material changes in the experience of work. On this matter, Steinfeld notes that even after the statutes legislating freedom came into effect, 'on entering employment ... a worker's labor still became the employer's. While the relationship continued, the employer was legally entitled to command that labor as if it were his [sic] own. And in the same way that the fruits of his own labor were his, so too were the fruits of his employee's labour' (ibid.:156).

Seeing the free employment relationship as normative came about not only by reference to those labour practices it was understood to include but also by the institution of slavery and indentured labour by which it was contrasted. And in this regard, freedom was highly dependent upon both one's racialized and nationalized classification. As Patterson (1982: 96-7) writes, '[freedom] ... an ideal cherished in the West beyond all others emerged as a necessary consequence of the degradation of slavery and the effort to negate it. The first men and women to struggle for freedom, the first to think of themselves as free in the only meaningful sense of the term were freedmen. And without slavery there would have been no freedmen.'

Thus, it was not the *eradication* of unfree forms of labour that caused the emergence of free labour but the *continued* presence of unfree employment relationships that allowed for the imagining of free labour. The process by which free labour was normalized, therefore, was both relational and highly ideological as it was founded in the emergence of national, liberal styles of governance.

Conclusion

While it is clearly necessary to blur the distinctions between free and unfree in order to examine how they are mutually constitutive, at the same time, it is important to understand how some workers remain free while others are rendered unfree within nationalized labour markets. In order for us to make *good sense* of the construction of migrant worker as a category in Canadian society during this latest period of capitalist restructuring, then, we need to account for changes not only in public policies or material conditions but also in the way that social relations in Canada have been organized. We need to untangle how the category of migrant worker operates as an 'ideological narrative' (Smith, 1990:92). What are the technologies used to deny a group of people organized as migrant workers the rights held by Canadian citizens and permanent residents with little, if any, threat to the legitimacy of the Canadian national state, these categories, or to commonsensical understandings of the character of 'Canadian society' and its supposed 'values' of freedom?

To answer this question, we need to begin by taking up Patterson's (1982:97) request to 'challenge our conception of freedom and the value we place upon it' and examine its link to the creation and reproduction of national state forms of governance, in particular, the idea of civil society which reinforces the limits of national boundaries. Nation-building projects, thus, not only continuously construct 'imagined communities' governed by the apparatus of states, they also render people as governable subjects or objects. Debates structured between various, elected political representatives of the Canadian state are particularly instructive in examining the discursive efforts to continuously reinforce a Canadian identity and, therefore, a non-Canadian one. Next, I will examine the significance of the discursive practices of parliamentarians in Canada's House of Commons to the realization of the category of migrant worker.

4 Canadian Parliamentary Discourse and the Making of 'Migrant Workers'

In the late 1960s and early 1970s the territorial as well as ideological boundaries of the Canadian nation and its state were imbued with great import. In this period, widely recognized as the beginning of the most recent phase of capitalist globalization, ideas of freedom became more strongly linked to those of nationness – and therefore to foreignness. It was in the interplay of these two ideas that the differential allocation of existential as well as material resources was organized according to ever more delineated categories of (im)migration status. While presented as disconnected from the other significant policy changes taking place, the major shifts in state policies concerning citizenship and immigration were informed by the restructuring of Canadian public policy in all areas that affected the relationship between state, capital and labour.

Concomitantly, the reorganization of state policies took place within a broad, international environment of increased competition for capital investment and growing trade liberalization. It was an environment that Canadian state policies helped to organize. In particular, by restructuring key pieces of legislation shaping trade and investment, Canadian state practices not only responded to but *facilitated* a growth in international competition for capital investments. Indeed, substantial material and political aid was organized through Canadian state practices for capital investors operating both within and outside of Canada, including tax breaks, capital grants, changes in regulations governing the sale of labour, and the introduction of the Canadian Export Development Corporation that insured capitalists' investments.

It is within the nexus of these restructurings that the category of migrant worker was consolidated and legitimized, and the people made to live and work as migrant workers were rendered homeless in Canada. The making of migrant workers, however, cannot be understood wholly through an analysis of the political economy of late capitalism. Instead, we need to link changes to the material structure of how capitalism was done at this time to how it was understood and how it was legitimated. For this, we need to examine the discourses that organized the governance of people as migrant workers in Canada and how this was related to the governance of Canadians.

A common theme in all policy changes at the time was the emphasis on shifting the multiple meanings of national membership in ways that helped to legitimize greater competition within global markets for both capital and labour. Whether one was considered inside or outside of Canada and its markets for capital investment and labour, or whether one was embraced by its liberal democratic principles, law had little to do with whether one actually lived within the boundaries established by the Canadian state or outside of them. Instead, global relationships of racism, imperialism, and patriarchy shaped how differently categorized people were socially and legally positioned both within and outside of Canadian society and the claims they could make on the state. These relationships were brought together within the ideological frame of nationalism so that the organization of discriminatory treatment of people on the basis of their (lack of) immigrant status was naturalized and, therefore, depoliticized.

In the five-year period preceding the introduction of the NIEAP (1969 to 1973), debates among parliamentarians helped to organize a major discursive shift regarding who was and was not a member of the Canadian national community. The constitution of current processes of globalization was accomplished, therefore, not only through a restructuring of the global political economy but also through the legitimization of a different rationality of national state power – one that worked to restructure the criteria of membership in the nation. This is evident in the discursive construction of the need for an expanded and consolidated foreign migrant workers program in Canada – the Non-Immigrant Employment Authorization Program (NIEAP) introduced on 1 January 1973 – in Parliament.

For this reason, rather than taking a 'case study' approach to understanding migrant workers in the labour market in Canada, it is important to shift the investigation onto the cultural level and examine both the making and *making sense* of the overarching category of migrant worker. Examining the cultural level in which the category migrant worker is organized helps to explain *how* it is that the Canadian government can create a category of non-citizens, such as migrant workers, who are legally positioned as unfree, indentured labour, with relatively little outcry, even tacit or explicit support, from much of the rest of the population living and working in Canada.

Such an investigation necessarily begins from the starting point that people categorized as migrant workers do not enter a 'neutral ideological context' when coming to Canada (Miles, 1982). Rather, the ideological practices mobilized by the category migrant worker connect to already existing ones concerned with putting different people in their place in Canadian society. The articulation of various ideological practices legitimates the subordinate positioning of migrant workers in Canada in such a way that the relations of ruling are reconfigured for changing circumstances. Examining the rhetorical process by which certain people and certain kinds of social relations are made into problems for Canadians while certain legitimate solutions are also constructed within the parliamentary debates helps to reveal the character of these new realities.

A textual analysis of these debates shows that one of the greatest problems discursively produced in Parliament in the five years preceding the 1973 introduction of the NIEAP was the problem of foreigners and the damage done to the 'prosperity of Canadians' by their competitiveness with Us in various markets – markets for capital, for labour, and for 'national cultural capital,' that is, the requisite criteria for being recognized (socially and legally) as belonging to the Canadian nation (see Hage, 2000:52). Foreigners, it was said, made it more difficult to fulfil the state's goal of attracting and/or retaining capital investments in its territory. Constructing foreigners – either foreign national states or more likely foreign workers – as *the* problem facing the Canadian nation allowed the various parties in Parliament to place this goal itself out of the arena of contestation.

Paradoxically, a key solution to the presence and competitiveness of foreigners *within* Canadian national state territory was to make foreigners out of the majority of migrants entering Canada to work. That is, the problem with foreigners in Canada was that they had become too Canadian. Shifting the immigration status of a large portion of people helped with this problem, since non-immigrant or migrant workers, unlike immigrants entering Canada with the rights and entitlements of permanent residents, were both discursively *and* legally made into 'foreign workers.' With no legitimate claims to being at home in Canada, those made into migrant workers also had no legitimate claims to make on the Canadian national state. Occupying the physical space of Canada but expunged from its ideological space, they were a vanguard of the emerging post-Fordist labour force – flexible, competitive, and readily disposed of.

The Parliamentary Production of Globalization

Analysing debates regarding the work of the newly merged mega-ministry of Industry, Trade and Commerce provides an important geo-political context for understanding the construction of the migrant worker category. In 1969 the new minister, Jean-Luc Pépin, back from a recent meeting of the Organization for Economic Cooperation and Development (OECD), reiterated agreements made there by the representatives of the Canadian state. He informed Parliament that the three priorities of Canada and the OECD were to respond to the expansion of international trade, the simultaneous growth in multinational corporations and the mobility of capital investments, and shifting 'relations with developing countries' (*Hansard*, 18 February 1969: 5635–6).

The Canada Export Development Corporation (CEDC) was heralded as one way for this ministry to respond to all three priorities. By enhancing state assistance to capital investors, the CEDC helped to restructure the global capitalist economy towards export-led growth. Designed to financially assist private enterprises in the hopes of making Canada more 'internationally competitive,' its first task was to insure exports from Canada, especially those to developing countries. Exports from capitalists operating in Canada were initially insured for up to $750 million, to be increased to $850 million by 1973.

The CEDC was also designed to ensure that capitalists based in Canada profited from the production of commodities *in* developing countries. In discussing this feature of the CEDC, MP Otto E. Lang, speaking for the Minister of Industry, Trade and Commerce, stated:

> The [Canada] Export Development Corporation will be the focal point for the government's interest in the financing of exports and in the insurance of private investments abroad. In succession to the export Credits Insurance Corporation, it will administer new and expanded facilities for export credits, export credits insurance and guarantees, and will encourage and facilitate the provision of private financing for export. It will be charged with responsibility for the insurance of private Canadian invest-

ment in developing countries. This entirely new facility is being added in the belief that such investment can make a meaningful contribution to our international development effort and at the same time improve the competitive position of Canadian firms in world markets, and should therefore be facilitated. (*Hansard*, 14 April 1969:7474)

By insuring Canadian investors in the global South for hundreds of millions of dollars against loss of profits, parliamentarians made the Canadian state liable for producing stability for capital investments in these countries. Thus, political and military intervention in the policies of other states, especially those in the South, was legislated as part of the work the Canadian state was authorized to perform. In keeping with the prevalent discourse on aid, and demonstrating its relationship to private profitability, doing this in the name of aid to developing countries helped parliamentarians represent such state practices as benevolence to impoverished people in the South instead of investors based in Canada.

The expanded scope of the CEDC, and the greater mobility it provided for the capital of investors, is one example of how parliamentarians provided mechanisms that structured greater global competition for investments. Such legislation established the framework through which Canada needed to become more globally competitive. Calls for reductions in so-called non-tariff barriers, such as higher levels of wages and corporate taxes in Canada, soon followed, resulting in cuts in corporate tax rates and arbitrary freezes of wages in union collective agreements (alerting us to the fact that current state practices in this regard are not new).

Alongside shifts in state practices supporting export-led capitalist development, there were concomitant shifts in state *ideological* practices. Parliamentary discursive practices, by producing a particular framework to make sense of these changes, helped to abstract people's consciousness of the restructuring of both their subjectivities and their material reality. These ideological practices worked to reframe state practices that led to greater power for investors and variously less for different groups of workers as necessary for what John Turner, then Minister of Finance, called 'Canadian prosperity' (*Hansard*, 2 March 1973:1833).

The ability for parliamentary discursive practices to produce the commonsensical ideal that globalization, or as it was then known, 'the need to be internationally competitive,' was of ultimate benefit to the

Canadian nation rested on the construction of a zero-sum game between Us-Canadians and those rendered as the foreign-Other. In tried and true fashion, by conflating the interests of capitalists with those of the imagined community of Canadians, parliamentarians used nationalist ideologies to abstract or objectify the ongoing reproduction of ruling relations. Parliamentary practices that worked to bring about further capitalist globalization with its increased competition for investments, therefore, rested on the performance of state practices as a *nationalist* response to foreigners. In the process, space was bifurcated into two ideologically discrete national and international (later to be called global) units resulting in a reconstitution of the Canadian nation on whose behalf state power was supposedly wielded.

Nationalist ideological practices were legitimized through a three-fold process. The first one predated British prime minister Margaret Thatcher's campaign slogan that claimed 'there is no alternative' to becoming more internationally competitive. The second was to expand the definition of 'Canadian capitalist.' The third was to problematize foreign workers in other countries. All three were mobilized to help make common sense of the increasing competitiveness of markets for capital investment and growing attacks against the security of workers in both the global South and North. Significantly, in Canada, competition was defined as *'foreign'* rather than *systemic* to capitalist social relations, thus making the antagonism between Canadians and foreigners appear natural and depoliticizing critiques of what MPs called, the 'new reality.'

In the early part of the period that I study (1969 to 1973), Canada's New Democratic Party, supported by MPs from the Quebec-based Ralliement Créditiste, were champions of what I call the 'Canada for Canadian capitalists' approach (Sharma, 2000a:166–8). However, this was soon eclipsed by the governing Liberal party's notion that 'all capitalists are (at least potentially) Canadians' (ibid.:169–71). The first approach centred on the position that capital investments in Canada should be owned and controlled by Canadians lest We lose control over the political machinery of the state. Those adhering to the second 'all capitalists are Canadians' view held that all investments made in Canada and even those investments made outside of Canada with the assistance of the Canadian state ought to be considered Canadian. The latter came to dominate. In one example, when discussing whose businesses were eligible for state-funded financial grants, a governing party MP stated, 'the eligibility criteria are concerned with the nature of the firm's business and prospects and not with the country of residence of its principal or owner' (*Hansard*, 1 April 1970:5878).

Such a shift constituted a movement away from Keynesian-style ideological state practices that emphasized the strengthening of national capitalists who were understood to exist in inherent conflict with foreign capitalists. In the representation of all capital as potentially Canadian, the nationalist framework was not eclipsed however. The prosperity of the national economy remained the focal discursive point. Moreover, with the redefinition of who constituted a Canadian capitalist, the focus was ideologically shifted so that foreign competition became a competition between workers rather than between capitalists or even national states. In the organization of globalization, it was only workers in other nationalized spaces, and not capitalist investors, who were imagined as a foreign threat for Canadians.

It was these workers against whom the borders needed to be maintained and even strengthened. This was especially pronounced in regard to workers in the global South who were said to be victimizing Canadians. Workers who had had the worth of their labour devalued by colonialism, racism, and sexism – as well as the commodities produced through their exploitation – were cast as the villain in the nationalist trope of global capitalism. International differentials in wage scales came to be regarded as 'unfair competition' (instead of just unfair) and, following 1970, parliamentary discourse came to be centred on the issue of what the proper solution to this *foreign* competition was.

Two opposing positions came to the fore but both were based on the assumption that foreign workers were indeed the collective problem of the nation. A growing number of MPs complained about the negative effects on Canadians arising from the import of goods made by low-waged workers outside of Canada. Thus, one solution was to penalize the products entering Canada made by people who came to be objectified as 'cheap foreign labour.' Along with the inclusion of concessional financing, Canadian state practices shifted to include products made by cheap labour to the definition of actions that constituted 'dumping.'

Demands for the restriction of imports from 'low wage countries' were made within the nationalist discursive framework that posited such actions as necessary for preventing foreign workers from taking jobs from Canadians. Significantly, agreement on this solution crossed class and party lines. For instance, one MP raised a concern expressed by both the Canadian Association of Chemical Producers and the International Garment Workers Union. Both wanted to know what parliamentarians intended to do about the threat that increased imports from low-wage countries posed to 'Canadian jobs' (*Hansard*, 5 February 1970:3238).[1] Indeed, it was around the issue of *who* was entitled to work that the problem of foreigners was most vociferously organized. For instance, NDP MP Harold Winch argued: 'thousands are out of work there [Vancouver] because as a result of the severe winter logs are not available to meet the needs of the sawmills and processing plants. Yet ships are today loading unprocessed logs there to be exported to other countries [for processing] ... The key to the Canadian economy lies in ... seeing that *Canadians are employed first* before *we* export raw materials, that *our* manufacturers are assisted first' (*Hansard*, 14 April 1969:7488, emphasis added).

The argument for Our-people-first policies naturalized the power that capitalists (reframed as Our capitalists) exercised. While Winch's statement is one example of the 'Canada for Canadian capitalists' approach, more importantly, it produced the ideological notion that Canadians were becoming increasingly unemployed *because* Our resources were being taken by foreigners to be processed by foreign workers. A corollary to this argument centred on concerns over the movement of production and assembly sites to where labour power and other costs of production were cheaper (see *Hansard*, 5 February 1970). In this scenario, too, foreign workers were constructed as the problem that threatened Our prosperity.

Importantly, in both cases while the notion of who constituted a Canadian capitalist was debated in the House of Commons, the idea of foreign workers being our collective problem went unchallenged. Either way, foreign workers were represented as taking Canadian jobs. The production of the notion that Canadians were first and foremost entitled to jobs helped to further entrench the ideological contention that while markets for commodities were global, labour markets remained national. And it was the Canadian state's responsibility that things remain this way.

This can be seen when in a spectacular display of double standards MPs of all political parties decried the imposition of tariffs on products made in Canada while arguing for the imposition of similar tariffs on products entering Canada that they deemed to be produced through 'unfair' means, that is, lower production costs, cheaper labour, and so on. For example, at the same time that charges of dumping were levied and higher tariffs placed on the import of textiles from Mexico, parliamentarians argued that the Mexican government must reduce tariffs on exports of highly state-subsidized agricultural products from Canada (*Hansard*, 5 December 1969:1634; 4 December 1970:1759). Indeed, throughout the period of my study, Canadian parliamentarians consistently asserted the sovereign right of the Canadian national state to impose whatever measures it deemed necessary while simultaneously putting into place practices that challenged or destroyed this same right of other national states, further demonstrating the ideological dimension of the concept of state sovereignty.

The second, related solution to the problem of foreign workers discursively organized through the parliamentary debates was making Canadian workers more competitive with foreign ones. This was to be done by simultaneously decreasing wages and weakening both minimum standard and collective bargaining structures in Canada. By 1969 discussions on the importance of wage and price controls in Canada had begun (see *Hansard*, 8 May 1969:8465–6). This is evident in the commissioning of research on comparative labour costs per unit of output in 1969 by Minister of Finance Lloyd Benson. Speaking within the context of the problem of decreasing business investments, Benson discussed the report's finding that, since 1965, labour costs in Canada were consistently higher than in the United States (*Hansard*, 3 June 1969:9492).[2]

The Minister of Finance linked higher wages to the winning of increased wage rates by unionized workers in Canada. Benson stated that 'negotiated increases in average annual wage rates under major collective agreements (excluding construction) rose from 5.7 percent in 1965 to 8.7 percent in 1967, moderating only slightly to 8.1 percent in 1968' (ibid.:9489). The growing influence of monetarist policy, which presented inflation as a threat to the 'Canadian public,' helped to legitimate decreases in wage levels and other solutions that negatively affected both the living standards and power of workers: 'we agree the time has now come to establish a yardstick against which to measure the reasonableness of wage and salary increases in relation to productivity and other relevant factors in an effort to end the relentless and damaging cost-price spiral which continues to plague the economy. Equally important is the fact that such guidelines would provide the Canadian public with a yardstick against which to judge the reasonableness of future wage and salary settlements in relation to the public interest' (Benson, *Hansard*, 8 June 1970:7818). The Finance Minister added: 'there is a considerable danger that a continuation of the current substantial increases in wages and salaries will seriously undermine the initial progress we have made in slowing down the rate of price increases ... Dr John Young, Chairman of the Prices and Incomes Commission, proposed to ministers that the federal and provincial governments join in supporting the adoption of guidelines to establish reasonable upper limits on wage and salary increases in present economic circumstances' (ibid:7818).

By identifying increases in workers' wages as a major cause for the supposedly collective problem of inflation, parliamentary discursive practices produced the notion that workers refusing to take pay cuts were working against the collective interests of Canadians. Thus, at the same time that state financial (and other) aid to capital investors was growing, Finance Minister Benson urged 'all Canadians to be modest in their demands on the economy, and not take more out of it than is being put in through increased productivity' (Hansard, 11 July 1969:11098).[3] While this solution challenged the so-called post–Second World War compromise of increased wages for unionized workers in exchange for their compliance with state legislation limiting the power of organized labour, it was presented as strengthening the nation's ability to be internationally competitive (see Hansard, 25 November 1970:1461).

When trade union organizations, such as the Canadian Labour Congress, did not consent to being 'modest in their demands' for higher wages and other protections gained through collective bargaining, most parliamentarians presented this position as unpatriotic. The position of unions was portrayed as signifying a lack of cooperation in the supposedly collective project of fighting inflation. Hence, Benson stated, 'we have been greatly disappointed that the leaders of organized labour have declined to join representatives of other sectors of the economy in helping to work out the terms of an agreed approach' (ibid.:7818).

In his response, Benson indicated his commitment to the reorganization of global capital along monetarist (later neoliberal) lines. Indeed, the Canadian state response was not out of line with much of the global North at this time. Shortly after Canada's move to limit wage increases for unionized workers, in September 1971, U.S. President Richard M. Nixon imposed a wage freeze (see Hansard, 13 September 1971:7743). Aside from showing how such domestic public policies were not specific to any one nation-state but extended throughout the North, these approaches also highlight how the restructuring of ruling relations at this time was centred on ensuring the existence of a certain type of relationship between employers and workers – one that gave employers both greater control over workers and a larger profit margin. Indeed, a wide range of shifts in Canadian state practices at this time can be attributed to the restructuring of the employment relationship.

This was apparent even in 1969, the year seen as the high point of the Canadian welfare state (McBride, 1992). At this time Prime Minister Pierre Elliot Trudeau laid the groundwork for future cuts in state assistance to social programs and stated: 'There will be a definite program of expenditure cuts that will have to be discussed with the provinces in order that they realize that some of the important programs will have to be curtailed. It is a matter of cutting into expenditures and programs which are now in existence and which will have to be curtailed. If we want to make cuts everywhere except where farmers, fishermen, urban dwellers and old age pensioners are affected, it will be difficult to fight inflation; this is a perfect example of the vested interests in the opposition' (*Hansard*, 9 May 1969:8515). Not only were these cuts, which had the effect of both reducing living standards and options to paid employment for a wide array of producers, portrayed as necessary for the prosperity of the nation, opposition to them was tantamount to having 'vested' interests rather than the national interests that the prime minister stated were his and that of Parliament. Moreover, by continuously conflating the interests of business with the interests of some imagined group called Canadians, calls to assist investors were portrayed as that which the state owed to the nation.

To summarize the argument advanced thus far, within the seemingly contradictory solutions to making Canada more 'internationally competitive' (increasing financial and political aid to capital investors and dismantling the institutions of the Keynesian welfare state) the discourse of Us-Canadians versus Them-foreigners was mobilized. In each scenario it was the foreigner who represented the greatest threat to Canadians and Our collective prosperity and against whose competitiveness the imagined community had to rally. However, the problematization of foreigners occurred in opposing directions: capital was increasingly freed, not only to cross nationalized borders but also increasingly freed from nationalized identities. For workers the opposite occurred: greater boundaries between the subjectivities of 'domestic' and foreign work forces were constructed.

In essence, nationalized boundaries became even more permeable for capitalists: no capitalists could be defined as foreign if they operated within Canada or with the assistance of the Canadian state. Foreign national states were judged – and periodically problematized – on the grounds of whether they were better or worse than Canada in attracting investment. They were also evaluated on whether they acquiesced to fully embracing the capitalist market system and its restructuring through the embrace of export-led development aggressively being advanced by Northern-dominated institutions such as the Organization for Economic Cooperation and Development, the International Monetary Fund, the World Bank, and the United Nations (Tomlinson, 1991). However, it was foreign workers who were consistently problematized as Our greatest threat, primarily for being 'too competitive.'

The antagonism between Canadians and foreigners was organized by simultaneous references to sameness and difference. Equating capitalists' interests with the interests of Canadians was one way sameness was reimagined. The creation of the problem of foreigners that debates in Industry, Trade and Commerce helped to organize, were indicative of the social organization of difference between workers in various national states. Through this two-fold process, the idea of a naturally existing Canadian nation itself was reproduced. In this sense, through their discursive portrayal of themselves as representatives of the People, parliamentarians re-enacted the nation and through this re-enactment, legitimated the performance of state power. Indeed, the discursive practice of constructing that which was Other and foreign and that, therefore, which was Canadian was a significant aspect of how state practices were able to situate Canada as a continuing site for capital investment.

Together, then, changes in both Canadian public policies and the organization of a nationalized common sense of this reorganization drove 'globalization.' Intensifying capitalist competition by restructuring economies in the South away from import-substitution towards export-driven models and the dismantling of the welfare state in Canada were all put together during the period I have examined. Not coincidentally, corporate profits rose. It was enthusiastically reported in Parliament that by the third fiscal quarter of 1973 corporate profits had risen by almost 60 per cent from 1968 (*Hansard*, 2 November 1973: 7476).

The Foreign Threat Within

In the parliamentary debates of this period (1969 to 1973), the foreigners said to be threatening Canadian prosperity did not exist *outside* of Canada alone. Rather, parliamentarians also helped to organize a problem of foreigners existing *within* the space occupied by Canadians and ruled over by the *Canadian* state. This was nowhere more evident than in the debates on immigration policy. This is because such policies, more than others, relied on tropes of nationhood and nation-state sovereignty for their legitimization.

By linking the existence of a foreign presence in Canada with a 'weak' immigration policy and associating the presence of 'new immigrants' with both the lessening of the quality of life for Canadians and a threat to Canada's national sovereignty, a common sense was organized that produced immigrants, all of whom were given permanent residence status upon entry to Canada, as foreigners residing in Canada. Throughout my period of study, the recasting of the problem of the foreigners-within as a problem of *immigration* was racialized. That is, the dual construction of a homogeneous White national identity and a homogeneous non-White immigrant foreignness was realizable only through the discursive production of racialized difference, one, however, that relied on nationalist tropes of natural homelands for variously racialized populations.

Parliamentary discursive practices related the problem of foreigners-as-immigrants to the removal in 1967 of the previous 'preferred nationalities and races' policy that favoured European, especially White British and other White northwestern European, immigrants. After 1967 non-Whites were not only allowed to enter Canada but to enter as *permanent residents.*[4] Prior to 1967, many non-Whites had indeed entered, worked, lived, and died in Canadianized space; however, many did so without receiving the formal rights of permanent residency or citizenship. It was shortly after the 1967 elimination of explicit racialized/nationalized entry criteria for non-Whites that the legal term, 'immigrant' was ideologically reframed as a negatively racialized social category – and a major social problem. Of course, this carried great consequences for the category of Canadian as well.

The following remark points to how parliamentarians produced a racialized common sense that these immigrants were the collective problem of Canadians. MP Steven E. Paproski, in responding to Immigration Minister Allan MacEachan, a Cape Breton MP, who had just presented his annual report to Parliament concerning the immigration numbers for 1969, stated:

> The Cape Breton mountain has laboured and brought forth a West Indian mouse. I would be the last person to criticize, on grounds of race or colour, an immigration policy that emphasized the bringing in of West

Indian and Asiatic immigrants. But I do believe it is legitimate to criticize a policy that concentrates on immigrants who, by reason of climatic conditions in their country of origin and by reason of their standards of skill and training, inevitably pose great problems for everyone concerned with their relocation in a radically different, highly sophisticated, industrialized, urban society such as ours. (*Hansard*, 16 December 1969:2013)

Paproski presented a highly racialized reading of the effects of immigration policy, clearly relying on various pseudoscientific, racist theories of White supremacy whereby entering Canada was akin to becoming modern. However, more importantly, immigration policy at this time did *not* actively give legislative preferences to people from particular countries (as it did for people from northwestern Europe prior to 1967). Instead, the elimination of racist criteria simply allowed non-Whites who were previously denied on the basis of these criteria to be accepted as immigrants. Moreover, the interest of White immigrants to enter Canada had decreased in the post–Second World War era due to the expansion and enrichment of European and U.S. labour markets for these workers. However, by stating that the Minister of Immigration '*emphasized* the bringing in of West Indian and Asiatic immigrants,' Paproski presented the operation of Canadian immigration policy as if it was completely disconnected from these and other factors and that it did actively recruit non-Whites in particular.

Together, Paproski's discursive strategy of using blatantly racist statements as well as misrepresenting the factors leading to shifts in who entered Canada as immigrants, helped to reorganize the existential constitution of the category of people named as immigrants. In this sense, the ending of racialized and nationalized criteria for immigration, because it ended the legal protection of state-organized racist nationalisms, led to the accentuation of discursive strategies such as Paproski's to socially position negatively racialized people as a national problem. Again, this process of racialization[5] was organized by both producing difference and similarity.

In examining those who were represented as being the same as Canadians, it is clear that this consisted of White Europeans or White members of other White-settler societies, such as the United States or Australia. During my period of study, there was never any question about whether *these* people should be welcomed (or even encouraged) to immigrate to Canada. Despite the formal elimination of the 'preferred races and nationalities' criteria of Canadian immigrant recruitment policy, then, Whites were still constituted within Parliament as 'preferred' people. This was apparent in the juxtaposition of two separate questions in Parliament concerning two racialized groups of people, one Scottish and the Other so-called gypsy. The first case concerned two men from Scotland, James and Alex Donald, and their families, all of whom were living in Canada without legal documentation. MP G.W. Baldwin asked the Minister of Manpower and Immigration to legalize the stay of these two men and their families in Canada (*Hansard*, 23 May 1972: 2456). Bryce Mackasey, the Minister of Manpower and Immigration at the time, responded to this request instantly and positively. He stated, 'I can think of nothing that would give me more pleasure than nine more Scots in Canada as landed immigrants and future citizens, so I will personally intervene' (ibid.). Consequently, the Donald families were given legal authority to reside in Canada as permanent residents.

Throughout the five years of parliamentary debates that I analysed, this swift and joyful intervention by the minister to aid undocumented (im)migrants was otherwise unheard of. Indeed, the Donald case stands in stark contrast with the following case where the people in question were presented as 'gypsies' from Europe. MP Craig Stewart asked: 'It [the question] arises from the entry into Canada in late April of a group of gypsies [*sic*] from Europe. As these gypsies have victimized people in rural areas of western Canada – amounts as high as $6,000 are involved – will the minister order their deportation immediately so as to protect Canadian citizens?' (*Hansard*, 26 June 1973:5059). Robert K. Andras, minister of manpower and immigration, responded by stating that although there was no proof of any wrongdoing on the part of the people in question, he would 'certainly pay very careful attention to the representations made by the honourable member' (ibid.).[6] The difference in both the discursive and physical treatment of the Donald families and this particular group of 'gypsies' *with legal documents* shows that the *immigration* of people to Canada – documented or undocumented – was not *in and of itself* the problem. Rather, the problem was the entry and residence of *certain* peoples – racialized as non-Whites – who were presented as not belonging.

Through the parliamentary debates, 'new immigrants,' an ever-increasing number of whom were non-Whites arriving from 'non-traditional source countries,' were discursively produced as a national security threat. In the period that I have examined, they were consistently presented as responsible for the existence of unemployment, violence, and crime, for increasing state expenditures, and for the supposed moral decline of the Canadian nation. While these discursive practices were not always distinctive to the late 1960s and early 1970s, they did involve a rearticulation of these discourses with new meanings and implications.

Non-Whites had always migrated to Canada. What had changed from previous periods in Canadian history was that after 1967 non-Whites were able to enter as permanent residents. By the end period of my study (1973), there was general consensus in Parliament that the 1967 changes had left the Canadian immigration system 'out of control,' thereby creating problems for Canadians. Not coincidently, it was also in this period, in 1974, that non-Whites first came to constitute the majority of immigrants to Canada. In this historical juncture, then, discursively producing immigration as the *cause* of various problems relied on the organization of a moral panic about the *permanent status* of non-Whites in Canada and the consequences of this for the 'character' of Canadian society. After the post-1967 abolition of legalized racism as a selection criterion for immigrants, the problem of immigration, now associated fully with the entry of non-White people, was represented as a problem of having a group of non-Whites who could neither be readily deported nor legally subordinated. A group of non-Whites, who, in fact, could begin to feel at home in Canada because, unlike previous non-White migrants, they held certain rights and entitlements due to their status as permanent residents.

The way the problem was discursively framed in Parliament, however, rested on the production of a border that was 'out of control.' Although there certainly were explicit calls to return to the pre-1967 'preferred nationalities and races' selection system that favoured Whites made by members of opposition parties, these did not comprise the dominant frame for immigration policy changes to come. Rather, the dominant frame utilized for regaining order at the border was the need to reverse some of the key aspects of the 1967 changes while leaving the (supposedly) 'non-discriminatory' features for selecting immigrants in place.

The changes sought in Parliament, then, were those that removed certain rights for both temporary and permanent (im)migrants. In announcing some of these changes only a scant six years following 1967, Minister of Manpower and Immigration Robert K. Andras gave a clear signal that the liberalization of Canadian immigration policy was coming to an end: 'I know there are some who would say that we should have acted two or three years ago, and certainly I will say that with the benefit of hindsight ... But I think many of us felt that the act and the regulations of 1967 had been a noble experiment, liberal with a small 'l,' and certainly represented the consensus of all groups in the House at that time. I think perhaps it was typical of the Canadian concern for people of other lands which has led this country, for example into so many peacekeeping missions, some of them under conditions which more coldly calculating people might have rejected out of hand' (*Hansard*, 18 June 1973:4952). One of the cornerstones of the new 'get tough' attitude in immigration policy, then, was the simultaneous portrayal of the 1967 changes as harmful and the production of Canadians as a generous bunch that had had enough.

While the 1967 changes were presented as having granted 'too many rights' to those categorized as 'visitors,' this, too, was linked to the problematization of the permanent status of new immigrants (read: non-Whites). Visitors (under which legal category non-immigrants or migrant workers were placed) were produced as a problem in so much as they had been granted in 1967 the possibility of remaining in Canada permanently. In June of 1972 legislation (Bill C-197) was brought in to eliminate the ability of visitors to apply for permanent resident status from *within* Canada. That is, once a person was within Canadian territory, he or she could not shift his or her status from temporary to permanent resident.

The minister couched the newly worded legislation in the discourse of having to protect Canada's borders against those who would 'defy' immigration policy. In keeping with the emerging discourse of Canadians as a generous group, the minister added that the legislation was for the *benefit* of the people who might otherwise engage in migration: 'I would also draw to the attention of honourable members the danger of the exploitation of many innocent people by unscrupulous so-called immigration counselors, who could take the substance of these decisions [people applying for and gaining permanent residency from within Canada] and convince innocent people to come to Canada, many of whom in countries we can all name and who would do anything to come to this country to get away from the circumstances in which they are presently living' (ibid.:5810).

Even though those 'who would do anything to come' to Canada were not specifically named, the commonsensical association of desperation with the global South, that is, 'in countries we can all name,' discursively organized the necessity of preventing non-Whites from applying for permanent resident status from within Canada, for their benefit, of course. This solution undoubtedly affected some Whites in the visitor category as well. Nevertheless, the expressed need to 'restore order' to Canada's borders was deeply linked to the problematization of non-White immigrants in Canada in this period and collapsing the category of non-White into that of immigrant.

The problem of Canadian national borders being 'out of control' was made commonsensical, in part, through the discourse that Canadians should not be made to be 'responsible' for just *anyone* who sets foot on 'Canadian soil' (*Hansard*, 18 June 1973:4951–2). As one Member of Parliament stated: 'a nation's first responsibility was to its own people' (*Hansard*, 22 June 1973:5028). Hence, immigration policy changes taking place in the latter period of my study were produced by parliamentarians as necessary in order to clarify the 'obligations' of Canadians to those constructed as falling outside of the scope of the nation.

The articulation of such discourses was part of the project of White nation building at this time, a project that relied not only on inferiorizing non-Whites in Canada but also on rendering them as *undesirable* (see Hage, 2000). It was they, the post-1967 immigrants (and visitors) who were making Canadian borders 'unmanageable.' How to make these undesirable non-White immigrants manageable, however, without jeopardizing Canada's new image as a 'tolerant' society, remained a tactical problem for parliamentarians keen on reversing the 1967 changes. Removing certain rights available to those the state categorized as non-immigrants (i.e., 'visitors'), therefore, came to occupy centre stage in the Canadian state's display of toughness.

Removing the right of visitors to become permanent residents from *within* Canada ensured that those entering the country as migrant workers would not be able to change their status once inside the country. Thus, shortly after the legislation to remove this right, the previously more limited policy of admitting people as temporary migrant workers within specific sectors of the labour market, such as domestic or farm workers, was expanded into the much broader 1973 Non-Immigrant Employment Authorization Program (NIEAP) that more efficiently recruited and monitored increasing numbers of people for a wide array of occupational 'labour shortages' in Canada. The result, as we shall see in Chapter 5 was that migrant workers became thoroughly integrated into the Canadian labour market and no longer worked only in certain niche markets. Together, these changes reversed large parts of the liberalization of Canadian immigration policy that took place in 1967.

In this regard, it is important to keep in mind that parliamentary debates on trade and investment took place at the same time as the ones on immigration policy. Taken in conjunction, nationalist ideologies that supported capital accumulation relied upon racist ideologies to make common sense of the negative duality between Canadians and foreigners. Racialized parliamentary debates that organized the presence of non-Whites as the collective problem of Canadians also helped to discursively construct a supposedly homogeneous White Canadian nation *for* whom state practices were carried out. Indeed, racist ideologies can be seen as a key part of *how* national state practices concerning all manner of things were legitimated at this time. Seen in juxtaposition with policies designed to increase the international competitiveness of businesses in Canada, we see that while there was an expansion in the criteria of Canadian capitalists, greater restrictions were erected for the cross-border migrations of non-White people. Through these restrictions, a migrant, indentured labour system was further entrenched within Canadian national society.

Yet, it was also during this time that the notion of Canada as a tolerant and even a 'just' society was being organized. Indeed, one of the striking features of immigration policy-making at this time was the practically simultaneous liberalization and restriction of access to Canadian citizenship. On the one hand, the Canadian government removed *explicitly* racist restrictions on immigration from the South in 1967 through regulatory changes (see Satzewich, 1989b). On the other hand, in 1973 the NIEAP was introduced which served to deny many migrants access to the entitlements of or permanent residency and, therefore, Canadian citizenship while recruiting them to work in Canada under conditions deemed unconstitutional for Canadians.

This was accomplished through a three-fold process including the further exploitation of the valuable currency of liberal philosophy already embedded within notions of Canadian democracy, selectively reporting accounts so that the NIEAP was rendered more or less invisible while the supposedly tolerant Canadian society was highlighted, as well as reproducing (and reworking) nationalized notions of the entitlements of Canadianness (and, hence, the disentitlements of non-Canadianness) established over time. Indeed, key to the organization of legitimacy for coercive state actions against migrants at the time the NIEAP was introduced was the reshaping of an identity that was tolerant but still very much entitled to exclude Others.

Important to this work were the ways in which certain groups of people continued to be excluded from the definition of Canadian yet how their exclusion was concealed through the organization of an ideological 'virtual reality' (Smith, 1990:62). The erasure of the colonial and racist foundations of Canada was a key, initial step in the presentation of Canada as a tolerant society. The construction of Canadianness during this period was one where the Canadian national state was represented as having been founded by an *overthrow* of colonialism. This anticolonial struggle was waged by the two 'founding' races/ nations of Canada: the French and the English. In this account, the reality of Canada being built on the *colonization* of diverse indigenous peoples and their traditional lands by those with a privileged position *within* the French and British empires was rendered invisible.

This virtual reality was presented in the House of Commons equally well by members of all the various political parties represented there. The following quote from David Lewis, MP from York-South and soon to be leader of the federal New Democratic Party, was representative of how Canada came to be constituted as a previously *colonized* – not *colonizing* – national state. In speaking to the importance of establishing good relations with 'developing' countries in order to foster 'international competitiveness,' he stated, 'From all our contacts and all our reading *we know* Canada has a special place of trust among the developing nations. We emerged as an independent nation almost a century before them, but we also emerged out of colonial status. We have never had an imperial goal or imperialistic intentions' (*Hansard*, 20 January 1969, emphasis added).

Another discursive flight shaping this virtual reality was found in the following statement by Conservative Party MP Heath Macquarrie, who in speaking in support of creating Canada Day (1 July) as a new statutory holiday, stated, 'A national day in any country reverts back to a time of great achievement ... The great moment in Canadian history, one which reflects its unique character among nations, is surely that it has achieved nationhood by peaceful means, by the *getting together* of different communities' (*Hansard*, 17 February 1970:3702, emphasis added).

Again, the violence of colonialism against Indigenous people was erased in favour of a Canadianness represented as 'peaceful.' Macquarrie's comments organized a particular kind of knowledge whereby the English and French empires did not colonize indigenous peoples but 'got together' with them. This allowed for an ideological reading of being Canadian, one that obscured the substandard conditions under which most indigenous peoples continued to live in Canada and one which removed any responsibility for this reality by those who colonized them (see Frideres, 1988; Goodleaf, 1995). The work that these texts, in part, did then was to have their readers come to know Canada (and, hence, Canadians) as bearing no responsibility for the existence of certain oppressive and exploitative social relations.

Significantly, part of the creation of the tolerant Canadian nation at this time was the omission of references to race (at least for the most part). This was particularly significant in relation to the racialized category of White. In the parliamentary debates of this time, nowhere was the term 'White' attached to being Canadian. This was key to the process of ruling in this period of Canadian society, as it allowed the transition of Canada being an intolerant society to becoming a tolerant one. The most effective organization of racist ideologies in the discursive practices of parliamentarians, therefore, was achieved by mobilizing nationalist tropes of better managing the presence of foreigners. The differential understandings of and material realities associated with Whiteness and non-Whiteness were reframed as necessary acts in the defence of the nation. Discrimination against foreigners was presented as its exact opposition – as Our national duty to protect citizens. Thus, since the legitimacy for the existence of the Canadian nation was never questioned in the parliamentary debates, discriminating against non-Canadians could not be imagined as such.

Since the Canadian-Self was not identified explicitly as White within parliamentary debates, an agreement could be struck between the producers and (some of the) readers of these texts that allowed reference to the 'tolerant Canadian society' to work ideologically to maintain existing relations of ruling while denying them all together. Not naming who benefited – socially, economically, and politically – from the existence of Canada allowed for the continuation of these relative privileges while working to delegitimize complaints from those who were kept from them. And since negatively racialized people remained objectified as outsiders within Canadian national space, they were constructed as falling outside of the scope of national subjecthood.

Thus, as Hage (2000) has correctly pointed out, although the transition from Canada being an intolerant society to becoming a tolerant one was presented as a break from the past, the *objects* of toleration – non-Whites, including Indigenous people, in this case – continued to be the objects upon whose bodies national subjects could act. The lives of those positioned as non-Canadians were seen as legitimately managed by Canadians. Within the new tolerant Canadian society, then, the concerns of Whites remained central and their supposed natural right to make decisions for the nation remained unquestioned. But precisely because this was done through the trope of 'tolerance,' and perhaps even 'inclusion,' it became necessary to *not* identify Whiteness. Omitting reference to racialized classifications, while doing nothing to eliminate racialized differences in power, wealth, and belonging, therefore, worked to create the tolerant society *and* to do its work of maintaining racialized criteria of national belonging. Tolerance and intolerance coexist with one another, and both aim to maintain the marginalization of dominated groups (ibid.).

Liberal rhetoric aside, then, the racialized meaning(s) of Canadianness *remained* embedded within ideas of Canadian nationhood. This is evident in the following comments by then Prime Minister Trudeau on a report of the Royal Commission on National Security. In addressing Parliament at a time when the immigration of non-Whites was steadily increasing and commonsensical ideas of being an immigrant became thoroughly racialized, he said:

> As the commissioners have stated, and I quote: 'Canada remains the target of subversive or potentially subversive activities, attempts at infiltration and penetration, and espionage operations' and they emphasize that: 'the duty of the state to protect its secrets from espionage, its information from subversion and its policies from clandestine influence is indisputable; what are matters for dispute are the organizations and procedures established by the State to meet this responsibility in an area which can touch closely upon the fundamental freedoms of the individual' ... [This requires] a careful and methodical build-up of modern technical facilities directed toward the detection and prevention of large scale organized crime, as well as the provision of information which the government requires in order to ensure the security and integrity of the state ... For this reason ... the government ... has decided to accept the commissioners' recommendation for the establishment of a Security Review Board ... It is their opinion that such a system of review might be required in the *three areas of employment, immigration and citizenship*. (*Hansard*, 26 June 1969:10636–7, emphasis added)

Trudeau's comments signalled that citizenship and immigration, particularly in relation to policies on employment, had been elevated to being considered as national security issues for Canadians. However, Trudeau was careful to recognize, and emphasize, *liberal* notions of individual freedoms within the context of selecting entire groups, that is, immigrants (increasingly read as non-Whites), for special attention. Without saying 'Canadians are under threat from non-White immigrants who will take away Our jobs,' Trudeau was able to racialize the problems facing Canadians and their potential solutions while maintaining a public image of tolerance. This was done by making immigration a problem for the security of the nation as well as by neglecting to make any positive comments regarding immigrants and immigration in his larger speech (ibid.).

To understand the way that readers can read such notions from the text, it is crucial to remember that each such statement was not made in isolation from previous ones. Images of which racialized and gendered bodies belonged in Canada and which did not are littered throughout the history of governing Canada (see Ward, 1978; Creese, 1988; Bourgeault, 1989). Parliamentary discourse can 'quietly borrow' (to use a term of Dorothy Smith's) from this history to frame the topic of the entrance of certain people as a problem worthy of being called a national security issue. In identifying the processes of citizenship and immigration as national security issues at this particular historical juncture when non-Whites were rapidly becoming the majority of immigrants (i.e., new permanent residents), and when immigrants were being associated with many of the ills plaguing Canadians, the risk identified by parliamentarians was the security of a *White* identity for the imagined Canadian nation. Significantly, one of the features of being Canadian was being free. Some MPs began to question this association.

This is evident in the following discussion that took place in Parliament under the topic of 'Manpower: Use of unemployed and students instead of West Indians to pick fruit.' MP Gerard Laprise (Abitibi) stated, 'Mr Speaker, I have a question for the PM. A few days ago, the Minister of Manpower and Immigration announced that seasonal workers from the West Indies would be hired this summer to help in picking and canning fruits and vegetables in Ontario. Could the PM then consider the possibility of assigning this work to our unemployed or to our students who for the most part will not find jobs this summer? (*Hansard*, 23 March 1971:4508)?

Through his choice of words, Laprise operationalized the negative dualities of Us-Canadians / Them–West Indians or Them–migrant workers. As we will see later, it was also of great import that Laprise used the word 'assign.' Trudeau responded by stating, 'Mr Speaker, this is a perennial problem and it must be recognized that this is a type of work that very often students or unemployed will not do. This is why the Department of Manpower and Immigration is admitting *foreign workers* on *our* labour market. Should students be willing to undertake this work, they would certainly have the preference. I am not cognizant with the specific case the honourable member is referring to, but I know that this is a problem which comes up year after year with respect to certain types of work' (*Hansard*, 23 March 1971:4508, emphasis added).

The problem, then, was at least partly identified as one of filling jobs that We Canadians do not want. The PM's statement once again operationalized binary notions of us/them. He also activated notions of the *legitimate* substandard treatment of and lower entitlements for migrant workers from the West Indies. To his response, the following exchange occurred:

Mr Laprise: Would the PM consider inviting the young people to do that work during the holidays, not only in Ontario where fruit and vegetables are grown, but in every province? This would be much more efficient than having them travel.' (*Hansard*, 23 March 1971:4508)

Mr Trudeau: Mr Speaker, I agree with the honourable member on that score. The purpose of the Manpower Centres is to send the unemployed or the students to take part in this work. But, once again, facts reveal that there are in Canada some types of work which the unemployed and the students refuse to do; this proves, by the way, that the rate of unemployment is at times somewhat artificial.' (ibid.)

Once again, the comments by the prime minister helped to ideologically reframe the recruitment of migrant workers as coming to work at jobs that Canadians would not (normally) take. Why were these jobs unfilled year after year? Because of low wages, unsafe and substandard working conditions, the seasonal character of the work, etc. (see Wall, 1992). However, this reality was eclipsed by a virtual one so that the nationalized segregation of the labour market in Canada was naturalized. As a result, the fact that such nationalized segregation was a result of state practices that legally allowed for the denial of certain labour market rights and entitlements to those with a migrant workers status was ideologically concealed.

The NIEAP, then, ensured the recruitment of people from outside of Canada for jobs that Canadians consistently refused both because, unlike foreign workers, *they legally could* and also, unlike foreign workers, because they had *options* to not working and instead accessing unemployment insurance or social assistance.[7] The NIEAP, ultimately, was structured to recruit workers through a category – non-immigrant– that rendered those brought through it as legally *unfree*. Thus, migrant workers were not only recruited when and where there was an actual *shortage* of workers in Canada. Instead, much of this shortage was qualitative: migrant workers were (and are) recruited for those jobs that were (and are) not qualitatively 'attractive' to those not legally indentured to perform them.

Indenturing workers therefore is one of the paramount meanings attached to the classification of some people as foreign workers. The suturing of notions of Canadianness onto notions of freedom as well as the articulation of ideas of foreignness with ideas of unfreedom are mobilized through the operation of the NIEAP. Having the ability to work within free employment relationships becomes a characteristic of being Canadian: the opposite applies to those categorized as migrant workers. The facticity organized by this binary code that separates migrant workers from Canadians organizes the expectation that differentiated categories of people will, in reality, be treated quite differently by the Canadian state. This is well reflected in the following exchange:

Mr Roch La Salle (Joliette):	... In view of the statement by the PM to the effect that some unemployed people would refuse to perform such work, would the PM consider *compelling Canadians* to work if they receive any social benefits? Would the government favour legislation requiring any government pension recipient to work? (*Hansard*, 23 March 1971:4508, emphasis added)
Right Hon. P.E. Trudeau (PM):	No, ... the government will not commandeer the work force. *The whole political philosophy of the government is based on freedom of choice for citizens to work where they want.* (ibid., emphasis added)

This statement highlights what is, ultimately, the crux of the issue from the standpoint of those made into migrant workers. The prime minister acknowledges that the Canadian state cannot indenture those who it has categorized as *its citizens* and as the beneficiaries of the existence of Canada itself, at least not without raising serious questions about the entire process of governance. Thus, in the framework of Canadianness it just does not (yet) make common sense to compel Canadians to work where they do not wish to.

Importantly, however, within this same ideological framework it does remain *permissible* to exploit people as indentured labour in Canada with no 'freedom of choice ... to work where they want.' To maintain the liberal democratic framework of Canadian society therefore requires that the state render those who are made unfree as 'foreign workers.' Consequently, with the non-immigrant (or migrant worker) category in place, a system of indentured labour in the Self-defined liberal, tolerant Canada can proceed. With the organization of national difference through state categories, the Canadian national state, as all others, can be simultaneously a liberal democracy and an authoritative state.

The state's action of indenturing migrant workers, then, is organized through what is both legally and socially possible at the time. It was simply not legal to make unfree those who fell into either the citizen or permanent resident category. At the same time, it was seen as within the purview of legitimate state action in Canada for parliamentarians to indenture those categorized as 'non-immigrants,' as 'foreign workers' in Canada. Both these acts were organized through the internationally recognized sovereign right of national states to deny rights and entitlements to those named as non-citizens and non-permanent residents. It was not a social problem for those working in the state to declare that Canadians had no responsibilities or obligations to 'foreign' migrant workers.

In this context it is crucial for us to note that nowhere in the preceding debate within Parliament were any objections raised as to the indenturing of 'foreign workers' in Canada. The fact of a person working as unfree labour was never, in and of itself, the problem. The problem instead was *who*, citizen or non-immigrant, was going to be made unfree. The nationalization of this discrimination so that 'foreigners' could be indentured to employers in Canada relied upon racist imagery, as the following statement by MP H.W. Danforth (Kent-Essex) demonstrates. In it, he presents as natural, and therefore as unworthy of debate – that We-Canadians get Those-Foreigners to do undesirable work because, in part, it is natural for Them to do it:

> The attitude of this government has been that if you do not want to work, you should not have to do so. I raise this matter because the PM reaffirmed the position of the government that a Canadian should not have to work if he [*sic*] does not want to. Mr Chairman, many people do not like to work in agriculture. They do not like the monotony, the conditions and the fact that you work sometimes in heat and sometimes in cold. That is all right; they do not like it and they should not be forced to work at it. We all agree with that ... How [then] do they [farm owners] obtain labour? Many of them have encouraged offshore labour over the years which comes from three sources, the Caribbean, Portugal and Mexico. We need this labour ... and these people are used to working in the heat. They are used to working in agriculture, and they are satisfied with the pay scale ... Everybody is satisfied: the workers are satisfied, the primary producers are satisfied and the consumers of Canada are satisfied because we are getting the crops harvested ... I feel that Canadians should provide work for Canadians wherever possible; Canadians should have the first opportunity to work. But ... if Canadians do not want to work at this job – many of them do not, and have expressed this feeling in no uncertain terms – then I say that the producers of this nation are entitled to offshore, competent labour from wherever it may come, if these people are willing to work under the conditions prevailing in Canada today and produce crops for Canadian consumers. (*Hansard*, 20 July 1973:5836)

This statement worked to depoliticize the very real differences *legislated* to exist between those discussed as 'offshore labour' from the Caribbean, Portugal, and Mexico and the Canadians (employers or consumers) for whom they were said to labour. Their bodies became legitimate sites for coercive state actions. Moreover, the discursive organization of this statement concealed the social practices that brought certain groups of people to work in clearly substandard (in relation to Canadians) working conditions and pay scales. Rather than revealing the state practices that organized these differences, these material practices were mystified through parliamentary practices that reproduced the ideologies of racism and nationalism that helped to hold in place commonsensical notions about the supposedly natural labour market capacities and desires of differentiated groups of people.

When examining the construction of binary codes that organize difference, it becomes apparent that categorizing a person a citizen or a migrant worker was an ideological practice that carried great material force. The exploitation of migrant workers was concealed and reproduced through the notion that citizens could and should expect certain rights and entitlements that non-citizens could not and that this situation was perfectly legitimate. The notion that some people *just were* citizens and Others *just were not*, even though they shared the same physical space, came to be a normative stance. The fact that these were realized through the social organization of human relations in a particularly exclusionary and exploitative way was concealed. As a result, it appeared perfectly ordinary and right that those categorized as migrant workers would be legally denied the same rights and protections that Canadian citizens are seen as solely entitled to. Why should migrant workers get the same rights as citizens? They were, after all, migrant workers. The circularity of the argument ensnared migrant workers (and others classified as non-citizens) in a particularly vicious way.

In this regard, it is important that even while the Other is *ideologically* differentiated from the norm, the construction of binary codes is intimately connected to the establishment and reproduction of unequal materialities so that those who are categorized as different (from Canadians) *do* become truly differentiated in relation to resources and power, as is the case with migrant workers. This gives social meaning, and not a small modicum of plausibility, to notions that actual differences exist. Our consciousness of ourselves and Others and our respective places in the world is shaped through the fact that we can see that there are tangible consequences stemming from belonging to differently constructed group categories.

The liberal framework that emphasizes freedom and citizenship, then, can actually be said to strengthen the racist meanings of concepts of Canadianness for they work to naturalize the very categories of national difference that organizes injustices. Within the liberal framework, legitimacy is secured by enshrining the rights of those who are placed (and have placed themselves) within categories of citizenship that privilege them in relation to Others placed within far more inferior categories, such as that of migrant worker. Liberal practices allow for the protection of individual freedoms but only for those whose protection the state is seen to exist. Those falling outside of this category are then seen as being *legitimately* denied the state's protection. Indeed, they become not only the social but also the legal-juridical foreigners *from* whom We are to be protected. It thus becomes acceptable that these Others become the targets for state coercive practices designed to strengthen Us.

Conclusion

A documentary analysis of Canadian parliamentary debates from 1969 to 1973 reveals how the migrant workers category was a legal *and* a social category, one given material force through racialized, nationalist ideologies. There were no questions or disagreements concerning the fundamental construction of this category or what it accomplished, that is, an indentured labour system in Canada. Instead, there was complete coherence within the debates about indenturing people categorized as foreigners. Consequently, following the changes in immigration policies of the late 1960s and early 1970s, the racialized criteria of admittance in Canadian immigration policy was shifted from the pre-1967 categories of 'preferred races and nationalities' onto the new category of non-immigrant or migrant worker that also relied on a racist nationalism but in a wholly new guise. 'Undesirability' came to be distinguished by people's categorization into highly subordinated state categories of entry and the lack of the right of permanent residence.

The discursive practice of continuously reconstructing the White Canadian nation was a significant aspect of how state practices were able to situate Canada as a continuing site for capital investment, for being non-Canadian, indeed, being a non-immigrant ensured a worker's competitiveness in the labour market in Canada. Nationalist ideologies were therefore a consistent part of parliamentary discursive practices that helped to organize processes of capitalist globalization. The process of restructuring was ideologically reframed as a *national* response to foreign threats. Thus, growing transnational integration occurred alongside a strengthened nationalization of territory and imagination or what Alexander T. Aleinikoff (1998) calls a 'tightening circle of membership' where distinctions between Us and Them were sharpened. There was a simultaneous dismantling of barriers to becoming Canadian for capital investors and the strengthening of boundaries of Canadianness against certain (im)migrants during this period. In this sense, the NIEAP was a legal tool that helped to define unequal social relationships of nationality within Canada, and a manifestation of how the national state was organized and understood in the late twentieth century.

While there were differences between different articulations of Canadian nationalism, within the discourse of the parliamentarians, whether left, centre, or right, it was foreigners who became the central problem of the period and not the social relations of capitalism. The organization of a common sense around the existence of supposedly distinct and separate national states, with the state acting as the representative of the nation or civil society, worked to legitimate this ideological practice. The legitimacy attached to national states (as compared with particular governments that come and go) helped to ensure that these ruling structures and ideologies were maintained. The material force exerted by these discursive strategies is what organized the state category of migrant workers. I now turn to a closer examination of the regulatory program that organized the state category of migrant worker: the Non-Immigrant Employment Authorization Program.

5 Canada's Non-Immigrant Employment Authorization Program (NIEAP): The Social Organization of Unfreedom for 'Migrant Workers'

Since 1973 the Non-Immigrant Employment Authorization Program (NIEAP) has facilitated a growth in the numbers of people made to work as migrant workers in Canada. The daily operation of the NIEAP organizes and enforces restrictive conditions of entry, residence, and work. Through it, the majority of people migrating to Canada to work labour in unfree employment relationships. Examining the specific features of the NIEAP points to the character of the contracting process within such relationships. When reviewing the labour contracts that govern the lives of migrant workers it is clear that the outcome is decidedly in favour of both the Canadian state and employers. The NIEAP permits state officials to save substantially on the costs of training and services for those brought in through it. Meanwhile, the program gives employers greater flexibility in meeting their labour needs by securing a more disciplined, often cheaper, post-Fordist workforce.

This is evident in the stipulations regarding the criteria for admittance under the NIEAP, which include the preauthorization of a number of employment conditions prior to entering Canada. The employer, location of employment, type of employment, condition of employment, and length of employment must be prearranged and stated on the worker's temporary employment authorization document (CIC, 1994g). Migrant workers cannot change the conditions of their authorization at any time without prior written permission from an immigration officer.

Temporary migrant workers are told that they, 'must follow the terms of your employment authorization while in Canada. If you do not, you may be asked to leave the country' (ibid.). In other words, if a worker employed on a temporary employment authorization leaves the stipulated employer, changes occupations, or takes on additional work without the approval of an immigration official, she or he is subject to deportation. The worker is therefore bound to 'work at a specific job for a specific period of time for a specific employer' (ibid.). Hence, workers entering under the NIEAP are denied mobility rights both in the labour market and, by virtue of being tied to their employer, geographically as well. They are not free.

Relatedly, the NIEAP operates as a forced *rotational* system of employment. Workers are not permitted to exceed the length of time stated upon their temporary employment authorization. However, the only temporary feature of this program is the individual worker contracted to work in the country for a particular period of time.[1] Through the NIEAP, the state recruits people to work for a pre-specified period of time after which they may be replaced with other workers. The availability of unfree workers is itself a permanent feature of the labour market in Canada.[2] The program has, thus, operated as a 'revolving door of exploitation' (Ramirez, 1982:17).

The categorization of a person as a migrant worker profoundly shapes how that person experiences life in Canada. Making a person into a migrant worker powerfully delimits her or his life. Much of these limitations are shaped by processes of racialization, the type of job a person works at, the wages prevalent in that occupation for migrant workers, and so on. The lived experiences of migrant workers, therefore, are shaped both by the organization of social relations within the space occupied by Canada and by the conditions applied to their lives and their sale of labour by the NIEAP.

There is a developing body of literature that has documented the everyday lived experiences of those categorized as migrant workers. Much of this work has examined the lives of women working as migrant domestic workers who are required to live in the home of their employers as a condition of their temporary employment authorization (Silvera, 1983; Arat-Koc, 1992). Their lives are shaped daily by interlocking practices of nationalism, sexism, and racism that assume that non-White women from the global South (who are the majority of domestic migrant workers throughout the period I examine) naturally occupy the most unattractive, least paying, and most difficult jobs (Silvera, 1983).

Aside from the fact that the stipulations of their labour contract are rarely enforced on their behalf, migrant domestic workers – like all migrant workers – face enormous disadvantages *because* they are indentured to their employers. Noreen, a migrant domestic woman interviewed by Makeda Silvera, in her 1983 pathbreaking oral history of domestic workers in Canada, sums up this dilemma: 'You know sometimes I feel like a slave, sometimes I dream about freedom. You know, I wish I could move where I want to, work in whichever job I want, and have a little apartment on my own' (ibid.:20). Molly adds, 'If I had my landed, though, I would feel much better because then I could go any place. I cold look any job I wanted ... It would be so nice to feel free ... Free to go anywhere I want to go. Free to look for any kind of job I want' (ibid.:70, 72). Almost twenty years following Silvera's interviews, the migrant domestic workers that Sedef Arat-Koc interviewed shared similar sentiments. One woman states, 'Without landed status, you are always scared ... You are afraid to terminate your contract with your employer ... You can't just work anywhere. I feel like I am in a cage' (in Arat-Koc, 2001:37).

The unfreedom of migrant worker affects every other aspect of their lives in Canada – whether they can seek unpaid wages, challenge the conditions in which they work, or question an employer's demands or their living conditions. The diminishment of their ability to resist poor wages and working conditions rests not only in the interpersonal relationships between migrant workers and their employers but in the unfree employment relationship they find themselves in. This is clear in a comment made by Savitri, another migrant domestic worker interviewed by Silvera (1983:47): 'I keep quiet, because I don't want to move around too much, I don't want to create any bad feeling with the immigration officers.' Molly adds, 'I needed to be in a job or they would deport me (ibid.:67). Molly's need to keep her job at all costs and Savitri's experience of being silenced is organized through the operation of the NIEAP. Migrant workers must strive to keep both their employers and immigration officers dealing with their case happy or else face deportation. As Primrose states, 'I know she [her employer] is a problem and I can't get on with her, but I also know that Immigration is another problem. So what can I do?' (ibid.:93).

This does not mean, of course, that migrant workers do not resist the injustices imposed upon them. They too are human subjects with agency, however much their agency is constrained. Yet, because the NIEAP renders them unfree, migrant workers remain unable to challenge the *structural* aspects of what creates unsafe and substandard employment conditions for them. The NIEAP very clearly organizes the cheapness and weakness of those workers brought through it.

Often, employers are matched with workers by overseas agencies set up to recruit potential employees in their country of last residence (Dias, 1994:140).[3] If this fails, employers can rely on visa officers at Canadian government offices abroad to help them recruit temporary migrant workers (CIC, 1994a). The role of these offices is to provide employers with advertising, interviewing facilities, and advice on local laws and immigration processing times (ibid.). Employers who require a large number of workers are able to arrange for blocks of labour through bilateral agreements between the governments of Canada and other national states (Cornish, 1992).

Officially, the Canadian government states that 'a temporary foreign worker will be considered if the job is temporary or is permanent, but an employee is needed to bridge the gap until a Canadian worker can be recruited or trained' (CIC, 1994a:3). To recruit workers on temporary employment authorizations, employers must therefore apply for permission from the nearest Canada Employment Centre (CEC; previously Canada Manpower Centre), administered by the Ministry of Human Resource Development Canada. Officials within the CEC are charged with carrying out an employment validation process (EVP) to determine if there is indeed a 'temporary shortage' of Canadian workers for the job(s) that the employer needs filled (CIC, 1994a). If the CEC affirms that there is, employers are then permitted to recruit temporary migrant workers.

We need to pay close attention to the notion of labour *shortages* that the NIEAP mobilizes. This is for two reasons. First, the EVP – considered one of the key innovations distinguishing the NIEAP from previous migrant worker recruitment schemes – is said to ensure that migrant workers do not take the jobs seen as belonging to Canadians. As such, the EVP helps to legitimize the notion that only when Canadians refuse a particular job should a migrant worker be able to take it. This reinforces the nationalist view that jobs in Canada belong, first and foremost, to Canadians. Such notions help to construct the common sense that there exist two labour markets in Canada – one that is Canadian and another that is foreign – each with their differential entitlements and rights.

In this way, the EVP works to conceal the ongoing disparities between the working and living conditions of workers with citizenship or permanent resident status and those brought in as migrant workers. Through the EVP, the argument that migrant workers are admitted to Canada only because the jobs for which they are recruited face *tempo-*

rary vacancies (supposedly employers continue to search for Canadian workers) lends legitimacy to the temporary, rather than permanent, residence of migrant workers and their resultant lack of rights. The fact that in many sectors of employment, employers rely on migrant workers to fill shortages year after year after year remains unaccounted for in these kinds of calculations.

Brought in as a result of pressure from groups representing Canadian workers as well as the complaints of some parliamentarians demanding that Canadians rather than foreigners fill any and all job vacancies in the country (see *Hansard*, 2 June 1971:6293), the EVP does not even function as designed. Approximately *80 per cent* of temporary employment authorizations issued in Canada in any given year are made exempt from the EVP (Interviewee A, 1998; Interviewee B, 1998; Interviewee C, 1998).

A second problematic aspect of the notion of labour shortages filled by migrant workers lies in the meaning of *shortage* itself. William Marr points to a 1975 report to Parliament by the Special Joint Committee on Immigration Policy. This report highlights the government's stated need to continue the program of temporary labour recruitment where a continual demand for labour arises which 'Canadian citizens or landed immigrants are unwilling to fill' (1977:49–53). The emphasis placed by the Committee on the *unwillingness* of citizens or permanent residents to take up certain jobs is highly significant and points to the double meaning that the idea of labour shortage has with regard to the implementation of the NIEAP.

As Saskia Sassen (1988:27) notes, for both employers and the state, shortages are often defined not by the absence of actual workers ready and able to work but by the existence of particular characteristics of the labour supply that impede the process of capital accumulation. In Canada, such characteristics include relatively high wage rates, access to social programs that help to decommodify workers, and workers' protections and their collective bargaining rights – exactly the characteristics of the labour force in Canada much bemoaned by business leaders during the period when the NIEAP was implemented and after (see Swanson, 2001).

Shortages, then, rather than reflecting purely *quantitative* gaps within the Canadian labour market are defined *qualitatively* as well. What there is a shortage of is a particular *kind* of workforce that can be filled by unfree, contract labour. In other words, in Canada, there are shortages of cheapened and politically subjugated labour power.[4] Workers employed on temporary employment authorizations, in contrast to citizens and permanent residents, are unable to competitively enter labour markets for opportunities to negotiate their wages or working conditions. Neither are they able to decommodify themselves by accessing social programs and services that offer an alternative to paid employment. Instead, many are forced to accept the conditions offered by employers or face deportation to the very countries they left in their need to secure new livelihoods.

In one government document, it is stated that 'the recruitment [of temporary migrant workers] is ... examined to determine whether it will strengthen the company's competitiveness in the international marketplace' (CIC, 1994a:1). The NIEAP allows employers to tap into the broader world market for labour and secure workers who come with conditions of unfreedom imposed on them. Such terms give employers access to an internationally competitive labour force. The need to organize employers in Canada as internationally competitive thus is a key consideration – and key accomplishment – of the NIEAP. As a result, employers remain under no pressure to improve wages, working conditions, or pay rates.

Many employers naturalize such legal restrictions by embodying migrant workers with certain traits seen to be non-existent in Canadian, that is, free, workers – traits such as being 'reliable,' 'caring,' or 'docile' (see Silvera, 1983; Basok, 2002).[5] As discussed in the previous chapter, these ideological practices are informed both by nationalist discourses that see foreign bodies as less deserving than citizens of certain rights and entitlements in Canada as well as by racialized and gendered tropes of certain bodies being seen as naturally suited to substandard work and working conditions. The fact that migrant workers face greater pressures and far fewer options than other workers in Canada is concealed by such ideologies. As a result, there has been startlingly little attention paid to the NIEAP and how it has come to be one of the major avenues for migrants entering Canada. This may, in part, be because those brought in under the NIEAP are not included in the government's annual report on immigration numbers, for they are legally classified as 'non-immigrants.' However, the greater reason is that having an unfree migrant labour force simply does not disrupt dominant discourses in Canada.

The Making of 'Migrant Workers'

The most striking evidence of the expansion of the use of unfree labour power is revealed in statistics on the NIEAP (some not made readily accessible to the public) collected by various departments responsible for immigration. Not only the increase in numbers, but also the continuity, indeed expansion, of the program over the last thirty-plus years attests that it has become a permanent component of recruiting unfree workers for ever longer periods of time and for expanding types of occupations in Canada.

The significance of the NIEAP to the reshaping of the labour supply available to employers in Canada is made clearer when comparing the number of migrants entering Canada as landed immigrants with permanent residency rights and those entering as migrant workers through the stipulations of the NIEAP.[6] Of particular importance is the comparison between those workers specifically recruited for entry into the Canadian labour market as either 'independent' class landed immigrants or as temporary migrant workers. Such a comparison reveals that during the last decades of the twentieth century (1973–2004), more than three-quarters of (im)migrant labour recruitment to Canada constituted unfree labour.

Before directly comparing immigrant workers with non-immigrant, or migrant, workers, a brief review of the total number of landed immigrants brought to Canada for social and humanitarian reasons (including those in the family and refugee category) as well as those brought to Canada for other economic reasons (including entrepreneurs, investors, the self-employed, and assisted relatives) is useful. While the 'classes' of landed immigrants shown in table 5.1 are admitted for various social, economic, and humanitarian reasons, all permanent residents have access to the labour market as free workers. That is, they are not legally restricted to certain occupations, employers, or geographical location.

Upon entry to Canada, each immigrant is asked to indicate whether he or she intends to enter the workforce (MIC, 1974). Those who indicate 'yes' are classified as 'destined' (to the labour market) and are considered immigrant 'workers' by the government. However, while all landed immigrants can enter the labour force, only 'independent' class immigrants are *specifically* recruited to work (ibid.:1). Independent class immigrants are admitted through the 'points system' that emphasizes, indeed requires, particular labour market skills. Unlike those in the family class, refugee class, or retired class, they are not recruited for social or humanitarian reasons. Unfortunately, the data from 1980 to 1993 and the data from 1994 to 2004 are not wholly comparable, since from 1994 onwards, the category of 'skilled workers' is intro-

TABLE 5.1
Permanent Residents to Canada, Class by Year of Landing, 1973–2004[a]

Year	Family	Refugee/ Protected Persons	Assisted Relative[b]	Entrepreneur	Self-Employed	Investors	Retired	Independent/ Skilled Workers	Total[c]
1973	—	—	—	—	—	—	—	—	184,200
1974	—	—	—	—	—	—	—	—	218,465
1975	—	—	—	—	—	—	—	—	187,881
1976	—	—	—	—	—	—	—	—	149,429
1977	—	—	—	—	—	—	—	—	114,914
1978	—	—	—	—	—	—	—	—	86,313
1979	—	—	—	—	—	—	—	—	112,093
1980	51,039	40,348	13,531	719	4,397	—	1,548	31,549	143,133
1981	51,017	14,979	17,590	900	5,128	—	2,063	36,941	128,618
1982	49,980	16,925	11,948	1,475	4,889	—	2,252	33,678	121,147
1983	48,698	13,967	4,997	1,865	4,360	—	2,094	13,176	89,157
1984	43,814	15,342	8,167	3,555	2,705	—	2,313	12,343	88,239
1985	38,514	16,760	7,396	4,959	1,522	—	2,100	13,051	84,302
1986	42,197	19,147	5,890	5,866	1,629	23	1,833	22,634	99,219
1987	53,598	21,565	12,283	8,440	2,313	316	2,662	50,921	152,098
1988	51,331	26,836	15,567	11,372	2,712	1,028	3,177	49,906	161,929
1989	60,774	37,004	21,520	12,984	2,309	2,271	3,565	51,574	192,001
1990	73,457	39,689	25,393	12,263	1,974	4,208	3,534	53,712	214,230
1991	86,378	53,401	22,247	9,901	1,953	5,189	4,215	47,497	230,781
1992	99,960	51,875	19,880	15,697	2,818	9,628	5,479	47,505	252,842
1993	111,670	30,262	22,738	16,644	3,362	12,630	7,723	49,292	254,321
1994	94,195	19,778	n/a	14,201	2,745	10,480	7,436	69,906	224,400
1995	77,386	27,794	n/a	11,429	2,854	5,160	304	81,734	212,868

TABLE 5.1 (Concluded)

Year	Family	Refugee/ Protected Persons	Assisted Relative[b]	Entrepreneur	Self- Employed	Investors	Retired	Independent/ Skilled Workers	Total[c]
1996	68,359	28,356	n/a	11,911	4,376	6,176	147	97,916	226,073
1997	59,979	24,226	n/a	10,404	3,927	5,595	46	105,648	216,038
1998	50,897	22,796	n/a	6,618	2,625	4,534	8	81,268	174,199
1999	55,276	24,379	n/a	6,155	2,599	4,265	9	92,505	189,966
2000	60,614	30,083	n/a	6,186	2,527	4,951	0	118,598	227,465
2001	66,794	27,912	n/a	6,093	2,158	6,339	0	137,231	250,637
2002	65,300	25,110	n/a	4,482	1,907	4,638	1	123,317	229,042
2003	70,721	25,983	n/a	2,982	1,425	3,695	0	106,893	221,355
2004	63,507	32,670	n/a	2,477	1,190	6,090	0	113,945	235,708

Source: EIC, 1974–93; CIC, 1994b; 2005.

[a] Unfortunately, for the years 1973–1979, information is not provided for the immigration class breakdown of landed immigrants. This lack of information, thus, affects the information provided in here and in table 5.2.

[b] After 1994, the 'assisted relative' class of immigrants are absorbed either into the 'skilled workers' class or the 'family' class, depending on whether they claimed they were 'destined' to the labour market in Canada or not.

[c] The total does not always equal 100% of the other categories. This is because those admitted as permanent residents under the following categories are not included for the totals for 1994–2004: Live-in Caregiver Program (those.landed through it), backlog (refugee cases), humanitarian and compassionate, deferred removal order class, post-determination refugee claimant, and temporary resident permit (landed through it).

duced which includes immigrants selected under the 'assisted relative' class. This inflates the number of people specifically admitted to Canada to work as permanent residents (table 5.2).

It is also useful to note the various groups admitted under the auspices of the NIEAP. It needs to be clearly stated, however, that not all persons admitted to the country under this program can be considered unfree wage workers and that the NIEAP should not be considered as *only* a labour recruitment program (Wong, 1984; Michalowski, 1993). Instead, it is heterogeneous in nature. For instance, a large number of the people admitted stay only for a very short period of time to do work that normally crosses many national borders, such as sports figures and performing artists.[7] They do not receive permanent residence status but neither can they be considered unfree workers since the very character of their business (or labour) crisscrosses national borders in a highly transitory manner.

The inclusion of people admitted under these categories in the data on migrant workers has been cited as a reason to dismiss claims that the NIEAP operates as a system of forced, rotational, unfree contract labour recruitment (Boyd, 1986). Therefore, for the purposes of the present study, out of the total number of people annually issued temporary employment authorizations, those admitted under such occupations are omitted from any statistics presented (table 5.3). Once removed from the data, though, it becomes evident that the NIEAP *does* produce a significant number of people in Canada who labour as unfree, temporary migrant workers. Thus, while not all are recruited to work as unfree wage labour within the Canadian labour market, we see that for the majority of the years under study, *most are.*

In 1973, 69,901 temporary employment authorizations were issued to those who can be properly designated as unfree migrant workers. In 1983 this number reached 87,700. By 1993 the number stood at 153,988, more than double that of twenty years earlier, and by 2004 the number had again increased, to 228,677. The high-mark for the number of people entering the country on temporary employment authorizations is 2004. However, there are other years in which the numbers approached or surpassed 200,000 (1988, 1991, 1992, 2000, 2001, 2002, and 2003).

The data show, then, that there has indeed been a consistent and continuous supply of migrant workers to employers in Canada. In fact, the numbers of workers admitted under the NIEAP has been growing, with intermittent decreases, since the program's inception in 1973. In this regard, it becomes useful to compare the number of workers who

TABLE 5.2
Persons Admitted under the Independent/Skilled Workers Class: Number (and Percentage) of Destined Category, 1973–2004

Year	Independent/ Skilled Workers	Other Destined[a]	Total Destined[b]
1973	–	–	92,228
1974	–	–	106,083
1975	–	–	81,189
1976	–	–	61,461
1977	–	–	47,625
1978	–	–	34,762
1979	–	–	47,949
1980	31,549 (50)	31,930 (50)	63,479 (100)
1981	36,941 (65)	19,735 (35)	56,676 (100)
1982	33,678 (61)	21,345 (39)	55,023 (100)
1983	13,176 (36)	23,364 (64)	36,540 (100)
1984	12,343 (33)	25,125 (67)	37,468 (100)
1985	13,051 (35)	23,898 (65)	36,949 (100)
1986	22,634 (36)	40,845 (64)	63,479 (100)
1987	50,921 (90)	5,755 (10)	56,676 (100)
1988	49,906 (68)	23,228 (32)	73,134 (100)
1989	51,574 (55)	42,838 (45)	94,412 (100)
1990	53,712 (49)	56,128 (51)	109,840 (100)
1991	47,497 (37)	80,373 (63)	127,870 (100)
1992	47,505 (35)	89,855 (65)	137,360 (100)
1993	49,292	n/a	n/a
1994	39,890 (36)	69,275 (64)	109,165 (100)
1995	47,197 (43)	62,740 (57)	109,937 (100)
1996	56,278 (47)	62,447 (53)	118,725 (100)
1997	58,637 (53)	52,780 (47)	111,417 (100)
1998	45,568 (50)	45,198 (50)	90,766 (100)
1999	52,926 (53)	47,820 (47)	100,746 (100)
2000	68,460 (57)	52,396 (43)	120,856 (100)
2001	77,665 (59)	53,934 (41)	131,599 (100)
2002	69,564 (59)	48,583 (41)	118,147 (100)
2003	62,585 (53)	55,052 (47)	117,637 (100)
2004	64,374 (52)	60,505 (48)	124,879 (100)

Source: EIC, 1981–93; CIC, 1994b; 2005.

[a] The 'other destined' category is comprised of people who indicate that they intend to enter the Canadian labour market upon admittance to the country. They enter Canada under the following classes of immigration: family, assisted relatives (until 1994 after which destined assisted relatives are classified as skilled workers), refugees, self-employed, and retired. For the years after 1994 (inclusive), the people included in this category change somewhat. In addition to those categorized as retired, refugees, and those in the family class, there are also the following: business, those landed from the Live-in Caregiver Program, and provincial nominees.

[b] Those admitted under the entrepreneur and investor classes are excluded since they are employers, not workers, within the Canadian labour market.

TABLE 5.3
NIEAP, Total Number of People Admitted to Canada with Temporary Employment Authorizations, 1973–2004

Year	Migrant workers[a] (non-immigrant)	Entrepreneurs	Artists/entertainers	Sports, etc.	Not stated/open employment authorization[b]	Total
1973	69,901	122	12,432	1,259	132,317	216,031
1974	71,773	242	13,276	1,185	154,066	240,542
1975	77,149	211	17,464	1,198	175,133	271,155
1976	69,368	216	19,379	1,886	188,917	279,766
1977	67,130	249	19,945	1,861	179,901	269,021
1978	14,459	37	4,958	131	30,644	50,229
1979	31,996	117	21,371	1,336	14	54,834
1980	98,681	n/a	n/a	n/a	n/a	n/a
1981	96,750	147	32,063	1,889	1	130,850
1982	90,182	65	33,826	1,812	2	125,887
1983	84,184	45	34,731	2,151	19	121,130
1984	108,735	170	32,591	1,962	3	143,461
1985	128,692	495	28,277	1,827	5	159,296
1986	143,534	316	26,101	1,655	123	171,729
1987	149,603	146	24,864	1,683	19	176,315
1988	186,398	111	25,431	1,868	39	190,959
1989	160,162	87,724	27,254	1,730	40	276,910
1990	165,643	19,000	27,503	1,964	8	214,118
1991	182,771	20,916	25,466	1,890	26	231,069
1992	174,312	27,892	26,171	2,072	0	230,447
1993	151,890	15,493	24,949	2,117	50	194,499
1994	n/a	n/a	n/a	n/a	n/a	n/a
1995	124,371	16	14,853	1,421	29,108	169,769

TABLE 5.3 (*Concluded*)

Year	Migrant workers[a] (non-immigrant)	Entrepreneurs	Artists/entertainers	Sports, etc.	Not stated/open employment authorization[b]	Total
1996	110,871	252	14,648	1,536	41,719	169,026
1997	132,765	141	16,326	1,536	13,380	164,148
1998	150,149	3	17,771	1,516	0	169,439
1999	166,439	3	18,340	1,717	0	186,499
2000	179,569	3	19,235	1,668	0	200,475
2001	188,610	7	19,423	1,643	0	209,683
2002	196,409	9	13,638	1,490	0	215,546
2003	202,509	9	9,165	1,477	0	213,160
2004	228,677	32	8,185	1,199	0	238,093

Source: EIC, 1981–93; CIC, 1994b; 1995; 2005.

[a] The worker category represents the number of people admitted under the NIEAP as unfree wage labour with temporary employment authorizations within the following categories: managerial, administrative; natural sciences, engineering and mathematics; social sciences and related; religion; teaching; medicine and health; clerical; sales; service; farming, horticultural, and animal husbandry; fishing, hunting, and trapping; forestry and logging; mining and quarrying, including gas and oil; processing; machining; fabricating, assembly, and repair; construction; transport equipment operating; material handling; and other crafts and equipment operating.

After 1995, Citizenship and Immigration Canada changed the way that it classified data on the occupations for which people were issued temporary employment authorizations. Thus, for the years after 1995 (inclusive), the migrant workers (non-immigrant) category is inclusive of all categories listed under the National Occupational Codes, except the following: entrepreneur; circus performers; choreographers; conductors, composers, and arrangers; actors; musicians and singers; buskers; magicians and illusionists; models; puppeteers; athletes; coaches; sports officials and referees; and all those issued 'open' employment authorizations that were unrestricted to occupation or location. This way of accounting for the number of workers brought in through the NIEAP underestimates their numbers, as certain people who fall into the various occupational categories of artists/entertainers are, in fact, workers in the sex industry.

[b] After 1995 (inclusive), the category 'not stated' no longer appears. Instead, there is a category 'any occupation – open employment.' The numbers of people issued temporary employment authorizations who have no specified employer or occupation on it have been excluded from the total number of people considered as 'migrant workers' under the NIEAP.

are admitted with landed status with those entering under temporary employment authorizations. Landed workers have virtually the same rights as Canadian citizens while those classified as temporary migrant workers do not.[8]

Before we can make an accurate comparison of those landed immigrants indicating their intention to work in Canada (i.e., 'destined') with those non-immigrants recruited as unfree wage workers, it is necessary to include those workers recruited as domestic servants in Canada (table 5.4).[9] Until 1995 they were not included in the overall numbers of workers admitted with temporary employment authorizations. They, too, enter the country as non-immigrants under temporary employment authorizations and, therefore, ought to be included in the category of non-immigrant, or migrant, workers (until 1995, after which time, I have not added them to the total).

If we categorize the number of destined immigrants and those given temporary employment authorizations to work in Canada as the total number of *(im)migrant workers* admitted into the country, then the proportion of destined workers (those given landed status) accounts for 57 per cent of all workers entering the country in 1973 (see table 5.5). By 1993, 65,130 permanent immigrants were considered as 'destined' to the labour market while 153,988 were admitted under temporary employment authorizations. This means that of the total number of (im)migrant workers admitted to Canada in 1993 (219,118), only 30 per cent received landed status while 70 per cent came in on temporary employment authorizations. By 2004, 65 per cent of all (im)migrant workers entered as migrant workers while only 35 per cent received landed status.

Indeed, soon after the NIEAP was introduced, *most* (im)migrant workers began to enter Canada as unfree wage workers. Temporary migrant workers, from constituting a minority of (im)migrant workers entering Canada in 1973, made up the majority of all (im)migrant workers for all except six of the past thirty-one years (1973, 1974, 1975, 1978, 1979, and 1996) of the operation of the NIEAP. Since that time, anywhere from 57 to 78 per cent of all workers entering Canada have done so under the unfree conditions regulated by the NIEAP. In some years the number of non-immigrant workers has even exceeded the *total* number of landed immigrants in Canada ('destined' workers in all classes of immigration *plus* family class *plus* refugees *plus* entrepreneurs – see table 5.1). This occurred most recently in 1988 when 161,929 landed immigrants entered Canada while 194,454 workers entered on temporary employment authorizations (see tables 5.1 and 5.5). It occurred

TABLE 5.4
Persons Admitted to Work as Domestic Servants in
Canada with Temporary Employment Authorizations, Foreign Domestic Movement Program (1982–
1991) and Live-in Caregiver Program (1992–2004)

Year	Total
1982	11,327
1983	3,506
1984	4,562
1985	5,475
1986	6,933
1987	7,889
1988	8,056
1989	8,842
1990	10,734
1991	8,621
1992	3,968
1993	2,098
1994	n/a
1995	7,781
1996	7,400
1997	7,472
1998	7,685
1999	7,834
2000	8,124
2001	10,531
2002	13,464
2003	15,657
2004	19,820

Source: INTERCEDE, 1993; 1994; CIC, 2005.

most dramatically in 1986 when over 50,000 more unfree wage workers were admitted than the total of landed immigrants.

As table 5.5 shows, the significance of unfree wage workers is most marked in the period between 1983 and 1986 when the levels of the permanent component of immigration decreased substantially (Michalowski, 1993:75). It was during these years that the high mark in the proportion of workers admitted on temporary employment visas was reached. In 1983, 71 per cent of all workers were admitted under the unfree conditions of the NIEAP. In 1984 the percentage was 75. In 1985 the percentage reached its all-time high of 78. It remained high in 1986 at 70 per cent, in 1987 at 74 per cent, and in 1988 at 73 per cent. In 2004,

TABLE 5.5

Total Number (and Percentage) of (Im)migrant Workers in the Canadian Labour Market by Calendar Year, Permanent Residents Destined to the Labour Market, and Temporary Migrant Workers, 1973–2004

Year	Destined (Immigrant Workers)	Visa[a] (Non-Immigrant, or Migrant, Workers)	Total (Im)migrant Workers[b]
1973	92,228 (57)	69,901 (43)	162,129 (100)
1974	106,083 (60)	71,773 (40)	177,856 (100)
1975	81,189 (51)	77,149 (49)	158,338 (100)
1976	61,461 (47)	69,368 (53)	130,829 (100)
1977	47,625 (41)	67,130 (59)	114,755 (100)
1978	34,762 (71)	14,459 (29)	49,221 (100)
1979	47,949 (60)	31,996 (40)	79,945 (100)
1980	63,479 (39)	98,681 (61)	162,160 (100)
1981	56,676 (37)	96,750 (63)	153,426 (100)
1982	55,023 (35)	101,509 (65)	156,532 (100)
1983	36,540 (29)	87,700 (71)	124,240 (100)
1984	37,468 (25)	113,297 (75)	150,765 (100)
1985	36,949 (22)	134,167 (78)	171,116 (100)
1986	63,479 (30)	150,467 (70)	213,946 (100)
1987	56,676 (26)	157,492 (74)	214,168 (100)
1988	73,134 (27)	194,454 (73)	267,588 (100)
1989	94,412 (36)	169,004 (64)	263,416 (100)
1990	109,840 (38)	176,377 (62)	286,217 (100)
1991	127,870 (40)	191,392 (60)	319,262 (100)
1992	137,360 (43)	178,280 (57)	315,640 (100)
1993	65,130 (30)	153,988 (70)	219,118 (100)
1994	109,165	n/a	n/a
1995	109,937 (47)	124,371 (53)	234,308 (100)
1996	118,725 (52)	110,871 (48)	229,596 (100)
1997	111,417 (46)	132,765 (54)	244,182 (100)
1998	90,766 (38)	150,149 (62)	240,915 (100)
1999	100,746 (38)	166,439 (62)	267,185 (100)
2000	120,856 (40)	179,569 (60)	300,425 (100)
2001	131,599 (41)	188,610 (59)	320,209 (100)
2002	118,147 (38)	196,409 (62)	314,556 (100)
2003	117,637 (37)	202,509 (63)	320,146 (100)
2004	124,829 (35)	228,677 (65)	353,506 (100)

Source: EIC, 1980–93; CIC, 1995; 2005; INTERCEDE, 1993, 1994.

[a] 'Visa' refers to the number of people admitted to Canada and working in Canada during the calendar year recorded. The total number of migrant workers includes 'workers' (table 5.3) plus those in the Foreign Domestic Movement Program (1982–1991) and those in the Live-in Caregiver Program (1992–2004) (table 5.4). For the years 1989–1993, the category 'backlog clearance,' given to refugees granted temporary employment authorizations while waiting for their status to be determined, is also excluded

[b] This category includes all those entering Canada under the above 'destined' and 'visa' categories.

65 per cent of (im)migrant workers entered Canada on temporary employment authorizations.

The economic recession of the late 1970s and early 1980s, combined with pressures placed upon the state by anti-immigration forces, led to a reduction in the number of landed immigrants (Berdichewski, 1991). However, we see that the *total* number of workers entering Canada was sustained. Thus, while employers were able to continue recruiting an (im)migrant workforce during this time, the overwhelming majority were obliged to work as unfree contract labour as a condition of entry to and residence in Canada.

It appears then that the permanent component of Canadian immigration policy is subject to greater fluctuation from economic, social, or political forces than is the NIEAP. Whether the number of landed immigrants admitted annually is high or low, the number of temporary migrant workers continues to grow – or at least remain steady. Indeed, except in 1978 and 1979, the *proportion* of workers admitted on employment authorizations has never fallen below 1974 levels.

As a reflection of the demand for unfree contract labour, these figures indicate that so-called shortages in the Canadian labour market are not as temporary as the federal government states (MIC, 1974). Indeed, it is useful to highlight the comparison between (im)migrant workers *specifically* recruited for the Canadian labour market – independent class immigrants/skilled workers who are free wage workers and those admitted as unfree workers under the NIEAP.

Table 5.6 indicates that of all (im)migrant workers recruited for labour market needs, over three-quarters were employed as unfree wage labour in Canada in 2004. In some years the proportion has reached 90 per cent of all those recruited (1984 and 1985). Over the past thirty-one years, the lowest proportion of unfree migrant workers to independent or skilled workers class immigrant workers has been 66 per cent in 1996 (when those admitted as assisted relative class immigrants were included along with independent class immigrants in the new skilled workers class) The significance of the NIEAP can perhaps be better visualized by examining figure 5.1.

It should, by this point, be clear that unfree forms of labour migration dominate in the recruitment of (im)migrant workers to Canada. Since 1980 the proportion of unfree to free wage (im)migrant labour has never fallen below 66 per cent. The average proportion of unfree wage to the total of all (im)migrants specifically recruited to the labour market in Canada in the period 1980 to 2004 has been 77 per cent. In

TABLE 5.6

Labour Recruitment to Canada from Abroad, Number of Persons (and Percentage) Admitted as Independent Class Immigrants and Temporary Migrant Workers, 1980–2004

Year	Independent/ Skilled Workers[a]	Visa[b]	Total
1980	31,549 (24)	98,681 (76)	130,230 (100)
1981	36,941 (28)	96,750 (72)	133,691 (100)
1982	33,678 (25)	101,509 (75)	135,187 (100)
1983	13,176 (13)	87,700 (87)	100,876 (100)
1984	12,343 (10)	113,297 (90)	125,640 (100)
1985	13,051 (9)	134,167 (91)	147,218 (100)
1986	22,634 (13)	150,467 (87)	173,101 (100)
1987	50,921 (24)	157,492 (76)	208,413 (100)
1988	49,906 (20)	194,454 (80)	244,360 (100)
1989	51,574 (23)	169,004 (77)	220,578 (100)
1990	53,712 (23)	176,377 (77)	230,089 (100)
1991	47,497 (20)	191,392 (80)	238,889 (100)
1992	47,505 (21)	178,280 (79)	225,785 (100)
1993	49,292 (24)	153,988 (76)	203,280 (100)
1994	39,890	n/a	n/a
1995	47,197 (28)	124,371 (72)	171,568 (100)
1996	56,278 (34)	110,871 (66)	167,149 (100)
1997	58,637 (31)	132,765 (69)	191,402 (100)
1998	45,568 (23)	150,149 (77)	195,717 (100)
1999	52,926 (24)	166,439 (76)	219,365 (100)
2000	68,460 (28)	179,569 (72)	248,029 (100)
2001	77,665 (29)	188,610 (71)	266,275 (100)
2002	69,564 (26)	196,409 (74)	265,973 (100)
2003	62,585 (31)	202,509 (69)	265,094 (100)
2004	64,374 (22)	228,677 (78)	293,051 (100)

Source: EIC, 1981–93; CIC, 1994b; 1995; 2005.
[a] This category is the 'Independent' category seen in table 5.2.
[b] This category is the Visa category in table 5.5.

other words there has been a ratio of almost 4:1 in favour of the recruitment of unfree wage labour during the period under study.

While the Canadian government states that the NIEAP is used to meet temporary shortages within the labour market, the *qualitative* nature of these labour shortages is emphasized when we take a look at Canada's official unemployment rates during the time of the program's implementation as well as in its operation in successive years. The official unemployment rate in Canada in 1973 was 5.5 per cent. In

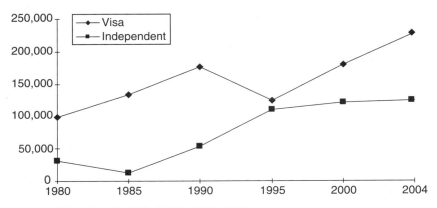

Source: EIC, 1981–93; CIC, 1994b; 1995; 2005.

Figure 5.1   (Im)migrants Specifically Recruited as Workers: Independent / Skilled Workers Class Immigrants and Temporary Migrant Workers, 1980–2004

this year 69,901 people were admitted as migrant workers. The top three broad occupational groupings employing unfree contract labour were service (17.2 per cent), farming (13.3 per cent), and fabricating, assembly, and repair (11.4 per cent). Together these three occupations accounted for approximately 42 per cent of all jobs filled that year (CIC, 1995).

Ten years later, in 1983, the official unemployment rate had skyrocketed to 11.9 per cent while the number of migrant workers had risen to 87,700 (EIC, 1984). In this year, service (29 per cent), farming (9.5 per cent), and fabricating, assembly, and repair (13.2 per cent) accounted for about 52 per cent of all migrant workers (CIC, 1995). In 1993 the unemployment rate remained high at 11.2 per cent while the number of migrant workers had again risen: this time by over 65,000, to reach 153,988 (CIC, 1994b). Again, service (11.3 per cent) and farming (14.1 per cent) were in the top three of all occupational groupings (CIC, 1995). Fabricating, assembly, and repair remained in the top five of all occupations employing unfree contract workers. The estimated unemployment rate for 2004 was 7.8 per cent while the number of migrant workers had grown to 228,677. Unfortunately, CIC stopped gathering data on the broad occupational categories of people on temporary employment authorizations after 1995 although occupations that would have been previously placed in the service sector, in fabricating, assembly, and repair, and in farming again top the list.

The demand for migrant workers in particular industries has, thus, remained steady. Yet, the Canadian government insists that employers in need of temporary migrant workers *cannot* recruit them 'if the job offers *reasonable prospects of continuity*' and must, instead, seek immigrants granted permanent residence rights in the country or citizens (CIC, 1994a:4, emphasis added). However, not only is it questionable whether there has been an actual *quantitative* shortage of qualified workers available for most positions filled by workers employed under temporary visas, it is also clear that jobs within these occupations do, indeed, 'offer reasonable prospects of continuity.' In fact, in some occupations, such as those in the farming sector, employers often hire the same employees every year for the same job (Wall, 1992; Basok, 2002).

While workers admitted under the unfree conditions imposed by the NIEAP comprise the majority of workers officially migrating to Canada, there is great variety in the composition of this labour force and in the kinds of jobs that they perform. Employees for both professional and non-professional occupations are sought.[10] Unlike professionals, though, workers admitted to Canada and classified as unskilled come largely through the NIEAP while those whose skills are officially recognized are, at times, able to gain access to permanent resident status in the country. Yet, even skilled workers are successively being shifted to entry under employment authorizations. Thus, while unskilled workers are disproportionately denied permanent resident status many of the skilled occupations increasingly rely upon workers admitted on temporary employment visas.[11]

For example, in the case of filling unskilled or semi-skilled occupations, in 1991, 1,974 persons were granted permanent resident status in Canada and stated their intention to work in the broad occupational category of farming. In contrast, in that year 13,868 people were admitted on temporary employment authorizations for farming occupations. Of all people entering the farming sector, therefore, 88 per cent entered under the unfree conditions imposed by the NIEAP (EIC, 1991). Likewise, in 1991, 9,922 people (22 per cent) were given permanent resident status for work in the service sector, while 34,648 (78 per cent) were admitted as unfree contract labour (EIC, 1991).

Importantly, workers who enter occupations normatively classified as unskilled, such as seasonal agricultural workers and domestic workers, are unable to enter Canada through *any* other avenue other than as unfree contract labour. For these occupations, temporary status is applied on a permanent basis (Arat-Koc, 1992:231). People applying for landed status from outside Canada to work in either seasonal farming or domestic occupations are categorically rejected. However, they make up a substantial proportion of workers admitted under temporary employment visas.

Reasons for the introduction of mobility restrictions upon these two types of work shed light on the purposes of the NIEAP. Prior to the imposition of unfree conditions, workers admitted to work in these two occupations sought other types of employment soon after arriving in Canada. This was because of the substandard working conditions and pay rates employers in the country provided. Workers were able to seek other employment, because they had the labour market and geographical freedoms associated with permanent residency. As a result, the turnover rate in these sectors was enormous (Arat-Koc, 1992). The introduction of temporary employment authorizations offered employers a solution to this problem. Hence, while the demand for workers in these areas has never abated, the supply has been ensured by the state by indenturing workers to their employer through the conditions imposed on the worker by their temporary employment authorizations.

We see a similar trend emerging for many other occupational groupings, including those normatively classified as skilled. Immigration statistics show that in the medicine and health sector, for instance, 5,281 people (66 per cent) were admitted as permanent residents in 1973 while 2,575 (33 per cent) gained entry under temporary employment authorizations. By 1991, however, an almost equal number of people were admitted on either basis: 3,573 (49 per cent) were given permanent status; 3,640 (51 per cent) were admitted on temporary employment authorizations (EIC, 1992). The state, thus, has used entry regulations to convert 'what otherwise might have been permanent settlers into a temporary transient labour force' (Bolaria, 1992:213).

While the number of people admitted for work in non-professional occupations continues to be the *main* component of the NIEAP, the number admitted for professional occupations is significant and this number has remained consistent throughout the period under study. In 1973, 23 per cent of all workers admitted under temporary employment authorizations fell within the professional category, in 1993, the percentage of professionals was 24 (CIC, 1995). Even though professional and relatively high-cost workers do not face the same degree of exploitation and subordination as low-cost labour, most of these work-ers are not the high-flyers touted as the future 'global worker' by some business pundits.

The vast majority of people admitted under temporary employment authorizations within the professional category, like their non-profes-sional counterparts, are unfree. They do not have the ability to choose whom to work for and where to work. Furthermore, much of the pres-sure to impose conditions of unfreedom upon their labour power comes from professional associations, like those governing doctors (Bolaria, 1992). These groups have successfully lobbied the state for a monopoly position with regard to assignment and a right to exercise 'closure.'[12]

For instance, instead of admitting licensed physicians as permanent residents and allowing them entry to professional organizations, the Canadian state annually admits well over 300 physicians to the country under temporary employment visas where they are used to meet needs in 'underserviced areas and in certain short supply specialties' (Joint Working Group, 1986:ii). Again, instead of seeing the shortages of phy-sicians in specific geographical or specialty-related areas as *quantitative,* it is more accurate to understand such shortages as largely qualitative, for they coincide with the least desirable jobs and the least desirable loca-tions in which physicians with citizenship or with permanent resident status prefer not to practise (Mick, 1975; Ishi, 1982). The reason for the low preference rate of these positions is that they offer relatively lower pay and lower chances for career enhancement (Bolaria, 1992:224).

While it is clear that low-cost and low-skilled as well as high-cost and high-skilled labour power (and various combinations thereof) are being imported as an unfree labour force, there are important gendered differentiations between those who fill such occupations. In 1991, the last year in which statistics are collected for employment authoriza-tions issued by broad occupational groupings and sex, we see that women are overrepresented in the service (89 per cent) and clerical (65 per cent) occupations. Men are strongly overrepresented in the natural sciences, engineering, and mathematics (89 per cent), managerial (83 per cent), and fabricating and repair (93 per cent) (EIC, 1992) sectors. Overall, men are highly overrepresented in professional occupations while women are concentrated and overrepresented in the service – particularly the personal service – occupations, such as domestic work (EIC, 1992). This is not atypical of the distribution of women and men within the Canadian labour market at large. Thus, it seems that the

NIEAP reflects and further entrenches the gendered division of labour already in operation in Canada.

In order to better situate workers admitted to Canada as unfree wage labour within the spatial allocation of wealth and power, and understand how the work that various migrant workers perform is racialized, it becomes necessary to examine the relationship between where in the world workers come from prior to entering Canada and examine how this may affect the type of occupation they are contracted to do. It is also important to examine the length of time that various groups of migrant workers labour under conditions of unfreedom in Canada. To do so, I have cross-tabulated data on country of last permanent residence with data on the broad occupational categorization of workers admitted under the NIEAP for the years 1973 to 1993 (CIC, 1995).[13]

From the information provided, the category of source region has been constructed from a collation of source countries. To best examine broader global trends, these source regions have then been collated into the categories of less economically developed countries (LEACs) in the global South and the economically advanced countries (EACs) in the global North. The reader should be cautioned, however, that this is a very rough accounting of global differentiations in the wealth and power of people in the countries of last permanent residence of non-immigrants since it inflates the numbers of people arriving from the EACs. This is because all those in Eastern Europe, which often occupies a middle area between EACs and LEACs, are included as EACs.[14]

Table 5.7 shows that of all professionals entering Canada through the NIEAP in 1973, 89 per cent were from the EACs. This is especially true in the case of management and administration jobs that are held disproportionately by people from the EACs (90 per cent in 1973). This fact has remained consistent. In 1993, 78 per cent of all professionals were from the EACs while 91 per cent of all managers and administrators were from these countries (CIC, 1995).

In contrast, within certain of the lowest paying occupations with the poorest documented working conditions, people from the LEACs, particularly women, predominate (Arat-Koc, 1992). For instance, in the occupation of domestic worker, over 80 per cent, 95 per cent of whom are women, are recruited from the LEACs (Cornish, 1992). Indeed, this proportion has progressively increased since 1973 (Arat-Koc, 1992; Cornish, 1992). These trends fit the worldwide pattern of migration

TABLE 5.7
Number of workers (and Percentage) Employed under Temporary
Employment Authorizations, within Professional Categories, Sorted by
Source Region (EACs and LEACs), 1973–1993

Year	EACs	LEACs	Total
1973	16,316 (89)	2,069 (11)	18,385 (100)
1974	18,442 (90)	2,081 (10)	20,523 (100)
1975	21,516 (87)	3,098 (13)	24,617 (100)
1976	20,787 (84)	4,006 (16)	24.793 (100)
1977	20,024 (83)	4,135 (17)	24,159 (100)
1978	4,208 (84)	799 (16)	5.007 (100)
1979	10,258 (92)	949 (08)	11,207 (100)
1980	n/a	n/a	n/a
1981	27,157 (79)	7,062 (21)	34,219 (100)
1982	25,371 (77)	7,516 (23)	32,887 (100)
1983	26,172 (77)	7,957 (23)	34,129 (100)
1984	26,857 (75)	9,090 (25)	35,947 (100)
1985	27,809 (75)	9,473 (25)	37,282 (100)
1986	28,517 (74)	10,200 (26)	38,717 (100)
1987	28,457 (83)	6,035 (17)	34,492 (100)
1988	31,260 (72)	12,742 (28)	44,002 (100)
1989	28,489 (66)	14,860 (34)	43,349 (100)
1990	29,111 (71)	12,009 (29)	41,120 (100)
1991	34,122 (75)	11,177 (25)	45,299 (100)
1992	28,758 (76)	9,079 (24)	37,837 (100)
1993	28,464 (78)	8,103 (22)	36,567 (100)

Source: CIC, 1995.

from the LEACs to the EACs, where because of the historical cheapening of the labour power of people from the LEACs, particularly that of women, it is more cost-effective to employ these workers. Moreover, these workers lives and ability to earn a living are more precarious, thereby weakening their ability to resist poor wages and working conditions. The Caribbean region sends the largest proportion of non-professional workers. For this area, throughout the period under study the percentage of non-professionals has averaged levels approaching 100 per cent (CIC, 1995).

When examining how the broad source region of migrant workers is related to occupational categories and length of stay, it becomes evident that workers from the LEACs, or what Hage (2000) terms 'Third

TABLE 5.8
Number of Persons (and Percentage) on Short-Term and Long-Term
Temporary Employment Authorizations: 1980, 1981, 1985–1988,
Including the Foreign Domestic Movement Program (1985–1988)[a]

Year	Short-Term	Long-Term	Total
1980	70,211 (71)	28,470 (29)	98,681 (100)
1981	102,893 (70)	43,853 (30)	146,747 (100)
1985	77,912 (52)	71,231 (48)	149,143 (100)
1986	99,697 (56)	79,517 (44)	179,214 (100)
1987	107,360 (52)	99,421 (48)	206,781 (100)
1988	112,404 (47)	126,428 (53)	238,832 (100)

Source: EIC, 1981; 1982; 1986; 1987; 1988; 1989.
[a] Workers entering under the Foreign Domestic Movement Program
  have been included in the long-term visa holder category, as they
  are admitted for a period of two years.

World-looking people,' find themselves largely within subordinate
occupational categories. Approximately 90 per cent of workers from
the LEACs are employed in non-professional occupations (CIC, 1995).
Since the vast majority of those within professional occupations arrive
from the EACs, it is clear that the NIEAP essentially mirrors – and further exacerbates – the racialized labour market already existing in Canada (Tomaskovic-Devey, 1993).

From the limited available data, it is clear that workers from the
LEACs work under the unfree conditions imposed by their temporary
employment authorization for *longer* periods of time than do their
counterparts from the EACs. The vast majority of workers from these
countries are employed in Canada on long-term temporary employment authorizations. It is workers from the EACs who are here largely
on a short-term basis. Importantly, for future trends, it appears that the
period of time that each worker is employed under unfree conditions
is increasing.[15]

Table 5.8 shows that from 1981 to 1988, while the overall number of
people admitted through the NIEAP has more than doubled, there has
been a significant shift in the proportion of short-term over long-term
visa holders. Moreover, these data do not exclude those who cannot be
considered to be migrant workers as other tables have done. Thus, the
number of short-term visas issued to sports figures and entertainers, for

instance, exaggerates the number of short-term visas issued. Nonetheless, in 1981, 71 per cent of temporary migrant workers entered under short-term visas. By 1988, 53 per cent of workers holding employment authorizations were in the country on long-term visas. This reflects Michalowski's findings that:

> overall, labour migration under the auspices of the Canadian [Non-immigrant] Employment Authorization Programme, although temporary in the sense of the legal right of persons to settlement, is in practice predominately long-term migration ... It is evident that, over time, migrant workers increasingly became long-term residents in Canada. Interestingly, this is a universal pattern of visa worker flows, regardless of origin. It is, however, especially reinforced among workers from all American sub-regions except North America [U.S. and Mexico]. At the end of the 1980s, close to 80 per cent of Caribbean workers and about 90 percent of those from Central and South America had resided in Canada for at least 12 months. (1993:11)

Given global disparities, it is not surprising to find that people from the LEACs are in a position where they must accept employment conditions which are unfree and temporary for longer periods of time than do people from the EACs. It is safe to say, then, that for many people from the LEACs, a temporary stay in Canada is becoming a much more permanent feature of their ability to live and work in the country. It is significant, therefore, that both the absolute numbers and the proportion of workers from the LEACs made to live and work in Canada under unfree conditions is increasing.

As we see in table 5.9, in 1973, 61 per cent of all unfree wage workers employed under temporary visas were from the EACs. This proportion drops to 43 per cent, however, by 1993. In 2004 the proportion of total temporary employment authorizations issued to people from the EACs is also 43 per cent. Conversely, the proportion of workers from the LEACs increases from 39 per cent in 1973 to 57 per cent in 1993 and 2004. There is, therefore, a clear trend towards the decrease in the number of people from the EACs and an increase in those from the LEACs. While working under conditions of unfreedom, by definition, denies workers from any country the ability to competitively enter labour markets to negotiate for better wages or working conditions, it appears that, over time, Canada has increasingly sought out sources of labour power that have been historically cheapened and weakened. This is even more

TABLE 5.9
Number of Persons (and Percentage) Admitted to Canada under Temporary Employment Authorizations by EACs and LEACs, 1973–2004[a]

Year	EACs	LEACs	Total
1973	42,385 (61)	27,516 (39)	69,901 (100)
1974	49,467 (69)	22,306 (31)	71,773 (100)
1975	55,458 (72)	21,691 (28)	77,149 (100)
1976	48,507 (70)	20,861 (30)	69,368 (100)
1977	46,610 (76)	20,520 (24)	67,130 (100)
1978	10,334 (71)	4,125 (29)	14,459 (100)
1979	22,814 (71)	9,182 (29)	31,996 (100)
1980	n/a	n/a	n/a
1981	61,657 (63)	35,093 (36)	96,750 (100)
1982	56,329 (55)	45,180 (45)	101,509 (100)
1983	55,338 (63)	32,362 (37)	87,700 (100)
1984	56,775 (50)	56,522 (50)	113,297 (100)
1985	66,265 (49)	67,902 (51)	134,167 (100)
1986	72,032 (48)	78,435 (52)	150,467 (100)
1987	76,507 (49)	80,895 (51)	157,492 (100)
1988	85,507 (44)	108,947 (56)	194,454 (100)
1989	70,866 (42)	98,138 (58)	169,004 (100)
1990	75,293 (43)	101,084 (57)	176,377 (100)
1991	76,721 (40)	114,671 (60)	191,392 (100)
1992	73,880 (41)	104,400 (59)	178,280 (100)
1993	65,594 (43)	88,394 (57)	153,988 (100)
1994	n/a	n/a	n/a
1995	92,541 (55)	77,212 (45)	169,753 (100)

apparent if we account for the inclusion of Eastern European countries, particularly the newly formed states emerging out of the collapse of the Soviet Union, in the broad category of EACs and remove these countries from that category (table 5.10).

When this is done, the proportion of workers from the EACs is reduced to 39 per cent in 2004. The increase in workers from more impoverished places in the world is accounted for by the absolute growth in numbers of workers coming from various Asian countries. In this regard, the Canadian national state has again conformed to worldwide patterns where the importance of Asia as a broad source of unfree contract labour has increased enormously over the last thirty-odd years (Appleyard, 1991:40–1). In 1973, fewer than 10,000 migrant workers arrived to Canada from Asia.[16] This figure remained fairly stable throughout the 1970s and 1980s. By 1993, however, more than

TABLE 5.9   (*Concluded*)

Year	EACs	LEACs	Total
1996	93,842 (56)	74,932 (44)	168,774 (100)
1997	95,536 (58)	68,381 (42)	163,917 (100)
1998	98,374 (57)	74,655 (43)	173,029 (100)
1999	108,953 (58)	77,543 (42)	186,496 (100)
2000	115,645 (58)	84,827 (42)	200,472 (100)
2001	111,121 (53)	98,555 (47)	209,676 (100)
2002	100,809 (48)	110,787 (52)	211,596 (100)
2003	92,745 (44)	120,406 (56)	213,151 (100)
2004	103,361 (43)	134,700 (57)	238,061 (100)

Source: CIC, 1995; 2005.

[a] For the years 1973–1993, the total number of people admitted from the EACs and the LEACs are workers as previously defined. However, for the years after 1995 (inclusive), I was not able to collect data that cross-tabulated country of last permanent residence with the National Occupational Code for people issued temporary employment authorizations. Thus, those who cannot reasonably be considered unfree migrant workers, such as entrepreneurs, artists/entertainers, sports figures, and those with any occupation – open employment work visas remain included in the total number of temporary employment authorizations issued. Not only does this mean that for the years 1995–2004, I am not able to calculate the number of workers admitted under the NIEAP by country of last permanent residents but that there is an over-inflation of the numbers of people admitted from EACs, since the vast majority of people admitted as artists/entertainers and sports figures come from the EACs. Moreover, since the category of EACs includes countries in Eastern Europe, the numbers of people from the EACs is also over-inflated.

45,000 workers arrived from various Asian countries representing more than 30 per cent of all workers employed under the unfree conditions imposed by their temporary employment authorizations (CIC, 1995). China and the Philippines were the main source countries for the majority of these workers. In 2004, while the total number of people from various Asian countries increased to more than 72,000 workers, their overall percentage remained approximately 30 per cent (CIC, 2005). The top three source countries in Asia in that year were the Philippines, China, and India.

With the increase in numbers of unfree workers and their subordinate working conditions, one might expect that coalitions between free and unfree wage workers would be formed. However, the rights and privileges available to unfree wage workers differ so drastically from others in the Canadian workforce that they have been constructed as

TABLE 5.10
Number of Persons (and Percentage) Admitted to Canada under Temporary Employment Authorizations by Eastern Europe, by Non-Eastern European EACs, and by LEACs, 1995–2004

Year	Eastern European Countries	EACs minus Eastern European Countries	LEACs	Total
1995	11,064 (7)	81,477 (48)	77,212 (45)	169,753 (100)
1996	8,032 (5)	85,810 (51)	74,932 (44)	168,774 (100)
1997	7,962 (5)	87,574 (53)	68,381 (42)	163,917 (100)
1998	8,786 (5)	89,588 (52)	74,655 (43)	173,029 (100)
1999	12,909 (7)	96,044 (51)	77,543 (42)	186,496 (100)
2000	16,954 (8)	98,691 (49)	84,827 (43)	200,472 (100)
2001	10,987 (5)	100,134 (48)	98,555 (47)	209,676 (100)
2002	10,790 (5)	90,019 (43)	110,787 (52)	211,596 (100)
2003	10,396 (5)	82,349 (39)	120,406 (56)	213,151 (100)
2004	10,296 (4)	93,065 (39)	134,700 (57)	238,061 (100)

Source: CIC, 1995; 2005.

occupying a wholly separate pool of labour. As already discussed, the overriding issue is the lack of both labour market and geographical freedoms available to them.

The very fact that workers on employment authorizations face restrictions upon their mobility allows employers that much more control over many aspects of their lives. For instance, for the thousands of farm workers admitted annually under the NIEAP, permission from the employer is required simply to leave his or her property (Wall, 1992:268). Likewise, domestic workers are forced to live with their employer as a condition of entry and continued residence in Canada (Arat-Koc, 1992).

Other methods of controlling or limiting the resistance of migrant workers rest on the fact that they encounter serious barriers to their ability to collectively bargain for improved working and living conditions. The very fact that this workforce is rotated hinders efforts to form collectives. As is the case for migrant domestic workers, who are forced to live in the residence of their employer, the ability to organize and ultimately strike is severely constrained by the fact that their place of work is also their place of residence. Furthermore, Wall has found that many temporary migrant workers, in their attempt to secure future employment in Canada, do not organize, because of fear of retaliation by the employer upon whom they pin their hopes for future work in the country. This is because 'eligibility for extended employment opportunities depends on whether employees are [seen as] desirable workers' (Wall, 1992:269). However, it is the fear of deportation if the employer is displeased in any way that is *the* overarching factor controlling these workers' militancy and should not be underestimated, particularly given the conditions that force many of these workers to migrate in search of employment abroad in the first place.

The lack of a legally binding contract further compounds the subordinate wages and working conditions experienced by workers admitted under the NIEAP. The problem of contract enforcement results, in part, from the prevailing (and convenient) division of power between the federal and provincial levels of government (Breti and Davidson, 1989). Migrant workers are caught in a double bind since they are, on the one hand, *bound* by employment agreements witnessed and enforced by the federal immigration department but they are not *protected* by the terms of such an agreement because labour legislation is under provincial jurisdiction. Indeed, federal employment agreements cannot be legally binding upon the employer since they are not considered labour contracts per se (CIC, 1994a). There are immigration contracts.

In examining these factors, one study conducted by AMSSA concludes that 'the agreement works out to be a "contract" with respect to the rights of the employer and the obligations of the employee, but a loose agreement with respect to the rights of the employee. Indeed ... workers are caught between a federal government which promises protection and provincial statutes which, either do not provide or are ineffective, in protecting foreign ... workers [sic]' (1993:9–10).

It is state regulations that render migrant workers socially and politically powerless in Canada – not any inherent qualities embodied in this workforce. Ultimately, it is the denial of citizenship or permanent resident status that differentiates migrant workers from others in Canada. Their non-immigrant status is used to deny them the rights normally associated with citizenship, that is, civil, political, and social rights. For instance, while federal and provincial human rights acts normally protect workers with respect to employment or any term or condition of employment because of the race, colour, ancestry, place of origin, political belief, religion, marital status, physical or mental disability, sex, or age, or because of a conviction for a criminal or summary conviction charge that is unrelated to the employment or to the intended employment of that person, it does *not* protect against discrimination on the basis of *nationality* (i.e., citizenship status) or a lack of permanent (or legal) resident status in Canada.

Workers admitted to Canada under the NIEAP are further differentiated from other workers with regard to their ability to access social programs. The Canadian government denies migrant workers access to many social services, such as unemployment insurance programs or social assistance. Only citizens and permanent residents are eligible for such programs in Canada. Again, since this group of workers does not have recourse to the social wage, not only is their comparable living standard considerably lower but they are also much more vulnerable to employers' demands than are workers who have the option of decommodifying themselves and standing outside the formal labour market through their access to social welfare provisions.[17]

The discrimination faced by workers admitted under the NIEAP with regard to social programs is further compounded by the fact that they pay fees and taxes to the government. Indeed, to enter Canada under the unfree conditions imposed by temporary employment authorizations, workers are charged a non-refundable 'processing fee.' In 1993 this fee was $100 (Serafico, 1995). Thus, the government received over $15 million from the 153,988 workers admitted to Canada under this program that year. Furthermore, in the years between 1973 and 1981, migrant domestic workers *alone* paid over $11 million into social program funds but were not eligible to make claims on these funds because of their non-permanent status (Arat-Koc, 1989).

The NIEAP therefore has allowed the state to have 'the maximal benefit of importing labour from all over the world without having to finance the overhead costs of labour reproduction' (Bolaria, 1992:212). Thus, the employment authorization program allows for the externalization to another state certain of the costs of labour force training as well as renewal (Buroway, 1976). Still, one might assume that with the extensive use of unfree labour power in Canada within many sectors of employment, governments and employers would face more questions and even resistance concerning the highly unequal treatment of migrant workers. As will be shown, however, the denial of citizenship rights, the non-immigrant labelling, and the invisibility of the program all contribute to the legitimation of their exclusion from the same protections available to permanent residents and citizens in Canada.

The NIEAP is probably one of the least discussed aspects of Canadian immigration policy. Foreshadowing the move to more and more regressive definitions of citizenship, the Canadian state labels those entering the country on temporary employment authorizations as *non*-immigrants,' thus providing the legitimacy for excluding them from statistics on *immigration* levels to the country. For most years migrant workers are excluded from annual statistics published by the department responsible for (im)migration. Indeed, it was not until 1980, a full seven years after the implementation of this program, that statistics began to be publicly disseminated by the government on the number of people entering Canada on employment authorizations.[18] Moreover, rather than providing public and easy access to such information, one often has to contact the department and request information, thus assuming a certain awareness of the program. This has led to the specialization of its study instead of enabling a popular understanding of the impact of the NIEAP upon Canadian society.

The more or less invisibility of this program promotes the notion that only landed immigrants account for the numbers of people migrating to Canada (Michalowski, 1993). Official levels of annual immigration into Canada *exclude* the number of people who enter on non-immigrant employment authorizations. Thus, for 1993, we are told that 254,321 were admitted to the country. If we add the total figure for workers entering on temporary employment authorizations (153,988), then the number of people entering Canada in 1993 as either permanent residents or as workers with temporary employment authorizations is, instead, 408,309.[19] Ten years later, in 2003, we are told that 221,352 people immigrated to Canada. However, this total excludes the 202,509 migrant workers who entered Canada that year.

Along with being labelled as 'non-immigrants,' workers admitted under the NIEAP are designated as 'temporary' persons within Canada. To define a human being as *temporarily* living in a particular situation has historically made it more palatable to deny her or him the same rights available to those classified as 'permanent.' The notion that some workers migrate to Canada only as 'sojourners' rather than with the intention of establishing permanent residency adds legitimacy to this unequal treatment, since it adds a voluntary veneer to the exploitation experienced (Chan, 1980).[20] Consequently, migrant workers have been excluded from any systematic or comprehensive demographic and socio-economic analysis of their impact on Canadian society. Yet, as Michalowski points out, 'it is easy to recognize ... that they contribute to the economy as they ... hold jobs and pay taxes. They are also consumers of goods and services, requiring housing, education and health care' (1993:62).

The supposed voluntary characteristic of the movement of migrant workers adds to the notion that temporary migrant workers are either fortunate to be able to work in Canada or that they themselves choose to work as unfree wage labour, thus, protests of substandard working and living conditions ought not be heard (see Withers, 1994). In Sedef Arat-Koc's view, 'in this discourse, immigration ceases to be viewed as a labour recruitment mechanism and becomes a system of "charity"' (1992:238). However, to describe the situation of unfree wage workers in Canada as privileged and fortunate seems somewhat perverse, for these are the same working conditions that citizens or permanent residents often find unacceptable.

Yet, many continue to consider those workers made to work under conditions of unfreedom within Canada as fortunate to be able to do so. It is at this point that the fact that it has been workers *migrating* to Canada who have been first targeted for the imposition of unfree conditions becomes significant. Indeed, in the economically advanced capitalist countries, it has always been those who can be easily described as a 'foreign' population who have been first targeted to work in unfree employment relationships (Carchedi, 1979; Jenkins, 1982). When the bodies of legal foreigners coincide with negatively racialized bodies of social foreigners, the effect on the lives of migrant workers is even more all-encompassing. This is because their agency is constrained in far deeper ways than that of those who do not have to accept conditions of unfreedom to escape conditions of poverty, despair, and war. *The NIEAP, therefore, should be considered as a means of institutionalizing nationalized discrimination informed by unequal relationships of racism and sexism.* It is a labour market tool more clearly understandable within the context of the global expansion of capitalist social relations and the discipline of both the capitalist marketplace and the capitalist national state.

Conclusion

The period in which the Non-Immigrant Employment Authorization Program was introduced (early 1970s) saw shifts concerning the free movement of both capital and labour. However, this has occurred in a non-complimentary fashion: as capital increasingly enjoys the right to national treatment, a growing number of migrants face the denial of such rights. Such denials are multifaceted. They have to do with the disciplining of labouring subjects, with the maintenance of nationalized binary identities of national subject and foreign object with all of their racialized and gendered components and with the expansion of global capitalism. It is within this matrix that we can best understand the NIEAP. Those who are made into migrant workers in Canada are an exemplar of a post-Fordist labour force that is rationalized through recourse to nationalist ideologies to allow employers in Canada greater flexibility and profit maximization.

Responding in this way to increasing pressures on people to move across nationalized space is part of the logic of late capitalism or the postmodern experience of global capital. As Bhagwati has noted, 'there is practically universal agreement, among modern states, that the free *flows of human beings*, no matter how efficacious for world efficiency, should not be permitted. Today, immigration restrictions are virtually everywhere, making immigration the most compelling exception to liberalism in the operation of the world economy' (cited in Zolberg, 1992:313).

In this period of capitalist globalization, there has been a shift in *who* is moving across nationalized borders. Unlike a hundred or so years ago when the majority of migrants were White, most people engaged in international migration after the 1970s are those who are negatively racialized as non-Whites. The imposition of restrictions that govern not only *if* they move but how they are positioned within the national states they move to does, however, reflect the labour recruitment practices of the nineteenth century. Like those non-Whites, mostly from Asia, who were moved throughout the British Empire (as well as into other colonized spaces) as indentured labour within the coolie labour system, a growing number of today's non-White migrants have little option but to surrender their freedom in exchange for a chance to earn a little 'hard' currency.

Greater constraints upon the growing movement of people across nationalized borders, then, are coupled with restrictions placed on their mobility *within* nationalized labour markets. Free movement in the labour market in Canada, as in many other nationalized spaces, is increasingly available only to those categorized as citizens or permanent residents. For many of those made into migrant workers, the difficulties faced when trying to cross into Canada are exacerbated by their complete inability to move within the labour market and, as a result, to move geographically within Canada as well.

Such constraint on their freedom makes common sense in Canadian society. Like their 'coolie' predecessors, migrant workers in Canada are defined as 'foreign workers.' This makes it very difficult, if not impossible, to have any desire they may have to make a new home within Canadian respected. After all, within the global system of national states, it is an oxymoron to insist that foreigners be at home in the nation. Migrant workers, then, are both legally and socially homeless in Canada even though this is a space in which they carry out their lives.

The distinctions of citizen/non-citizen as well as immigrant/non-immigrant, thus, serve to exacerbate inherent contradictions within a globalized capitalist system that relies on the equally global system of national states to regulate belonging, especially belonging in national-ized labour markets. Over the last thirty-odd years, these contradic-tions have been further entrenched. Mustafa Koc observes that 'among the unemployed, under-employed victims of economic restructuring and 'rationalization' in the Western world, globalization has strength-ened populist or nationalist movements tainted with anti-immigrant and racist tones' (1992:14). Racist, sexist, and imperialist ideologies as expressed through dominant notions of the inferiority of women or non-Whites and nationalized forms of discrimination that shape ideas of natural belonging and therefore natural not-belonging combine to create a situation where workers employed under temporary employ-ment authorizations face great disadvantages in Canadian society.

State immigration policies do more than reflect ideologies that help to legitimate unequal treatment, however. They also create the objective conditions for this discrimination to continue through the legislated denial of freedom. Thus, it is the social organization of both existential and material differences between citizens and migrant workers that has depoliticized the Non-Immigrant Employment Authorization Program in Canada. The ideologies that serve to make foreigners or non-immi-grant migrant workers more vulnerable than others in Canadian society are the very ideologies that help to legitimate their subordinate posi-tions. The notion that these people are *legitimately* discriminated against weakens attempts to strengthen their rights.

The ideology of nationhood allows for adherence to an imagined community of the nation to be given more saliency than to the emer-gence of a consciousness of shared exploitation. Since migrant workers are defined as non-members of the nation and foreigners labouring in a *Canadian* labour market, they are, incorrectly, perceived as insignificant in the struggles of other workers. While this does serve to legitimate the superordinate status of some citizens and permanent residents, ulti-mately, such a perception weakens the collective strength of workers everywhere, since the relative cheapness and structural weakness of any one group of workers contributes to the weakening of all producers. In the next chapter, I examine how the construction of *difference*, such as that between national subjects and their foreign objects is an integral part of how ruling projects retain their power to shape our lives.

6 Rejecting Global Apartheid: An Essay on the Refusal of 'Difference'

> There were the few ... who chose to do good ... those who never confused objects and humans, who knew the difference between naming and the named.
>
> Anne Michaels, *Fugitive Pieces*

The urgent question informing this book is one posed by the poet Minnie Bruce Pratt: *why are we in thrall to the institutions that oppress us?* In understanding the creation and legitimization of the Canadian state category of non-immigrant or migrant worker and the program, the Non-Immigrant Employment Authorization Program that orders their lives, this is an important question to ask. This question has driven my inquiry into the discursive production of 'lost Canadian state sovereignty' as the central problem in most left analyses of neoliberal processes of capitalist globalization. This question has also informed my investigation into how notions of freedom and its relationship to citizenship status has – and continues to – rely on the unfreedom of those othered by the ongoing project of White Canadian nation-state building. These, together with my examination of how the discursive production of certain 'national problems' by parliamentarians engaged in debates on immigration, international trade, and finance in Canada's House of Commons helped to produce migrant workers as one 'solution' to ensuring the 'prosperity of Canadians,' may, at first glance, be regarded as a disparate and disconnected set of topics. However, I believe, each on their own and in combination helps to bridge the gulf that often separates studies of ideological practices and their very real material effects on the lives of those who have been named as migrant workers.

Pratt's question has been the pivot on which my research has revolved because national state institutions, which initially were understood by many as an integral part of ruling relations, have, over time, become one of the main sources of identity and loyalty for many (even the majority?) who are oppressed and exploited. It is this hegemonic character of nationalized identities with their attendant organization of always-exclusionary homes and homelands that makes it important to investigate the articulation between forms of identity based on processes of social differentiation and the institutional form of nation-state rule. This is especially so in the context of the simultaneous and related phenomena of people's growing displacement and international migration. As more and more people depend on cross-border migration to try and survive the expansion and daily workings of global capitalism, we need to focus our attention on the interconnection between ideologies of nationness and the reorganization of material life.

As we have seen, how people are officially categorized shapes practically all aspects of their existential as well as material existence. The act of naming someone a migrant worker, as in naming citizens, permanent residents, or illegals, involves much more than simply describing a person's legal status in Canada. Instead, their categorization positions them within Canadian space in particular, always-hierarchically organized, ways. Indeed, in the modern (and now postmodern) world, nationalism is what organizes people's relationship between space, place and identity. For the remainder of this book, I clarify the relationship between the formation of national subjects and foreign workers and the exercise of state power. In particular, I examine the importance of questioning and undoing social practices of *difference-making* so that we can realize justice for migrants and for all of us on this planet. For this reason, this chapter takes a more philosophical approach to understanding how the category of migrant worker is made and how its existence is made possible.

The Nationalization of Spaces and Identities

Edward Soja's (1980:210) distinction between two different conceptualizations of space – contextual and created – is very useful in this regard. For Soja, *contextual* space is physical space and is only one small part of a spatialized politics of nationalist home-making practices. He argues that space is not merely a 'container' for society or only a 'context' in which it exists but is, instead, a *social* structure created out of extant power relations. Imagining Canada as one's homeland, in other words, requires that we mobilize the social relationships of nationalism and its never far away relationships of capitalism, racism, and sexism.

Nationalist ideologies are fundamentally aimed at asserting the relationship of the imagined community of the nation to a particular space and the resources (land, livelihoods, and so on) found there. The making of national space is therefore reliant not only on the construction of physical borders but also on the various social relationships organized through negative dualities. As such, nation-state practices have historically embarked on vigorous acts of *limité*: the structuring of strict differentiations that both organize and make common sense of systems of apartheid or the existence of two or more separate legal regimes and practices for differently delineated groups.

After all, it is not only citizens but also many foreigners who reside within the space of the Canadian national state. This is not new but has always been the case. National borders do not now, or in some mythical past, correlate with classifications of national membership. It is the nationalization of identity, and of society itself that takes place both through juridical-legal state practices *and* the everyday social practices that produce certain people as national-subjects and others as foreign-objects within the same territorial and legal space. As in any system of apartheid, people legally positioned as foreigners live and work closely together *with* the national subjects that they are ideologically separated from (Cock, 1980). Their interdependency and the closeness of their daily interactions, however, does not lead to ideas of sameness or to experiences of equality. Instead, within the global system of nationalized apartheid, those positioned in national states as the subordinated half of the member/non-member binary have, among other things, their labour cheapened and weakened as a result of the differential status imposed on them by the national state.

Thus, while a commonsensical understanding of apartheid is one where racialized classification schemes are the major makers of legal differences, historically many regimes of apartheid have depended on the difference of *citizenship* to make common sense of the gross inequalities organized through them. The system of 'reservations' in Canada, where diverse indigenous peoples renamed as 'Indians,' by the state were physically and socially segregated, relied, initially, on excluding them from Canadian citizenship. Likewise, the South African state's construction of a Bantustan system during the apartheid era designated these peripheral territories as the legal homelands of people categorized as Blacks. In this way, the South African state, like all national states, was able to define itself as only responsible for, and to, its citizens who, of course, were those categorized as White.

In both systems of apartheid, inequality was legitimized by discursively and legally producing different groups as racialized national subjects – national subjects that belonged to different nations – *not* Canada and *not* South Africa. This was *legally* manifested through the construction of differential citizenships. The South African example is clearer. In Canada, Indian reservations existed within Canadian national space, whereas in South Africa the Bantustans were seen as being wholly outside of South African jurisdiction (although, in reality, of course, completely governed and controlled by the South African state). In both cases, however, the justification of 'separate but equal' nations (each with its supposed sovereignty) – a founding ideology of the global system of national states – was the main rationale given for the continued existence of inequalities. As Hage (2000:87) would say, in each instance of apartheid 'a mode of domination [was] presented as a form of egalitarianism.'

Historically, then, citizenship has acted as a difference-making device. Far from being a progressive force throughout the history of the national state system (see Marshall, 1950), citizenship has constructed complex and layered levels of inequalities. These inequities are created in large part through national state categories of differential membership that accomplish, both materially and ideologically, the gendered racialization of class in Canada. Whether people can feed, clothe, and shelter themselves *or not*, decide where to live *or not*, receive health care, educational services, and other social services *or not*, be protected *or not* by state forces: all these are significantly affected by their differential placement in various state categories of citizenship and non-citizenship. Notably, whether one is a citizen, a permanent resident, or a temporary migrant worker is the most important factor in determining if a person will be free or unfree in Canada.

Yet, apartheid continues to be largely associated with race-based legal differentiations. And because such differentiations are, almost without exception, no longer an explicit part of most national legal systems, there is a strong tendency to deny that any form of apartheid exists at all. Not only does this legitimize global inequalities, it also renders as legal and legitimate the use of coercive state power against those defined as non-nationals. People differentiated on the basis of their nationality/citizenship status are told to rely on 'their own state' for protection, entitlements, and rights. In this sense, an important activity of the system of national states is the spatial definition and delineation of coercion.

For this reason, nationalist ideologies and the nationalists who utilize them are not only concerned with constructing a national community in contrast to a foreign exterior but also with securing the legitimate power to organize and materialize the difference between citizens and their Others *within* nationalized space. The specificity of modern forms of governmentality, therefore, lies in the convergence between the tremendous legitimacy of imagining *national communities* and the legitimacy of *national states* to uphold and defend the space occupied by the nation. In this sense, what we have usually understood to be nation-building projects are more accurately understood as *nation-state*–building projects. It is for this reason that borders – and the citizenship and immigration policies that enforce and regulate them – are the point where the nation's sovereignty finds its clearest expression (Sahlins, 1989:7).

Nationalism, thus, is not solely concerned with the construction of limited communities but, just as importantly, with the realization of the power of the state to control and regulate mobilities through and across nationalized space. The mobilities that national states attempt to manage consist not only of people trying to physically cross territorial borders but, perhaps more importantly, the geographical, labour market, and social mobility of differentiated groups of people *within* nationalized spaces. Consequently, it is often (but not always) people's need to migrate across national borders that places them in situations where they can be named as foreigners and denied the same rights that citizens lay claim to.

Thus, in contrast to John Holloway (1994:30), who argues that 'the destruction of personal bondage was also the destruction of geographical constraint,' it is clear that in present (and, in fact, past) movements of people, the existence of unfree labour is not predicated on people's spatial *immobility* but on exactly the opposite. In this sense, the process of migration for negatively racialized, gendered, sexualized, and classed bodies can be said to be 'a secular expression of ... inequality' (Petras, 1980:157). Anyone who can be categorized as a foreigner is seen to be *rightly* denied the various entitlements of membership in the nation. Consequently, within liberal democratic societies common sense is made of the state's protection of individual freedoms but only for those categorized as the citizens the state claims to protect.

The trope of citizenship works, therefore, to make freedom 'unpolitical' (Brown, 1995:14). Yet, it is clear that freedom within the global relations of ruling, rather than being a philosophical absolute, is the mark of a particular kind of relationship between citizens and their foreign Others (ibid.). In Canada freedom and unfreedom have been based on nationalized differences. Only citizens and permanent residents are legally recognized as having the right of free geographical and labour market mobility.

Indeed, the bounding of labour markets within nationalized space is a crucial aspect of how the global system of national states shapes, and depoliticizes, ideas of freedom and society. It also is a fundamental aspect of global capitalist competition. The ability of national states to shape domestic labour supplies plays a large part in shaping competition within what can only adequately be described as a world market for labour power (Potts, 1990). Indeed, the organization of competition between workers, both globally and within nation-states, can be said to be one of the key reasons for the formation of the nation-state system and the continued importance of national state practices within this period of capitalist globalization.

The common sensical character of notions of national entitlement is found in the idea that labour markets are naturally national. The circular argument exhorting that 'jobs in Canada are for Canadians' organizes a plethora of penalties for those differentiated as non-citizens. Unsurprisingly, then, national states have been intent on ensuring that the mobility of workers across nationalized boundaries remains within its disciplinary powers and does not act as a challenge to it. This is often done through a great deal of violence (Hardt and Negri, 2000:212). Such violence is materialized not only in how national states are able to prevent certain people's actual mobility into national space but in constructing certain people as falling outside the ideological – *but not territorial* – boundaries of this space. National states are therefore an important part of how inequalities are (re)produced not only *across* the global national state system but *within* what Mike Davis (2002:x) calls 'national real-estate.' In this way, the maintenance of national borders occurs not only at the boundary between one national state and another but also *within* national space. This is clearly manifested within the labour market where workers labour under highly differentiated state categories of residence.

Border Control as Ideology

Border control practices as well as national boundary maintenance practices are therefore manifestly *ideological*: they are less about restricting access to the territory of the national state than about differentiating those within it while obfuscating the source of the discrimination faced by workers named as foreigners. Following from Deleuze and Guattari (1987:174–91), border control practices are therefore best understood not as exercises in exclusion per se but as forms of *differential inclusion* for they organize the paradox that those who have been Othered are within the 'contextual' or physical space occupied by national society but positioned as definitive outsiders by its legal and social framework.

Border control practices, therefore, construct a global apartheid far more deeper than the one which divides the world between 'haves' and 'have-nots' where the former impose restrictive immigration policies in an attempt to *keep out* the latter (Richmond, 1994). Over the past thirty years, as international migration has grown at unprecedented rates, the absolute or relative *movement* of people across national borders has *not* been restricted. Instead, there has been a two-fold increase in global migration from the mid-1980s to the mid-1990s (Withers, 1994:311). The U.N. Population Fund (2003) officially estimates that about 175 million people now cross national borders every year. This figure is expected to double by the end of this decade. In absolute numbers, which are arguably important, this rate of migration is more than that which occurred in the late nineteenth and early twentieth centuries: the great 'age of mass migration' (Hatton and Williamson, 1998). Significantly, in contrast to the migrations of a century ago, when most migration was out of Europe, most cross-border migrants today are from the global South (Sutcliffe, 2001).

Restrictive immigration policies do not only restrict people's mobility. Although it is certainly the case that a greater number of barriers to migration have been erected,[1] the greater effect of restrictive immigration policies is to restrict migrants' ability to obtain permanent, full legal status in the countries in which they come to live and earn a livelihood. Not to underestimate the incredible toll on human life and dignity organized through restrictive immigration policies, however, these have done far more to restrict the *rights, entitlements, and freedom* of migrants than to halt their mobility. Limits to migrants' movements, then, lie in the ability to restrict certain differentiated people's mobility *within* nationalized space – not only across it. The border, therefore, is not just the physical boundary separating nationalized spaces but, perhaps more importantly, a *line of difference* that allows state authorities to carry out practices against non-nationals that are deemed unacceptable, even manifestly unjust and undemocratic, if they were to be carried out against citizens or perhaps even permanent residents. It is in such practices that we find one of the most important aspect of notions of Canadianness – the continuous construction of collective national subjects and foreign objects– that nationalist practices work to organize and operate.

The trope of nationalism frames migrant workers admitted through Canada's Non-Immigrant Employment Authorization Program as not at home, as existing in a separate society, a foreign space, and part of a foreign labour force. National demarcations of difference or zones of *limité* that structure the inferior legal status of migrant workers serves to construct them as naturally existing in the subordinated positions they are placed in by the state. This allows those who are national subjects to imagine that We hold no responsibility for Them. Indeed, if thought of at all, their existence in Canada is often regarded as an act of charity granted them by a generous citizenry (Arat-Koc, 1992).

Significantly, as I found in Chapter 4, the legitimacy of the migrant worker category rests on the production of social *illegitimacy* of negatively racialized Others placed in the category of *immigrant* (or permanent resident) in Canada, an illegitimacy organized in part by the discursive practices of Canadian parliamentarians. Quickly on the heels of the 1967 changes that removed the legal 'preference' for White immigrants from other White-settler colonies or Europe and allowed non-Whites to gain permanent residency in Canada, non-White immigrants were represented as posing serious threats to the character and security of the nation. Indeed, parliamentarians singled out 'weak immigration policies' as a major weakness in the ability of the nation to defend itself.

By 1973, and the introduction of the NIEAP, being non-White in Canada became tantamount to being a foreign presence. In the process, Canadians were once again interpolated as White. Being admitted as a landed immigrant to Canada did not, therefore, secure for non-Whites de facto membership in the Canadian nation. Yet, while they were discriminated against in many areas of life in Canada, as permanent residents they could not legally be denied all of the rights of membership in the Canadian national state.

In this regard, it is noteworthy that even though parliamentary debates that problematized the permanent residency of non-Whites in Canada *could* have led to the reinstatement of explicitly racialized and nationalized criteria for entry as an immigrant to Canada, this was not done. This is because it was also during this same time, the late 1960s and early 1970s, that the Canadian nation and state were being carefully constructed as a 'tolerant,' and, according to Prime Minister Trudeau's first campaign slogan, even a 'just' society.

It was in the nexus of the simultaneous production of Canada as a tolerant society *and* the representation of non-Whites as a *foreign* threat that legitimacy for categorizing people as migrant workers was organized. By problematizing the permanence of 'too many' non-Whites while shifting Canadian immigration policy away from admitting the majority of people as immigrants towards one that admitted people as migrant workers, the Canadian state was able to assert that it was simply protecting the integrity of the nation and the state. The making of migrant workers and the discrimination against them that resulted was effectively depoliticized, since discriminating against non-Canadians simply could not be imagined as such by most. Indeed, discriminating against foreigners was most often presented as part of the state's *duty* to its citizens.

In presenting themselves as the protectors and guardians of Canadians, parliamentarians continuously constructed the nation on whose behalf they were said to be acting. Certainly, in the late 1960s and early 1970s, the early period of this phase of capitalist globalization, the construction of immigrants (read: non-Whites) as a foreign threat was the *foundation* upon which parliamentarians performed the nation and enacted the legitimacy of state power. The Canadian national state was reinvented in this same process, reconstructed as the natural, even democratic, body existing to empower the wishes of the People of Canada. The area of citizenship and immigration, then, was the paramount arena through which processes of nation-state building – and global capitalist relationships – were restructured (see Hall and Jacques, 1989, regarding similar processes taking place in Great Britain around this same time).

In order to rule, the Canadian state required the existence of the *nation* for the realization of its own powers as well as for its ability to help in the reproduction of the capitalist mode of production. Border control policies served not only to strengthen the institutional apparatuses of the Canadian state but to also give greater meaning to the differences between citizens and foreigners. Nationalism organized the idea that if some people are said to belong together, then other people are meant to be apart. Hence, it was by *not* organizing the exploitation of migrant workers through overtly racialized state categories of exclusion but through the rationality of the national state system that ruling over migrant workers was accomplished – and the making of a global apartheid based on nationalist ideologies secured.

Representing the oppression and exploitation of migrant workers as simply the natural workings of national state policies that owed nothing – socially or legally – to foreigners was a more socially acceptable way to organize discrimination against the nation's Others, particularly at this historical moment when the Canadian state was distancing itself from its racist past and redefining itself as 'multicultural.' The use of nationalism to both organize and conceal racist practices was, thus, a significant part of the rationality of governance during this period. Nationalist discursive practices in Parliament helped to legitimize the very categories through which a highly racialized *non*-nationality was materialized.

People named as migrant workers are the very embodiment of the foreigner in that they can legally be denied many of the protections and entitlements offered by the state to its citizens. Indeed, it has been with the production of the category of migrant worker that the existential meaning of foreigner has been *fully* materialized within Canadian society.

Ultimately, legitimacy for the migrant worker category was secured by nationalizing entitlements to the benefits of being Canadian. That We have more benefits than Others in Canada was represented as positive, even progressive, and most certainly natural. It comes as little surprise, then, that migrant workers, unlike landed immigrants (and later, the category of people known as 'illegals') were not represented in Parliament as constituting a threat to the nation's security and identity.

And so it continues to this day. Successive changes to Canadian immigration policy have ensured not only the maintenance of the NIEAP but its expansion. Over the last thirty-odd years, various ministers of the Department of Citizenship and Immigration have pledged to increase the number of temporary, migrant workers available to employers. And they have delivered. This is evident in the regulatory changes accompanying the 2002 Immigrant and Refugee Protection Act whereby employers are granted even quicker access to people as migrant workers in order to remain 'globally competitive.'

Canadian state practices continue to be central to processes of globalization, therefore, *because* they are able to mobilize ideological concepts of national community. Herein lies the complicity of membership in the dominant half of negative dualities of power. Consent for the state's right of national sovereignty has worked to both operationalize and obfuscate the global cheap labour strategy of securing profits. Indeed, the rationality of globalization within Canada has been based on constant reference to the national interest against foreign ones. Nationalist practices, therefore, should not be seen as existing in opposition to or in conflict with processes of globalization. In Canada, at least, people working within state apparatuses not only have been very active participants in the organization of globalization but the hegemonic ideology of nationalism has profoundly assisted in the restructuring of the labour market along neoliberal lines.

In a world where the capital of investors has increasingly been granted 'national treatment' (i.e., citizenship) rights (as in Articles 301, 1102, 1202, 1405, and 1703 of the North American Free Trade Agreement; see Dillon, 1991:17), the denial of exactly this to people categorized as migrant workers is very much part of how state practices reconstitute competition between and within nationalized labour markets. Ideological state practices that are productive of the nation enable processes of globalization precisely because nationalist ideological frames not only organize the super-exploitation of foreigners but also conceal the otherwise obvious fact that both those represented as foreign-objects and those seen to be Canadian subjects work within the *same* labour market, a market made more competitive through the hegemony of nationalist ideologies. Thus, while notions of Canadianness continue to legitimize the rule of White Canadians over non-Whites and non-Canadians, other ruling relations are buttressed, including those social relations through which most Whites are themselves oppressed and exploited. In fact, the exploitation of all workers, including White workers in Canada, hinges upon the commonsensical acceptance of extra-coercive state action against those rendered as foreign-Others.

Nationalism therefore works to fragment what are in reality highly interdependent sets of social relationships. In doing so, nationalism abstracts the global character of relationships among people into particularized, more readily governable nations. In this regard, it is vitally important for us to expand our definition of nationalism to include any discursive practice that works to reproduce, ideologically as well as materially, the imagined community of the nation and present it as always realizable. This includes those practices that create and maintain nationalized boundaries and that organize discrimination on the basis of differentiated nationalities.

Nationalism, therefore, should not be seen as limited to those chest-beating exercises in which notions of national blood and soil are brought into play. As Billig (1995) well points out, 'banal nationalism' permeates our lives. It shapes our identities, the many social interactions we have on a daily basis, and our modes of thought. Therefore, to capture the significance of nationalism in our lives, we need to recognize that any and all ideas premised on the taken-for-granted assumption of the naturalness (if not always the beneficence) of the national state system with its separation of discrete national groupings are a part of the repertoire of nationalist discursive practice.

Nationalist ideologies further include those discourses that make common sense of social and/or legal distinctions between people *within* nationalized spaces and the discrimination faced by those named as foreigners. These two kinds of nationalist ideologies – the existence of nations and the existence of foreigners within them – are clearly related. The categorization of, and mobilization against, the threat of Other national states is intrinsically linked to the categorization and defence against the internal Other. The ideology of nationalism, then, ought to include those discourses that reinforce naturalized dichotomies between domestic and foreign spaces. Not only our notions of differences between national and international or between transnational and global spaces but also our ideas of difference within the homeland are formed through such negative dualities.

Lines of Difference

The existence of *differences*, far from being something to be valued and respected, is a fundamental part of ruling relations and, as such, needs to be eradicated. Lest this be taken as an argument for liberal univeralism, we need to distinguish between the *social process of differentiation* and the presence of actual *diversity* born of lived experience. Making such a distinction is not simply a semantic exercise but is, fundamentally, about creating the possibility for more effectively challenging ruling relations that oppress, exploit, and destroy most life on this planet.

Differences are socially organized divisions among people shaped by discourses and patterns of human action that work to create and/or preserve unequal relationships through the formation of hierarchically ranked identities and highly disparate material realities. *Identities based on difference are imposed identities, imposed in order to realize gross disparities in wealth and power.*

Ironically, but not contradictorily, the organization of differences has a *homogenizing* principle at its core. As exemplified by the ideas of universalism within western Enlightenment thought, a parochial interest is masked as a common one. Those who have been Othered are not only judged in relation to the norms, be they nationalized, gendered, racialized, classed, and/or sexualized, established by ruling groups, they are expected to conform to them as well. The social organization of differences, then, is a technology that creates the conditions for adherence not just to the demands of rulers but to their ways of living. How 'different' one is is always judged from the standpoint of those who rule.

Any deviance from their supposedly universal values is represented as a threat to civilization and the surest path to barbarism. Jean Baudrillard and Marc Guillaume (1992:5) discuss this in their *Figures de l'Altérité* when they argue, 'Western Societies have reduced the reality of the Other through colonization or through cultural assimilation. They have abolished what was radically heterogeneous and incommensurable in the other.' This heterogeneity has been replaced *both* with numbing conformity to ruling ideas and practices and the existence of numerous differences among us.

This nexus of homogeneity – difference organizes global society. Our very perception of space and time has been organized through the institutionalization of difference. We have local spaces, national spaces, domestic spaces; we have foreign spaces, global spaces, and the space of the universal; we have modern spaces, postmodern spaces, and cosmopolitan spaces, just as we have fundamentalist spaces, feudal spaces, and backwards spaces. How people are positioned in one or the other of these 'created' spaces is shaped by the 'degrees of deviance' one is seen to possess, relative to the universal norm (Deleuze and Guattari, 1987:178).

The social organization of difference affects not only the politics of identity but also how people are inserted into global markets of capital and labour. How one has been identified shapes a person's position within global capitalism. In the nascent days of capitalist globalization, the differential inclusion of indigenous peoples, Black slaves, and Asian coolie producers shaped the realization of capitalist investments as well as the formation of national states. The continued legitimacy of the differential valorization of people's labour power along the lines of how they have been categorized by the now well-entrenched national state form shapes contemporary ruling projects. In Canada the materialization of difference has led to the relative cheapness of workers who are women, people of colour, and foreigners in comparison with those seen to belong.

In the violent symbolism inherent to all relations of ruling, the very differences structured by modes of domination are tautologically reified as the *reason* for differences in lived experience: 'You are a migrant worker and because of this you are not a citizen.' Differences are therefore ideological. That is, they naturalize and depoliticize their material and social basis. Such differences not only create lines of difference, they also create lines of sameness: they shape where and with who our empathy lies. The creation of subjectivities based on difference and sameness is in part why differences organized through gross inequalities persist. Indeed, the ongoing maintenance of such subjectivities is essential to the global division of labour and power.

In contrast to the destructive practices of difference making, *diversity* is the necessary precondition for life on this planet. 'Diversity,' Vandana Shiva (1997:87) writes, 'is the key to sustainability.' Historically, the existence of biodiversity of plants and non-human animals has relied upon the existence of diverse human communities with diverse systems of production and reproduction that do not harm themselves or other living beings. As Shiva (ibid.:88) notes, 'self-organized and decentralized communities and ecosystems give rise to diversity.' Reciprocal interdependence and mutual coexistence, rather than hierarchical subordination is the basis of such modes of living.

It is not my intent to talk about such ways of living to romanticize past or present small-scale communities organized through practices of commoning (hunting, gathering, etc.) and/or farming and animal husbandry. Indeed, as Sylvia Wynter (1995) has well pointed out, to do so would inevitably lead to failure, given that since 1492 no one has been left untouched by either the destructive forces of capitalist colonization or its productive processes, that is, the processes through which new identities and ways of living have been constructed for the 'conscripts of modernity' (Scott, 2004). Instead, the goal is to recognize the modernist preoccupation with identities, most of which are imposed, and move *through* them so that we humans can reorganize ways of living that are not antithetical to continued life on this planet, not only for us but for all living beings.

In a world based on social relations of diversity, there are no sover-

eign entities of any kind but rather relative and overlapping boundaries subject to change. The boundaries of identity, of community life,
of productive capacities are understood as historically, socially, and
ecologically contingent. Each is fluid and responds to changes in everyday lived experiences: changes produced, for example, by migration.
As Hardt and Negri (2004) note, such relationships do not start with
identity. Instead, what is understood as being in common by people in
any social formation is produced through shared lived experience.

In other words, people's relationships to each other are *imminent*
instead of hinging on transcendent ideas and imposed identities of
race or nation. Empathies and connections are based in *practice* rather
than in identity (Chan and Sharma, 2004). Consequently, the recognition of commonalities shared among people, the common experience
of being producers, for instance, does not reduce them to the ideological singularity that notions of the People organize (Hardt and Negri,
2004:105).

For social relations reliant on maintaining differences, the multiple
and overlapping singularities found within systems based on diversity
are perhaps their greatest threat. Thus, unsurprisingly, differences are
organized specifically to destroy diversity and replace it with what
Salman Rushdie (1995) has called, 'the rule of One over Many.' The
unity of this One rests on the continued subordination of those who
have been made to be different. The making of this One, then, is a history of the simultaneous dislocation and differentiation of those who
have been Othered couched within concepts and practices of liberal
universalism – of the spread of 'democracy,' 'freedom,' and the 'rule of
law.'

We live in a world where diversity is increasingly bounded by differences and where diversity is grotesquely mimed as difference. Multiculturalist policies in Canada, for instance, exist in tandem with the rapid
loss of biodiversity and human diversity within the space occupied by
Canadians. The same is, of course, true globally. We can see this in the
rapid loss of diverse spoken languages. Linguists report that approximately 50 per cent of the approximately 6,000 languages spoken around
the globe are moribund, spoken only by adults who no longer possess
the capacity to pass them on to succeeding generations (Crawford,
2005). Another 40 per cent are under threat, as the numbers of people
learning them are in significant decline (ibid.). Thus, only 10 per cent of
existing languages are relatively secure (Robins and Uhlenbeck, 1991).
As English becomes further entrenched as the language of choice in the

global marketplace, it is the most protected but, even then, only the kind of English spoken by those represented as its 'natural' speakers.

The history of the making of this ruling One, then, runs alongside the history of capitalist globalization. The history of the last 500 or so years has been one of the erection of ever more rigid and immutable boundaries between Us and Them, the creation of different spaces and, eventually, the institutionalization of such differences through national border regimes. Other modes of production – and ways of being – have been, one after another, assimilated and destroyed giving rise to 'coercively controlled monocultures' (Shiva, 1997:102). New forms of representation are connected to new forms of exploitation and together these bring into being new political subjects and objects (Balibar, 1991:88; Wynter, 1995).

With the ascendancy of capitalism and the formation of national states, supposedly unified races and nations replace diverse and ever-changing human communities. As patriarchal relationships expand alongside capitalist ones, the entrenchment of sexualized divisions of labour have produced 'gender' with its unitary categories of man and woman. The organization of human sexuality in similar binaries has produced 'straight' people just as it has produced 'gays' and 'lesbians.' Maintenance of ruling practices through such identities is ensured through both physical and ideological methods. Difference is always imagined as one's relationship to the outside, whether that is the human's broad outside of all non-human life whereby humanity (especially Man) is held to be the *ens perfectissumum* of the 'Great Chain of Being' or the more narrow outsides peopled by nationalized, racialized, gendered, and sexualized subjectivities.

Nationalized societies, in particular, because they join particularist identities with territorial space institutionalize difference through the state by constructing 'zones of purity' that actively work against the creation of diversity (Rosaldo in Morley, 2000:6). Thus, in concert, the national state and global capitalism transform radical diversity and capture it within an exclusive community of rights bound within binary relations (Fiedler, 2002:4).

The postmodern organization of racism in Canada is very much reliant on practices of nationalism. Indeed, Hage maintains that contemporary racialized differences, as are evident in the construction of a migrant workers category, are best understood as nationalized differences, because what is at stake is the space of – and the rule over – the nation. Nationalist practices, since they are concerned with issues of the rightful spatial allocations of people across space and of various differentiated people within national spaces, privilege the relationship between a particular territory and those people defined as belonging there. Relationships shaped by such spatial politics are those of apartheid: each differentiated group in its place or, perhaps most precisely, people within each Othered category kept in their place while elites differently include Others in ways that suit their needs and desires.

Celebrating Difference?

What should we make, then, of those celebrations of differences not made from a liberal, multiculturalist perspective but from a more progressive position, one very much concerned with eradicating structural inequalities? Given the wide influence of the work of Iris Marion Young (1986) in this regard, I will spend some time examining it. For Young, the realization of equality rests on the development of a 'participatory democratic theory not on the assumption of an undifferentiated humanity, but rather on the assumption that there are group differences and that some groups are actually or potentially oppressed or disadvantaged.' She therefore argues that we need to foster a respect *for* difference, a respect based on 'an openness to unassimilated otherness' (in Morley, 2000:214). Young's 'unassimilated otherness' refers to the presence of people who are not like us *and* who have not been absorbed into contemporary relationships of power. Such people are thought of as differently self-determinate: able to effectively resist conforming to the views and practices of dominant groups. Such differences, Young argues, ought to be celebrated and structured into power. There are two major problems with this formulization of difference.

First, in Young's celebration of *difference* there is an equal, but largely implicit, celebration of *sameness*. As it is the uniqueness or discrete character of communities that forms the basis of people's existence in society, Young's work comes to reproduce two dichotomous discourses: one of purity and authenticity, the second a reification of separate and discrete groups that upholds tropes of difference and similarity (Haber, 1994:120, 126). Young's framework thus asks us to choose a liberal and not a transformative politics of plurality over an equally liberal politics of universalism.

A second and related problem contained within Young's conceptualization and celebration of difference is that in today's world, and arguably the world of the last several hundred years, it is simply not tenable to argue that an 'unassimilated other' exists *outside* of global capitalist social relations, with its attendant relations of colonialism, nationalism, racism, and sexism. Indeed, it has been a very long time indeed since anyone has been able to remain outside of these dominant and global relations of ruling. Today, with ever-accelerating flows of people, capital, information, services, goods, and ideas, as well as the growing proliferation of weapons of war, such a view of the world is even more fantastic. For instance, neither the people in Iraq nor the people in the United States – each imagined as sharing similarities within each nationalized identity and differences across these identities – exist in a state of 'unassimilation.' Rather, they are both caught up in the project of 'Empire,' with its goal of reducing complex and overlapping social relations to discrete hierarchical differences (Hardt and Negri, 2000).

Young's respect for differences, because it is conceptualized largely at the level of representation of identity (identities, no less, which have not been 'democratically' arrived at but imposed), creates her inability to account for the centrality of ruling relations in the creation and unequal lived experiences of differentiated groups even though this is one of her key aims. As a result, her respect for difference comes to sustain the very mechanisms by which Otherness is brought into being. There is simply no such thing as Others who are not severely constrained in both their identity and their actions by the homogenizing drive of making differences. This is what makes them different in the first place – their subordination to ruling groups. Thus, Young's call to create equalities by 'celebrating differences' leads us back to a liberal democratic framework in which the discussion of imposed identities is wholly eclipsed, while the centrality of identity itself is maintained.

Young's lack of questioning of the formation of differences is also evident in the work of those who, like H. Fern Haber, wishes to argue for a politics of sameness. Haber (1994:126, emphasis added) is sceptical of the project of celebrating differences, for she believes that in the 'universalisation of difference' is constructed a '*metaphysics* of difference' where any idea or feeling of identity or community is seen as inherently troublesome. Yet, as with Young's approach, this kind of analysis also suffers from the lack of distinction made between relations based on difference and relations of diversity based on reciprocal interdependence and shared practices rather than shared identities.

Haber's critique of difference, in the end, leads to the same problematic position evident in Young's work where there are only ever similarities *or* differences. This is tempered somewhat by her insistence that unity does not necessarily mean 'unicity' or 'the demand that we speak with one voice,' however, Haber (1994:120) ultimately calls for a 'repression of difference' but a repression whose negative results are supposedly mitigated by the recognition that identities are always provisional (in Morley, 2002:252). In the end, however much Haber tries to rescue the idea of unified communities by inserting an acknowledgment of historical contingency, she repeats the liberal call for universalism. Thus, though she believes in the possibility of unified communities that are not inherently oppressive, Haber, unlike Young, simply sees no intrinsic problem in similarities of identity because she argues that such similar identities will constantly shift.

This is similar to Arjun Appadurai's (1993) notion of the formation of a 'trans-nation' wherein 'bounded territories could give way to diasporic networks, nations to trans-nations, and patriotism itself could become plural, serial, contextual and mobile.' Appadurai (1993:804) thus establishes as his goal the granting of 'rights to the pursuit of cultural difference under public protections and guarantees' to different groups. In such formations, where supposedly transnational diasporas are respected, Appadurai sees the 'future of patriotism in a postcolonial world' (ibid.). Appadurai's call for transnational diosparic networks, like Haber's calls for unified communities, suffers from a lack of insight into how such identity-based communities are historically and socially organized and how they are structured through inequalities in power, inequalities that determine whose vision of sameness prevails.

Neither examines the fundamentally hierarchical architecture of nations with their patriotic subjects pledged to unity nor the architecture of transnations or diasporic communities with their hierarchical leadership structures. Lacking a distinction between difference and diversity, both fail to see that the social organization of difference is precisely aimed at homogenizing experiences of Self and Other in order to privilege those who are legitimately seen to belong in the space occupied by the community. At best, Appadurai tries to despatialize ideas of communities which, nonetheless, remain unified and loyal to established – and hegemonic – forms of community.

While this alone should give us great cause for concern, what is even more alarming is that, in the end, liberal arguments for difference or sameness do not diverge that greatly from the ideas of those who are *unconcerned* with social justice: those that argue, for example, that differences, especially in race, nation, and culture, are more or less natural (see Huntington, 1996). The only distinction between the two is their proposed strategy to deal with difference: respect it and enshrine such differences in law or prevent different peoples (or 'civilizations') from coming together in the first place so the supposedly inevitable 'clash' can be avoided.

In such sets of arguments, coming from either progressives or reactionaries, there is a failure to recognize that *differences* between people based on their religions, cultural practices, languages, national identities, and so on, are not pre-existing, natural social formations. This failure is evident in Appadurai's (1993:4) claim that unlike modern nation-states, 'language, blood, soil and race' are 'natural facts.' Yet, such identities are neither accidental nor inevitable. Rather, whether it is nations or languages, blood, soil, or races, communities based on each and every one of these markers of difference has been socially *imagined*. Moreover, in each case, one supposedly unified race or culture has been socially, economically, and politically positioned as superior to another. Thus, not only are hierarchies between different groups socially organized, the existence of homogeneity *within* differentiated groups is equally manufactured. There simply is no shared interest *within* differentiated groups because such groups are a *product* of, not the *precursor* to, the process by which they become social formations.

In this regard, it is especially important to note that the contemporary identities of oppressed and exploited groupings of people are as socially and historically constituted as are those of the groups that oppress and exploit them. The essentialization of subordinated groups, 'strategically' or not, to the realm of natural communities occurs, in some large part, because of the work done by those who position themselves as group representatives and community leaders (see Spivak, 1987). In their position as leaders, these representatives, much like the representatives of the nation, carry tremendous power in being able to set the criteria by which people belong to the community or remain outsiders to it. Often, their ability to lead is assured by silencing or marginalizing dissent both from within the boundaries of such identified groups and from those left out.

The promotion of certain people as the leaders of subordinated communities also occurs through the support of elites in dominant groups. This is evident in the financial, military, and moral support given to fundamentalists in places such as Afghanistan by the United States and other governments (Ali, 2002). Significantly, it is the supposed 'unassimilated otherness' of these Others –their seeming legitimacy to represent their own people – that becomes the very rationale for denying the charge of imperialism from those who have been ejected from the community or by those opposed to the political regimes installed through this leadership.

The organization of sameness, then, assures otherness and always within the matrix of spatialized ruling relations wherein certain identities accrue persons more privilege than others. Claiming that this otherness is 'unassimilated' because it is not culturally manifested in the same ways as in globally dominant groups is part and parcel of the work of Empire. The social organization of differences, thus, does not produce diverse and varied ways of living so much as it shapes our consciousness of the authenticity, and therefore naturalness, of parochial forms of power.

To eradicate inequalities it is these socially organized relationships of difference and sameness that must be questioned and transformed. It is only by recognizing that both similarity and difference have *homogeneity* as their overarching principle that allows for the realization that it is not differences but diversity that we should celebrate. Instead of Young's respect for 'unassimilated otherness' or Wilson's (1998:355) 'aesthetic of openness towards otherness,' we need to take seriously the fact that the existence of Others is not natural. It is the acceptance of essentialized or acculturated *otherness* that reveals the parody of hegemonic power relations evident in the supposed self-naming practices of oppressed and exploited people who seek the affirmation of the categorical identities imposed upon them. Not only are the names often the same – 'Black,' 'Brown,' 'Yellow,' 'of colour,' 'homosexual,' 'woman' – there is also little if any questioning of the bifurcating power mobilized by such identities.

In this the work of James Donald is important, for he questions hegemonic forms of community development. He asks whether 'community, the question of how we live together, must take the form of collective belonging, affiliation or identity' (in Morely, 2002:255). For Donald, community is never a fixed social unit but a continual negotiation of what he calls 'being in common' (in Morley, 2002:256). In his view, commonality is not based on ideas of origin, however. Likewise, it is not dependent on the organization of discrete groups of members and non-members. Instead, community is built through experiences of trying to negotiate alterity with our 'Noisy Neighbours' (Donald, 1999). Such discussions of alterity are certainly an advance on those that fail to question the social organization of otherness. Unfortunately, though, Donald does not contend with the issue of inequalities of power or governance. A noisy neighbour who will not be quiet, indeed, who will not negotiate, or whose noisiness is upheld by institutionalized power, is a possibility that needs to be accounted for.

One resolution to the binary of similarity/difference as the basis of social life lies in the recognition of diversity as simultaneously a lived reality, a goal, *and* an organizing strategy aimed at achieving social justice. Equally important to the recognition of diversity, though, is a serious reconsideration of people's relationships to the national state with its built-in machinery of difference making. In this, a rethinking – and a complete transformation – of the relationship between interiority and exteriority is crucial.

The concept of hybridity is somewhat useful in this regard, for it challenges the idea of there only ever being an inside or an outside – a world of Us and Them (be they assimilated or 'unassimilated'). In taking up this approach, Renato Rosaldo (in Morley, 2000:6) argues that in our everyday lives there are no 'zones of purity' but only an ongoing process of transculturation (versus the notion of *inter*-culturation that theories relying on difference produce). Pure communities exist only at the level of ideology. Hybridity, then, is the lived experience of crossings, multiplicities, and shifting non-unitary identities.

Yet, though it certainly is the case that a multitude of shifting identities, experiences, and interests are the actual lived experience of humans, the term *hybridity* and its subject, the hybrid, can be more confusing than clarifying of such experiences. This is because of the conceptual baggage the term carries as well as how it is often understood by those who use it. In both senses, the concept of hybridty continues to rely on tropes of purity for its very meaning. According to the *Oxford English Dictionary* (2003), a hybrid is 'anything derived from heterogeneous sources, or composed of different or incongruous elements.' Unsurprisingly, the first use of the term *hybridity* was by Charles Darwin in 1837. In the physical sciences, the study of hybridity was concerned with the cross-breeding of divergent animal species, but when used to describe *human* interactions it was informed by the emergent and burgeoning field of psuedoscientific racism in the nineteenth century, itself reliant on Social Darwinism. Thus the dominant idea of hybridity with regard to humans was that of race-mixing.

Today, hybridity continues to be understood as some combination of different types of humans and is most often spoken of in terms of the intermingling of races or cultures. The use of the concept of hybridity, thus, can be seen as part of a counterpoint to the rise of new forms of racisms, ones less centred on biological references and more on ideas of immutable cultures. But the reclamation of hybridized identities by scholars such as Homi Bhabha (1994) and Stuart Hall (1996) does not fundamentally alter the meaning of hybridity as a process in which one or more distinct groups interacts with others and that such a meaning is how hybridity gets taken up.

Emphasis on purity and its correlate of mixing is perhaps most evident in Appadurai's (1993) notion of a 'federation of diasporas' where a 'confederacy' of different diasporas negotiates the *sharing* of shared space. In Appadurai's theorization, diasporas are imagined in their original sense – as discrete communities rooted in shared ancestry, culture, nationality, religion, and geography that cross space and by so doing intermingle with the races and cultures they encounter to become something different than they once were. However great such shifts may be, though, *origin* remains the pivotal point on which such identities are (overtly) structured. In Appadurai's 'federation of diasporas' identified through their roots, the relationship between identity, space, and power is understood in ways not unlike Young's respect for 'unassimilated otherness.'

Moreover, when we speak of hybridity we usually only see certain people, communities, and spaces as hybrid while all others are not so conceptualized. This fails to account for the most powerful contribution of early theorists of hybridity: that there are not now, nor were there ever, any such thing as 'pure' communities based on sameness unaffected by shifts in cultural and material life. In other words, diversity of life is a general condition.

Lines of Flight: Towards a World without Borders

How then to theorize diversity, or the *simultaneous* existence of singularity and potential commonalities based on practice rather than fixed identity, in such a way that we avoid reproducing the binary trap of sameness/difference? In this, Doreen Massey's (1991) call to develop an 'extroverted' relationship to space is more useful than are concepts of hybridity. In her understanding of space and therefore of social relations and institutions, *each* place and person is seen as linked through numerous *mobilities*. Massey's conceptualization of home, therefore, is neither reliant on a singular, separated space nor is it structured through regressive claims of collective origin with their habitual dichotomy of sameness/difference. That is, both singularities and commonalities are recognized, commonalities, moreover, that are not based on identities but on shared human practices.

Through such recognitions, home is no longer seen as necessarily locale dependent. Massey's theorization of homeyness conceptualizes home the way it is *actually* experienced: as a *process*, a *practice*, and a *relationship* – not necessarily a place. Home is organized *in, through, and across* spaces and consists of various linkages and interdependencies.

Such a conceptualization helps us to shift both our material practices and our consciousness so that ideas of insides and outsides no longer determine our relationships with one another. It allows us to recognize how people occupy a multiciplicity of spaces and how our identities are continuously reformed through the shifting spaces that we inhabit. By acknowledging the transitory character of identities once imagined as fixed, we can perhaps learn to think beyond identity itself and start to focus on practice. After all, we live not only with the identities of gender, race, nation, and class (among others) imposed on us, we also have ways of knowing ourselves based on our diversre *lived experience* of our own and each others' mobilities. These mobilities are not only geographical but are also the mobilities of the various identities we take on throughout our lifetimes. Thus, while the constitution of society as national is currently the dominant way of organizing space, one that is 'a source of catastrophic exclusion' (Fiedler, 2002:1), there is nonetheless also an experience of the social that is materially constructed through our physical and virtual movements across and through both contextual and created space (Urry, 2000:2).

This is evident in an example provided by David Morley (2002:259) who cites 'one elderly woman's complaint, when confronted with the contentious dilemma of her community's identity [ethnic Hungarians living in disputed territory in southern Slovakia]. For myself, this woman stated, 'I do not want to be a pure identity person.' It is precisely the lived experience of being present in many spaces at once, often in a highly alienated way, that we need to draw upon to inform our strategies for transformative change (see Rouse, 1991:14).

Rather than bemoaning the lack of community and unity in some accounts of home (Haber, 1994) or seeing attempts to decentre the idea of original roots as leading to political immobility (see Yuval-Davis, 1996), it is important that we recognize that it is precisely by disconnecting home from ideas of sameness and difference (however formulated) that we can create the possibilities for collective, transformative change for justice. Indeed, as Gilles Deleuze and Felix Guattari (1987) have pointed out, conceptualizing human communities (and relationships) as founded on roots, what they call 'tree logic,' assumes a naturalized sameness that powerfully works to reproduce ruling relations. Instead of using the metaphor of roots, with its attendant notion of people being bounded to biological ancestors and to specific territories or communities, they use the notion of rhizomes to argue for the possibility of undoing ruling relations. Rhizomes are always on the move.

Rhizomatic relationships simultaneously incorporate the principles of connection *and* heterogeneity so that 'any point of a rhizome can be connected to anything other, and must be' (Deleuze and Guattari, 1987:7). Such notions of home are 'antigenealogy' (ibid.:21). Rhizomatic relationships are therefore imminent relationships – they are organized from *within* the world and do not rely on transcendent ideas of historical belonging. In such *experiential* appreciation of the social, home is delinked from our supposed mythical, internal connection to it. Furthermore, rhizomatic relationships are conjunctive relationships which hold the possibility for 'and ... and ... and' instead of either/or (ibid.:25). It is such conjunctions that can create the potential for a world where diversity is not constrained by the nexus of difference–sameness and where lived experiences are transparent rather than clouded by hegemonic discourses. In rhizomatic relationships, we can only be at home – both in social space and in our own skins – when both our distinctive characteristics and our mutual interconnectivity are truly respected and where commonalities are born of lived experience rather than imposed identities.

The current lack of such realizations of home helps to explain why many people do not feel 'at home' in the places they are born and/or live and/or die, why many people feel like perpetual strangers in society, indeed why so many people are counted out of society altogether and instead positioned only as risks to it, and why those of us who have been given subordinated identities often turn to reactive identities that are mirror opposites (and therefore constitutive) of the very identities that deny us dignity and Self-identification (I am a 'person of colour' rather than 'White'; I am indigenous rather than an immigrant; I am a woman rather than man, and so on). A political consciousness and practice based on the lived experience of *rhizomatic diversity* can help us to dismantle identities that simultaneously organize and conceal the social process of making differences.

It is the possibility of being at home anywhere (not to be mistaken for being a colonizer everywhere) that allows us to *not* essentialize it as a place of origin, or a place of similarity where our authenticity is what gives us shape and form as the People of 'distinct societies.' A corollary to this is the recognition that the reification of indigeneity as an ethnicized identity is itself a product of colonial relations and the arrogant power of colonizers to name those they denied political, economic, and social self-determination to. Decolonized relationships, therefore, would be ones that understood indigeneity as a social process rather than a biological one. People can *become* indigenous through their gathering of knowledge of how to live without destroying the multiplicity of life that shares any space.

Demanding the ability to be at home anywhere helps us to move away from ideas of homes as autonomous, discrete units. Only by not imagining (and realizing) home as an interior condition are we able to stop thinking of spaces that exist outside of us as being reserved for others, even if they are 'unassimilated.' It is only when everyone will be able to be at home anywhere, instead of only in particular places (or, indeed, only in our recreations of the past), that the idea of home will be liberated from its fantastic form.

A shift in thinking about home as a *process* contingent upon the existence of social justice forces us not only to deal with the important issues of representation but also on the need to change the *material* basis of life. In particular the recognition of home as a process demands that we deal with the situation of homelessness. Homelessness, rather than a state of being, is a relationship whose dominant inverse is that of homeyness. Indeed, the deadly turn that feelings of homeyness often take is productive of homelessness and destructive of those represented as being away from 'their own homes.' Thus, homelessness is not an experience of being placeless but one of being *kept in place*; it is an experience of being bounded and constrained by those who claim to be at home. In representational terms, being homeless is seen as being outside of society. People made into migrant workers in Canada are homeless in this sense, for they are coerced into indentured, unfree employment relationships on the basis of their placement outside of the categories of either citizen or permanent resident.

The ability to be at home anywhere, therefore, requires a politicization of ideas of belonging and not belonging. It is a process of valuing our lived relationships with many, many people here, there, and everywhere, for example, valuing our relationships with others who produce (as compared with those who appropriate) wealth. Being at home any-where requires from us the formation of diverse forms of living that respect, not disdain and assimilate, the multiplicitous forms that lives take. This is not a relativist call where producers are asked to be at home with exploiters or the colonized with the colonizers. Far from it: the call to base our feelings of commonness on shared experience makes oppressed and exploited people that much stronger in their abil-ity to overcome those who benefit from such arrangements while also transforming the social basis of life. Indeed, honouring and nourishing human diversity, the diversity of life, is the challenge to the continued brutality of socially organized differences. Being at home anywhere, then, is the only viable alternative to the terrifying spread of homeless-ness in which relationships of capitalist globalization are based.

While no one can – or should – have a singular blueprint for effective challenges to current global regimes of ruling, I do know, after having carried out this study, that, at minimum, the realization of social justice requires that we rid our imaginations of the negative dualities of always-colonizing systems and the identities that they produce. Con-cretely, with regard to responses to the current border security policies being undertaken to reproduce global capitalist relationships, espe-cially by states in the global North, we need to captivate people's imag-ination through the demand for two, critically associated conditions of non-oppressive, non-violent, non-dualistic self-determination.

First, we need to re-imagine and decolonize notions of *staying*. In a socially just world, people must have the power to *stay*; that is, people must have the power to prevent their displacement. Currently, the overwhelming majority of those forced to become (im)migrants have had to exercise their (always constrained) agency to flee war, poverty, economic restructuring based on trade liberalization, and world dis-parities in the ability to live in comfort, good health, and dignity. With-out having the power to ensure that such conditions do not exist, people's ability to be self-determine is meaningless.

Second, people must have the self-determinacy of *movement*. Indeed, the free and autonomous movement of people is a necessary corollary to the ability to *stay*. It is essential that people face no constraints in their mobility for two reasons: first, to ensure that local sites do not become holding pens for people who can be exploited because they are denied the option of leaving and, second, that extra-local sites not be able to discriminate against people said to belong 'back home.'

Just as borders and other social, economic, and political boundaries need to be imaginable, then, so does a world without them. The ability to actualize the power to stay and to move cannot be founded on a recommitment to abstract cosmopolitanism based on 'the [parochial] ideology of one (very powerful) traveling culture' (Clifford, 1997:36). Rather, it necessitates a radical deconstruction of the social practices that simultaneously create both homelands and homelessness and a radical reconstruction of a world where rhizomatic diversity is seen as necessary to maintaining life on this planet. Realizing the power to stay and move entails the condemnation of those social relations based on assumptions and lived realities of apartheid and the construction of the kind of multiple relationships that would allow the world to be a home for everyone. Together, the ability to stay and to move would redefine the terrain of society so that society, and membership in it, would truly be understood both as global and as site-specific.

In the making of such a world, those who are migrating cannot be essentialized as some sort of super-heroes – able to destroy borders by the sheer act of crossing them or able to forge new identities based on their dispersal from previous imagined communities. The majority of the world's migrating people are those who have been displaced and who need and desire new homes. Their struggles for new lives/livelihoods should not become a celebration of homelessness, for their desire to construct new homes is precisely what is denied to them through practices that categorize them as the anti-heroes of nationalist home-making practices. It is their placement in the various categories of foreigners that renders them extremely vulnerable to the authority of the state and the bosses.

The multiplicitous call to bring into being a world in which people are neither displaced nor constrained in (or by) their movements comes with the recognition that simply because the category of migrant worker can be – indeed must be – deconstructed theoretically, much work is needed before it can be dislodged materially. In order for those captured by the category of migrant workers to be freed from the constraints of nationalist identification schemes, our struggles must become imminent. That is, they must also be set *within* the lived experiences that have violently brought people together. In particular, our struggles must take great care to not merely mimic or simply turn the binary identities imposed upon us on their head.

These calls, therefore, are for a world where all human beings are able to gain the fruits of their constituent activity and live in a 'communism of singularities' where each is recognized as part of a global society rather than some partitioned part of humanity (Badiou, 1992:108). It is therefore, fundamentally, a call for a 'line of flight' (Deleuze and Guattari, 1987) away from ruling ideas and ruling processes of identifications and towards the ethical-political *reconstruction* of what has been called the multitude (Hardt and Negri, 2000, 2004; Linebaugh and Rediker, 2000).

The multitude is the manifestation of diversity. Each person is part of a global plurality and not just one part of a unified totality. At the same time, each person is singular and cannot be reduced to one part of the whole. Formed through the circulation of knowledge about – and resistance to – global capitalist relationships, the multitude is simultaneously anticapitalist and antistatist. The multitude is, as Sergio Fiedler (2002:3) puts it, 'the trauma of bourgeois society.' Its basis of solidarity is fluid. 'Fluid solidarities,' according to Mohammed A. Bamyeh (2002), are 'perspectively fragmented' and subject to self-reflective revision, rather than totalistic and, as such, are able to avoid the absolutism of ideological identities. Consequently, the multitude is capable of forming new forms of sociality based on cooperation *through and against* existing national borders and racialized communities. Hence, the power of the multitude lies in its democratic potential, its ability, if exercised, to refuse to succumb to the homogenizing dimensions of the national state's transcendent, 'sovereign' power and the deceit of identity politics of all sorts.

Notes

1 Home(lessness) and the Naturalization of 'Difference'

1 I have placed the idea of national communities within scare quotes to signify that I am interested in problematizing its naturalization. Because of my desire to trouble other depoliticized terms, concepts, ideas, and categories, such as state categories of migrant worker, illegal, foreign, race, nation, home or Canadian society, are similarly placed within scare quotes. However, for the sake of easier readability, I will only use scare quotes at the first mention of them.

2 The independent class of immigration recruits people as permanent residents through the 'points system' that evaluates applicants according to their occupation, educational qualifications, and English and French language skills, as well as 'adaptability' to Canadian society and then assesses applicants on their ability to meet a minimum number of 'points' in these areas.

3 Remembering that it is the global system of nation-states that organizes people as either citizens or (im)migrants, it is important to note that the imposition of unfree conditions upon those constructed as (im)migrants is part of a long historical trajectory. For instance, Richard Plender's research shows that the first instance of permanent immigration control, England's Alien Law of 1793, included the ability for the King to limit the spatial mobility of (im)migrants who could be forced to live in a specified district (1972:43). These laws, Petras argues, 'marked the decline of free movement and the establishment of the right of states to impose direct controls on alien immigration' (1980:166). It was during the earlier part of the twentieth century, however, that there was a marked increase in immigration legislation among nation-states. For instance, it was during this time that the international system of passports was first developed (Torpey, 2000).

4 Although traditional political science approaches see MPs of the governing party but not the opposition parties as part of the *government*, I believe it is more fruitful to view the MPs of all political parties as participating in state governance, especially in discursive activities concerned with legitimizing the existence of the state and its power.

2 Globalization and the Story of National Sovereignty

1 Joseph Schumpeter argued that the supply of innovation is central to capitalist growth dynamics (see Moss, 1996).
2 It is in this light that we can make sense of recent shift in trade union bodies, such as the Canadian Labour Congress, from calling for an *abolishment* of international trade agreements, such as the North American Free Trade Agreement (NAFTA) of 1994 to demands for a 'seat at the negotiating table' within international fora such as the Forum for Asia Pacific Economic Cooperation (APEC), WTO, Free Trade Area of the Americas (FTAA), and so on. Such a demand is part of the ongoing efforts of trade union leaders to reinsert themselves in a global North tripartite arrangement of regulating capitalism, supposedly for the benefit of their members.
3 In this sense, it is also important to see the politics of import substitution in the national states of the South as having contributed to the consolidation of the ideology of discrete and sovereign national economies.

3 Imagined States: The Ideology of 'National Society'

1 Historically, the concept of 'character' has been a key organizer of racialized notions of belonging to the Canadian nation. As Valverde (1991:104) notes in her study, 'white people were seen as having more character, as a group, than Native people or people of colour; and among whites, people of British descent were regarded as having the most character.'
2 During the time that White male workers were generally employed under unfree conditions, their status changed when they married and became 'heads' of their own households. Men who were married and heads of their own households could not generally be considered another's indentured servant. Unmarried White men, however, could continue to be subjected to forced employment until the mid- to late-nineteenth century (Steinfeld, 1991:59, 98). Women, regardless of whether they were married or not, continued to be considered as living under the tutelage of the male head of the household – whether father, husband, or son.

  It is important, especially for feminists, to understand how White women who were made to work under unfree conditions were simultaneously oppressed and exploited through sexist practices but were, nonetheless, still imagined as an integral part of the Canadian nation. Thus, though they were considered as belonging to the men of the nation, their gender relations with White men were constructed within the framework of White Canadian nationalism. This helps to explain White feminist arguments for being included in the Canadian franchise in the early part of the twentieth century *because* they were 'mothers of the race' (see Valverde, 1992).

3 Lydia Potts (1990:67) writes that 'during the 19th century and the first few decades of the 20th century, workers from India, China, Japan and Java were despatched to every continent with the exception of Europe [*sic*].' Within the space of less than a hundred years (1830–1920), it is estimated that anywhere from a minimum of twelve million up to thirty-seven million people from Asia were indentured through the coolie system of unfree labour (ibid.:73–4).

4 Rosa Luxemburg's theory of imperialism, in which she develops the idea of articulated modes of production, is a dualist one. She sees imperialism as a process by which the capitalist mode of production uses and continuously reproduces non-capitalist modes of production for its own benefit. For this reason, Luxemburg (1951:365) argues that 'since accumulation of capital becomes impossible in all points without non-capitalist surroundings, we cannot gain a true picture of it by assuming the exclusive and absolute dominion of the capitalist mode of production.' She posits that the very process of capitalist accumulation rests upon the procurement of labour power from non-capitalist modes of production. Luxemburg argues that capitalism, in and of itself, is not able to produce or reproduce *all* of the labour power which it needs and, thus, essentially 'raids' non-capitalist social formations for labour power.

5 Such an approach is also evident in the work of Perry Anderson (1992) who views the expansion of free wage labour as a process accompanying the development of capitalism. He argues that while unfree labour was indispensable in the 'early modern epoch,' it cannot be considered as a part of the capitalist mode of production. He (1975:403) maintains that 'all modes of production in class societies *prior* to capitalism extract surplus labour from the immediate producers by means of extra-economic coercion. Capitalism is the first mode of production in history in which the means whereby the surplus is pumped out of the direct producer is 'purely' economic in form – the wage contract: the equal exchange between free agents which reproduces, hourly and daily, inequality and oppression.'

Along the same lines, Beiguelman (1978:76) has shown that others have normally regarded the abolition of slavery in the United States as 'a progressive purification of capitalism. Since capitalism is a system based on free [wage] labour, slavery is sometimes considered to be a graft that commercial capitalism could originally tolerate, but which had to be eliminated at a more advanced state.' Again, the notion of 'purifying' capitalism by introducing free wage labour implies that this form of labour power defines capitalism.

6 Can we seriously consider the proposition that a person arriving to Canada from a precapitalist economy (the term 'pre-capitalist' itself is often left undefined) is carrying with her a non-capitalist mode of producing and reproducing her labour power while employed in Canada where production is organized by capitalist social relations? Furthermore, to argue, as Claude Meillassoux (1981) does, that the existence of unfree wage labour within the capitalist economies of the North can be understood by recourse to the source country of migrant workers is not grounded in fact. Clearly not all migrant workers come from countries that could be classified as pre-capitalist. Conversely, not all workers from countries considered pre-capitalist work as unfree labour within Canada.

7 C.B. Macpherson's work in uncovering the ideologies of 'possessive individualism' is a useful intervention in this line of thought. He points out that freedom for waged workers meant possessing the ability to 'choose' who to sell one's labour power to. Proponents of liberal democracies argued that 'what makes a man [sic] human is his freedom from other men. Man's essence is freedom. Freedom is proprietorship of one's own person and capacities' (1977:142). By employing classic liberal tenets in which it was argued that, under capitalism, workers were *free* if they were able to choose their employer and choose to quit their employer, one's own labour power came to be seen as something privately owned. However, in understanding workers' labour power as a form of private property that they held title to, the fetishizing of labour as a commodity was secured. Labour power was made into a commodity to be bought and sold.

8 Miles also views modern forms of unfree wage labour as a pre-capitalist form of acquiring labour power, since he does not regard it as fully commodified (1987:32). For Miles, what distinguishes slave labour from modern forms of migrant contract labour is the *partial* commodification of the labour power of the latter. By this he means that, while migrant contract workers receive a wage, they do not have *mobility rights* within the labour market. Thus, Miles (ibid.) argues that 'the essential criterion for the category of unfree wage labour is found in the existence of politico-legal restrictions on the operation of the labour market.' These restrictions are put into place by the state and regulated by it. Miles further argues that unfree wage labour exists *alongside* free wage labour. For him, the creation

and existence of this form of acquiring labour power is an 'articulation' of capitalism with pre-capitalist social formations. Miles's notion that unfree wage labour comes from pre-capitalist social formations hinges upon his assumption that unfree wage workers in Western Europe are a part of the displaced peasantry in their home countries. Suzanne Paine (1974), however, has shown that workers from Turkey, for example, who are forced to work as unfree wage workers in Western Europe come not from the peasantry but largely from the proletariat.

9 Marx recognized that the concept of freedom for workers under capitalism was ideological since workers were not free in the literal sense that they had no constraints upon them. Rather, they were *compelled* to sell their labour power by having had their own means of production taken away and placed under the ownership and control of capitalists. Marx largely conceptualized the term *freedom* to mean that the previously visible use of coercion involved in exploiting labour power was concealed with the use of free wage workers. This is evident in the following statement by Marx (1977:272): 'The owner of money must find the free worker available on the commodity-market; and this worker must be free in the double sense that as a free individual he [*sic*] can dispose of his labour-power as his own commodity, and that, on the other hand, he has no other commodity for sale, i.e. he is rid of them, he is free of all the objects needed for the realization of his labour-power.' In other words, Marx believed that free wage labour rested on the ability of a worker to 'decide whether, and to whom his or her labour power will be sold' (Miles, 1987:25).

10 Paula Beiguelman's work is also useful here. She moves away from the dichotomous view that slavery and capitalism are antithetical by pointing out that 'empirically and historically colonial slavery must be considered a constituent part of [capitalism] ... it follows that a process of progressive purification is not what happens since slavery does not represent a non-capitalist component ... but, on the contrary, constitutes a *capitalist creation*. Nor is it possible to speak, in this case, of the extension of the system to the periphery of the capitalist world, since slavery turns out to be the form in which capitalism is *realized* in the colonial economy' (1978:76–7).

11 Both Karl Marx (1977) and Max Weber (1927:277) viewed unfree labour as relatively uneconomical and inefficient. It is assumed that, as capitalist social relations are established and continue to expand, unfree forms of labour power will be successively replaced by free wage labour.

12 Douglas Hay (1989:8) shows that there was an actual increase in the number of incarcerations of workers who broke their employment contracts in the nineteenth century – the heyday of laissez-faire capitalism.

4 Canadian Parlimentary Discourse and the Making of 'Migrant Workers'

1 There were other such instances. See *Hansard*, 'Trade: Protection of Canadian textile and footwear manufacturers against imports from People's Republic of China,' 14 Oct. 1970:110; and 'Finance: Tariff Adjustments to offset foreign competition with certain industries,' 22 May 1970:7211.
2 Perhaps not coincidently, it was in 1965 that the Canadian state began a review of its investment policies. Significantly, there had been no discussion of amendments to the original Corporations Act of 1934 until parliamentarians began this review process. See *Hansard*, 10 Nov. 1969:703.
3 In this they received the support of the chairperson of the Prices and Incomes Commission, who in a statement to the Canadian Manufacturers Association said that there were 'only two means of fighting inflation, restrictions on salary increases and unemployment' (*Hansard*, 7 May 1970:6677).
4 These same parliamentary debates rendered gender largely invisible in this process, although we know that gender has been key to imagining who belonged and who did not in Canada (Iacovetta and Valverde, 1992).
5 Racialization is the processes of signification where human beings are socially constituted as belonging to one or another 'racial' group. Racialization, then, is an ideological practice whereby social meaning is attached to actual or attributed physical characteristics or specific cultural, religious, and linguistic histories, and where these attributes are seen as constituting social difference.
6 In a later exchange in Parliament, the reader (hearer) is told that the people in question have never been convicted of any criminal activity in Canada (*Hansard*, 27 June 1973:5121).
7 It is of great import that the ability for formal citizens to access these options is becoming more restrictive. However, while the content of citizenship may be becoming more hollow, the distinction between being a citizen and being a non-citizen within Canada is still of great significance for people's experiences in the labour force.

5 NIEAP: The Social Organization of Unfreedom for 'Migrant Workers'

1 In Canada, the figures presented on the NIEAP represent the number of people granted temporary employment authorizations rather than the number of visas issued. The numbers do not include multiple visa issuance to the same person (Michalowski, 1993:8–11). In other words, the number of people entering on temporary employment authorizations is recorded

and not the number of jobs employing unfree wage workers in Canada. Thus, the numbers are actually an *underestimation* of the demand for unfree wage labour as only the number of people granted employment authorizations are captured by the data.

2 The NIEAP is strikingly similar to many other contract labour recruitment programs elsewhere in this regard. Hassan Gardezi, in describing the situation of guest workers in the Persian Gulf states says that 'all of these States tie a migrant worker's residence permit to his [sic] work permit, restrict his work to one employer, and do not allow him to change employers unless he obtains the consent of the first employer and the Ministry of Work' (1995:7). These conditions are almost identical to the conditions imposed on workers employed under temporary employment authorizations in Canada.

3 Research has demonstrated the often abusive and highly exploitative conditions exerted against migrant workers by recruitment agents. As many workers have exhausted their search for other means of survival, they are convenient targets for these 'middle persons' who often represent the only means for workers to find prospective employers. These middle persons often exhort a hefty price from the migrant workers for this service (see Dias, 1994:140–6).

4 On average, workers in Canada have experienced a decline in wage rates and collective bargaining rights throughout the period under study. Furthermore, indigenous peoples, people of colour, and women have historically comprised the ranks of 'cheap' labour in the country and continue to do so. However, in comparison with those countries currently found to be 'attractive' to capital investors, Canada continues to constitute a 'high wage' country.

5 I would like to thank one of the anonymous reviewers of this manuscript for pointing this out to me.

6 Not all those admitted as permanent residents intend to work in Canada. It is, therefore, vital to separate out those who have stated that they will work from those that do not intend to. Furthermore, it is important to distinguish between those entering with temporary employment authorizations that essentially have similar freedoms as does free wage labour from those who work as unfree wage labour in Canada. For these purposes, the category of 'worker' has been constructed as the sum total of permanent residents from all classes of entry who have stated they intend to work (labelled as 'destined' to the labour market by CIC) and those persons employed under temporary employment authorizations *excluding* entrepreneurs, artists, sports figures, and those with 'not stated' occupations or 'open – any occu-

pations.' To best understand the Canadian government's *recruitment* of (im)migrant labour, the category of 'destined' is further deconstructed to examine those admitted within the 'independent' category, instead, for unlike the other classes of landed immigrants, they gain entry for labour market reasons alone.

7 Such people fall under the following occupational categories: entrepreneurs; artistic, literary, performing arts and related, and sports and recreation, as well as those with 'not stated' occupations on their employment authorizations.

8 Permanent residents have the right to access the same social programs as other citizens. However, those permanent residents who enter under the family class cannot access many social services without their sponsoring relative being subject to cost-recovery or without fear of deportation. Permanent residents work as free wage labour in the country. The rights not available to permanent landed residents are: voting rights in provincial and federal elections, jobs within the federal public sector, and the holding of political positions. However, all permanent residents have the right to apply for citizenship status after three years of continuous stay in Canada. Furthermore, they cannot be deported unless they have committed a 'major' crime while in the country or have falsified their application documents.

9 Following much work by various groups representing the interests of migrant domestic workers, the Canadian government introduced the Foreign Domestic Movement Program in 1982 followed in 1992 by the Live-in Caregiver Program. Domestic workers recruited under these programs are eligible to apply for landed status after two years of continuous employment as domestic servants in Canada. This right is not available to those who are admitted under the NIEAP.

10 For the purposes of this study two categories have been constructed from the broad occupational groupings of workers entering under the NIEAP for the years 1973–1993. After 1995, these broad occupational groupings were replaced with the National Occupational Codes that did not broadly categorize occupations. Those in the 'professional' category include: managerial, administrative; natural sciences, engineering, and mathematics; social sciences and related; religion; and teaching. 'Non-professionals' include: medicine and health; clerical; sales; service; farming, horticultural, and animal husbandry; fishing, hunting, and trapping; forestry and logging; mining and quarrying, including gas and oil; processing; machining; fabricating, assembling, and repairing; construction; transport equipment operating; material handling; and other crafts and equipment operating.

Medicine and health occupations have been listed in the non-professional category because past studies have shown that workers recruited for jobs in this category are overwhelmingly employed in non-professional occupations within this broad grouping (Bolaria, 1992).

11 Monica Boyd (1986) contends that Canada's NIEAP cannot be called a 'guest worker' program because of the large numbers of workers entering the country in professional occupations. She argues that the conceptualization of any labour recruitment program as a guest worker program should be reserved for programs that permanently recruit workers for low-skilled jobs that are situated among the lowest paying (1986:938–9). Boyd bases these arguments on the operation of guest worker programs in Western Europe. However, she makes assumptions about these programs that are largely incorrect. She assumes that such programs are solely designed to recruit labour for low-skilled jobs. However, many people who work under the auspices of these programs are employed in high-skilled jobs. For example, Corrigan has shown that, as in Canada, guest workers in Western Europe are employed in a variety of jobs, including skilled jobs in the advanced technological sectors, such as automobile manufacturing (1977:445). Likewise, Connell (1992) has shown that systems of forced rotational employment can encompass a wide variety of occupations and are highly subject to domestic economic needs and concerns. As such, it is not the occupation being filled that defines conditions of unfreedom but the lack of mobility rights imposed upon guest workers.

12 Sacks has defined closure as the process by which professions 'regulate market conditions in their favour, in face of actual or potential competition from the outside' (1983:5).

13 Unfortunately, this same dataset was not available for the years following 1994. This is because it was impossible for me to sort occupations by the same categories of professional and non-professional labour by country of last permanent residence.

14 The category of less economically advanced countries (LEACs) include the following source regions: Africa, Asia (excluding Japan), North and Central America (excluding the United States), the Caribbean, South America, and Oceania. The category of economically advanced countries (EACs) includes: Europe, Australasia, the United States, Israel and Japan.

15 Unfortunately, immigration statistics have not been kept on short-term and long-term employment authorizations throughout the years. Also, for the years that they have been kept, the classification of source areas has altered. For instance, in 1980, 1981, and 1985–1988 (inclusive), such statistics were gathered. However, in the years 1982–1984 and, 1991–1993 (inclusive), the

two types of temporary employment authorization holders were lumped together. This makes comparison very difficult. This is why I have made comparisons with source areas for the years 1985–1988. It was felt that comparing the numbers for four consecutive years would bring to light at least some of the changes under way.

16 The category of 'Asia' does not include Turkey, which the Canadian government has listed as under Europe. Neither does it include workers entering from Japan.

17 It is argued that any reduction or elimination of the social wage represents a wage cut for the affected worker. Indeed, social programs, such as health care, can be said to be part of the real income of workers. Thus, for workers employed under temporary employment authorizations, their lack of access to the social wage represents a lower wage rate than for those who do have access to social programs.

18 From 1980 to 1988 information is provided in the annual reports on immigration levels to Canada; however, beginning in 1989 no information is publicly disseminated until 1993, when limited information again begins to appear.

19 This total excludes people entering Canada on student visas, visitors visas, or as entrepreneurs, artists, sports people, refugees with generic visas, and 'not stated' visas within the NIEAP.

20 The myth of the sojourner has existed as an explanation for discrimination against certain groups of workers, especially workers from Asia, since Confederation. For example, while there is no doubt that some immigrants from both the EACs and LEACs intended to stay only for a brief period in Canada, it is workers from the LEACs who were categorized as temporary rather than permanent residents, and as such, the discrimination they faced was seen as legitimate by many. *Importantly*, the Asian population was singled out for the 'sojourner' label, because they were the ones most affected by the coolie system of labour recruitment, i.e., the system of indentured servitude characteristic of the international movement of labour in the period 1830 to 1920 (Potts, 1990:202).

6 Rejecting Global Apartheid

1 The national states of the global North have imposed visas for those from most, if not all, countries in the global South and Eastern Europe, as well as carrier sanctions, 'short stop operations,' training of airport or border police personnel, lists of 'safe third countries,' lists of 'safe countries of origin,' readmission agreements with neighbouring countries that form a

buffer zone around them, immigration intelligence sharing, reinforced border controls, armed interventions at sea and military interventions (Crépeau, 2003). Migrants are often 'funneled' into more dangerous routes and
the death rates of unauthorized crossings of national borders are increasing
everywhere.

References

Abele, F., and D. Stasiulis. 1989. 'Canada as a "White Settler Colony": What about Indigenous and Immigrants?' In *The New Canadian Political Economy*. Ed. W. Clement and G. Williams. Montreal and Kingston: McGill-Queen's University Press.

Action Canada Network (ACN). 1997. *A Question of Choices*. Ottawa: ACN.

Aglietta, Michel. 1979. *A Theory of Capitalist Regulation*. London: New Left Books.

Agnew, John, and Stuart Corbridge. 1995. *Mastering Space: Hegemony, Territory and International Political Economy*. New York: Routledge.

Aleinikoff, Thomas A. 1998. *Between Principles and Politics: The Direction of U.S. Citizenship Policy*. Washington, DC: Carnegie Endowment for International Peace.

Ali, Tariq. 2002. *The Clash of Fundamentalisms: Crusades, Jihads and Modernity*. London and New York: Verso.

Amin, Samir. 1974. *Accumulation on a World Scale: A Critique of the Theory of Underdevelopment*. Vol. 1. New York: Monthly Review Press.

Affiliation of Multicultural Societies and Service Agencies of B.C. (AMSSA). 1993. 'Foreign Domestic Workers on Employment Authorizations and Labour Legislation in British Columbia.' Brief presented to the Minister of Labour. Vancouver. Unpublished.

Anderson, Benedict. 1991. *Imagined Communities: Reflections on the Origin and Spread of Nationalism*. London: Verso

Anderson, Perry. 1992. 'Components of the National Culture.' Pp. 57–77 in *English Questions*. London: Verso.

Anthias, Floya, and Nira Yuval-Davis. 1993. *Racialized Boundaries: Race, Nation, Gender, Colour and Class and the Anti-Racist Struggle*. London and New York: Routledge.

Appadurai, Arjun. 1993. 'The Heart of Whiteness: Plurality, Diversity and Democracy in the United States.' *Post-Colonial Discourse*. 16:4, 796–808.

Appleyard, Reginald. 1991. *International Migration: Challenge for the Nineties*. Geneva: International Organization for Migration.

Arat-Koc, Sedef. 1989. 'In the Privacy of Our Own Home: Foreign Domestic Workers as Solutions to the Crisis in the Domestic Sphere in Canada.' *Studies in Political Economy* 28(Spring), 33–58.

– 1992. 'Immigration Policies, Migrant Domestic Workers and the Definition of Citizenship in Canada.' In *Deconstructing a Nation: Immigration, Multiculturalism and Racism in '90s Canada*. Ed V. Satzewich. Halifax: Fernwood.

– 2001. *Caregivers Break the Silence*. Toronto: INTERCEDE.

Ashforth, Adam. 1990. 'Reckoning Schemes of Legitimation: On Commissions of Inquiry as Power/Knowledge Forms.' *Journal of Historical Sociology* 3:1, 1–22.

Avery, Donald. 1979. *Dangerous Foreigners*. Toronto: McClelland and Stewart.

Backhouse, Constance. 1999. *Colour-Coded: A Legal History of Racism in Canada, 1900–1950*. Toronto: University of Toronto Press.

Badiou, Alain. 1992. *Manifesto for Philosophy*. Albany: SUNY Press.

Baines, Donna. 2002. 'Storylines in Racialized Times: Racism and Anti-Racism in Toronto's Social Services.' *British Journal of Social Work* 32, 185–99.

Baines, Donna, and Nandita Sharma. 2002. 'Is Citizenship a Useful Concept in Social Policy Work? Non-Citizens: The Case of Migrant Workers in Canada.' *Studies in Political Economy* 69 (Autumn), 75–107.

Bakker, Isabella. 1991. 'Canada's Social Wage in an Open Economy, 1970–1983.' In *The New Era of Global Competition: State Policy and Market Power*. Ed. D. Drache and M. Gertler. Montreal and Kingston: McGill-Queen's University Press.

– (ed.). 1996. *Rethinking Restructuring: Gender and Change in Canada*. Toronto: University of Toronto Press.

Balibar, Etienne. 1991. 'The Nation Form: History and Ideology.' In *Race, Nation, Class: Ambiguous Identities*. Ed. E. Balibar and I. Wallerstein. London: Verso.

Bammer, Anjelika. 1992. 'Editorial.' *New Formations* 17.

Bamyeh, Mohammed A. 2002. 'Fluid Solidarity.' Conference paper presentation, Nationalism and Globalism, University of Technology, Sydney, Australia, 15–16 July.

Bannerji, Himani. 1995. *Thinking Through: Essays on Feminism, Marxism, and Anti-Racism*. Toronto: Women's Press.

– (ed.). 1993. *Returning the Gaze: Essays on Racism, Feminism and Politics*. Toronto: Sister Vision.

Barlow, Maude. 1993. 'Competition: The New Global Gospel.' *Free Trade in Perspective* 3:2.

Basok, Tanya. 1996. 'Refugee Policy: Globalization, Radical Challenge, or State Control?' *Studies in Political Science* 50 (Summer), 133–66.

– 2002. *Tortillas and Tomatoes: Transmigrant Mexican Harvesters in Canada.* Montreal: McGill-Queen's University Press.

Bateson, Gregory. 1979. *Mind and Nature: A Necessary Unity.* New York: Dutton.

Baudrillard, Jean, and Marc Guillaume. 1992. *Figures de l'altérité.* Paris: Editions Descartes.

Berdichewsky, Bernardo. 1991. 'Multiculturalism and the Process Towards a Pluralistic Society in Canada.' Position Paper. Ottawa: Canadian Ethno-Cultural Council.

Bhabha, Homik. 1994. *The Location of Culture.* London and New York: Routledge.

Billig, Michael. 1995. *Banal Nationalism.* London: Sage.

Bina, Cyrus, and Behzad Yaghmaian. 1991. 'Post-war Global Accumulation and the Transnationalisation of Capital.' *Capital and Class* 43 (Spring), 107–30.

Bird, John, 1995. 'Dolce Domum.' In *House.* Ed. J. Lingwood. London: Phaidon.

Bolaria, B. Singh. 1984. 'Migrants, Immigrants and the Canadian Labour Force.' In *Contradictions in Canadian Society.* Ed. J.A. Fry. Toronto: Wiley.

– 1992. 'From Immigrant Settlers to Migrant Transients: Foreign Professionals in Canada.' In *Deconstructing a Nation: Immigration, Multiculturalism and Racism in '90s Canada.* Ed. V. Satzewich. Halifax: Fernwood.

Bolaria, B. Singh, and Peter S. Li. 1988. *Racial Oppression in Canada.* 2nd ed. Toronto: Garamond.

Bonacich, Edna. 1972. 'A Theory of Ethnic Antagonism: The Split Labour Market.' *American Sociological Review* 37 (Oct.), 547–59.

Bonefeld, Werner. 1993. 'Some Notes on the Theory of the Capitalist State.' *Capital and Class* 49 (Spring), 113–22.

Bonnett, A. 1998. 'How the British Working Class Became White: The Symbolic (Re)formation of Racialised Capitalism.' *Journal of Historical Sociology* 11:3, 316–40.

Bottomore, Tom, Laurence Harris, V.G. Kiernan, and Ralph Miliband (eds.). 1983. *A Dictionary of Marxist Thought.* Oxford: Blackwell.

Bourgeault, Ron. 1989. 'Race, Class and Gender: Colonial Domination of Indian Women.' In *Race, Class, Gender: Bonds and Barriers.* 2nd ed. Ed. J. Vorst et al. Toronto: Society for Socialist Studies and Garamond Press.

– 1992. 'The Struggle for Class and Nation: The Origin of the Metis in Canada and the National Question.' In *1492–1992: Five Centuries of Imperialism and*

Resistance. Ed. R. Bourgeault, D. Broad, L. Brown, and L. Foster. Winnipeg: Fernwood.

Boyce Davies, Carole. 1994. *Black Women, Writing, and Identity: Migratory Subjects.* London: Routledge.

Boyd, Monica. 1986. 'Temporary Workers in Canada: A Multifaceted Program.' *International Migration Review* 20:4, 929–50.

– 1996. 'Female Migrant Labor in North America: Trends and Issues for the 1990s.' In *International Migration, Refugee Flows and Human Rights in North America: The Impact of Trade and Restructuring.* Ed. A.B. Simmons. New York: Center for Migration Studies.

Brah, Avtar. 1996. *Cartographies of Diaspora: Contesting Identities.* London: Routledge.

Brand, Dionne. 1993. 'A Working Paper on Black Women in Toronto: Gender, Race and Class.' In *Returning the Gaze: Essays on Racism, Feminism and Politics.* Ed. H. Bannerji. Toronto: Sister Vision Press.

Brass, Tom. 1988. 'Review Essay: Slavery Now – Unfree Labour and Modern Capitalism.' *Slavery and Abolition* 9:2, 183–97.

Brecher, Jeremy. 1993. 'The Hierarchs' New World Order – and Ours.' In *Global Visions: Beyond the New World Order.* Montreal: Black Rose Books.

Breti, D., and S. Davidson. 1989. 'Foreign Domestic Workers in British Columbia.' Brief submitted to the British Columbia Human Rights Commission.

Brodie, Janine (ed.). 1996. *Women and Canadian Public Policy.* Toronto: Harcourt Brace.

Brown, Wendy. 1995. *States of Injury: Power and Freedom in Late Modernity.* Princeton, NJ: Princeton University Press.

Buci-Glucksmann, Christine. 1980. *Gramsci and the State.* London: Lawrence and Wishart.

Burchell, Graham, Colin Gordon, and Peter Miller (eds.). 1991. *The Foucault Effect: Studies in Governmentality.* Chicago: University of Chicago Press.

Buroway, Michael. 1976. 'The Functions and Reproduction of Migrant Labour: Comparative Material from Southern Africa and the United States.' *American Journal of Sociology* 81:5, 1050–87.

Burton, Antoinette. 1997. 'Who Needs the Nation? Interrogating "British" History.' *Journal of Historical Sociology* 10:3, 227–48.

Butler, Judith. 1992. 'Contingent Foundations: Feminism and the Question of Postmodernism.' In *Feminists Theorize the Political.* Ed. J. Butler and J.W. Scott. New York: Routledge.

Butler, Judith, and Joan Scott (eds.). 1992. *Feminists Theorize the Political.* New York: Routledge.

Carchedi, Guglielmo. 1979. 'Authority and Foreign Labour: Some Notes on a Late Capitalist Form of Capital Accumulation and State Intervention.' *Studies in Political Economy* 2:37, 37–74.

Carney, J. 1976. 'Capital Accumulation and Uneven Development in Europe: Notes on Migrant Labour.' *Antipode* 8:1, 30–6.

Carroll, William K. 1989. 'Neoliberalism and the Recomposition of Finance Capital in Canada.' *Capital and Class* 38 (Summer), 81–112.

Chan, Anthony. 1980. 'The Myth of the Chinese Sojourner in Canada.' In *Visible Minorities and Multiculturalism: Asians in Canada*. Ed. K.V. Ujimoto and G. Hirabayashi. Toronto: Butterworths.

– 1983. *Gold Mountain: The Chinese in the New World*. Vancouver: New Star Books.

Chan, Gaye, and Nandita Sharma. 2004. 'The Diggers: The Unmaking of Public Space.' *Chain*, no. 11, 69–76.

Chin, Ko-Lin. 1999. *Smuggled Chinese: Clandestine Immigration to the United States*. Philadelphia: Temple University Press.

Citizenship and Immigration Canada (CIC). 1994a. *Hiring Foreign Workers: Facts for Canadian Employers*. Ottawa: Minister of Supply and Services.

– 1994b. *Facts and Figures: Overview of Immigration*. Ottawa: Minister of Supply and Services.

– 1994c. *Highlights. Into the 21st Century: A Strategy for Immigration and Citizenship*. Ottawa: Minister of Supply and Services.

– 1994d. *Immigration Consultations Report*. Ottawa: Minister of Supply and Services.

– 1994e. *A Broader Vision: Immigration and Citizenship Plan 1995–2000. Annual Report to Parliament*. Ottawa: Minister of Supply and Services.

– 1994f. *Into the 21st Century: A Strategy for Immigration and Citizenship*. Ottawa: Minister of Supply and Services.

– 1994g. *Do You Want to Work Temporarily in Canada?* Ottawa: Minister of Supply and Services.

– 1994h. *Canada's Immigration Law*. Ottawa: Minister of Supply and Services.

– 1994i. *Hiring Foreign Workers: Facts for Canadian Employers*. Ottawa: Minister of Supply and Services.

– 1995. Information Management Data Warehouse Services. Hull.

– 2005. Information Management Data Warehouse Services. Ottawa.

Clark, G.L., and M.J. Dear. 1984. *State Apparatus*. Boston: Allen and Unwin.

Clarke, Rick. 1993. 'Full Speed Ahead Backwards.' *Free Trade in Perspective* 3:2 (Spring), 9–15.

Clarke, Tony, and Maude Barlow. 1997. *MAI: The Multilateral Agreement on Investment and the Threat to Canadian Sovereignty*. Toronto: Stoddart.

– 1998. *MAI, Round 2: New Global and Internal Threats to Canadian Sovereignty.* Toronto: Stoddart.

Clifford, James. 1986. 'On Ethnographic Allegory.' In *Writing Culture: The Poetics and Politics of Ethnography.* Ed. J. Clifford and G.E. Marcus. Berkeley and Los Angeles: University of California Press.

– 1997. *Routes.* Cambridge: Harvard University Press.

– 1998. 'Mixed Feelings.' In *Cosmopolitics.* Ed. P. Cheah and B. Robbins. Minneapolis: University of Minnesota Press.

Cock, Jacklyn. 1980. *Maids and Madams: A Study in the Politics of Exploitation.* Johannesburg: Ravan Press.

Cohen, Marjorie. 1994. 'Debt and Deficit: A Problem or THE Problem?' Speech given at the NDP Renewal Conference, 27–8 Aug., Ottawa.

Cohen, Philip. 1996. 'Homing Devices.' In *Re-situating Identities.* Ed. V. Amit-Talai and C. Knowles. Peterborough, ON: Broadview Press.

Cohen, Steve. 2003. *No One Is Illegal: Asylum and Immigration Control Past and Present.* Stoke on Trent, UK: Trentham Books.

Cole, Phil. 1998. 'A Game of Two Halves: "English" Identity Fifty Years after the Windrush.' *Soundings,* no. 10.

Cornish, Cynthia D. 1992. 'Unfree Wage Labour, Women and the State: Employment Visas and Foreign Domestic Workers in Canada.' Master's thesis, University of Victoria.

Corrigan, Philip. 1977. 'Feudal Relics or Capitalist Monuments? Notes on the Sociology of Unfree Labour.' *Sociology* 11:3, 453–63.

Corrigan, Philip, and Derek Sayer. 1985. *The Great Arch: English State Formation as Cultural Revolution.* Oxford: Blackwell.

Cox, Robert. 1981. 'Social Forces, States and World Orders: Beyond International Relations Theory.' *Millennium* 10:2, 126–55.

Crawford, James. 2005. 'Endangered Native American Languages: What Is to Be Done, and Why?' <http://ourworld.compuserve.com/homepages/JWCRAWFORD/brj.htm> (accessed: 26 Jan. 2005).

Creese, Gillian. 1988. 'Exclusion or Solidarity? Vancouver Workers' Confront the "Oriental Problem."' *B.C. Studies* 80 (Winter), 24–51.

Crépeau, François. 2003. 'The Fight against Migrant Smuggling: Migration Containment over Refugee Protection.' In *The Refugee Convention at Fifty: a View from Forced Migration Studies.* Ed. Joanne van Selm, Khoti Kamanga, John Morrison, Aninia Nadig, Sanja Spoljar Vrzina, and Loes van Willigen. Boston: Lexington Books.

Cresswell, Tim. 1996. *In Place/Out of Place.* Minneapolis: University of Minnesota Press.

Davis, Mike. 2002. 'Foreword.' In *Operation Gatekeeper: The Rise of the 'Illegal*

Alien' and the Making of the U.S.–Mexico Boundary. Ed. J. Nevins. New York and London: Routledge.

Dehli, Kari. 1993. 'Subject to the New Global Economy: Power and Positioning in the Ontario Labour Market Policy Formation.' *Studies in Political Economy* 41, 83–110.

De Lauretis, Teresa. 1986. 'Issues, Terms, and Contexts.' In *Feminist Studies, Critical Studies.* Ed. T. De Lauretis. Bloomington: Indiana University Press.

Deleuze, Gilles, and Félix Guattari. 1987. *A Thousand Plateaus: Capitalism and Schizophrenia.* Trans. B. Massumi. Minneapolis: University of Minnesota Press.

Deleuze, Gilles, and Claire Parnet. 1987. *Dialogues.* Trans. Hugh Tomlinson and Barbara Habberjam. London: Athlone Press.

Dias, Malsiri. 1991. 'Overview of Mechanisms of Migration,' In *The Trade in Domestic Workers: Causes, Mechanisms and Consequences of International Migration.* Ed. N. Heyzer, G. Lycklama a Nijeholt, and N. Weerakoon. London: Zed Books.

Dillon, John. 1991. 'Trade Talks Are Key to the "New World Order."' *Pro-Canada Dossier* 30 (March-April).

Donald, James. 1999. *Imagining the Modern City.* London: Athlone Press.

Donaldson, Laura. 1992. *Decolonizing Feminisms: Race, Gender, and Empire-Building.* Chapel Hill: University of North Carolina Press.

Doty, Roxanne L. 1996. 'The Double-Writing of Statecraft: Exploring State Respones to Illegal Immigration.' *Alternatives* 21, 171–89.

Drache, D., and M.S. Gertler. 1991. 'The World Economy and the Nation-State: The New International Order.' In *The New Era of Global Competition: State Policy and Market Power.* Ed. D. Drache and M.S. Gertler. Montreal and Kingston: McGill-Queen's University Press.

Dutton, Alan. 1984. 'Capitalism, the State and Minority Ethnic Relations in British Columbia.' Master's thesis, University of Victoria.

ECEJ (Ecumenical Coalition for Economic Justice). 1993. *Reweaving Canada's Social Programs: From Shredded Safety Net to Social Solidarity.* Toronto: ECEJ.

Elias, Norbert. 1978. *The Civilizing Process: The History of Manners.* Oxford: Basil Blackwell.

Employment and Immigration Canada (EIC). 1977. *1976 Immigration Statistics: Canada.* Ottawa: Minister of Supply and Services.

– 1978. *1977 Immigration Statistics: Canada.* Ottawa: Minister of Supply and Services.

– 1979. *1978 Immigration Statistics: Canada.* Ottawa: Minister of Supply and Services.

– 1980. *1979 Immigration Statistics: Canada*. Ottawa: Minister of Supply and Services.

– 1981. *1980 Immigration Statistics: Canada*. Ottawa: Minister of Supply and Services.

– 1982. *1981 Immigration Statistics: Canada*. Ottawa: Minister of Supply and Services.

– 1983. *1982 Immigration Statistics: Canada*. Ottawa: Minister of Supply and Services.

– 1984. *1983 Immigration Statistics: Canada*. Ottawa: Minister of Supply and Services.

– 1985. *1984 Immigration Statistics: Canada*. Ottawa: Minister of Supply and Services.

– 1986. *1985 Immigration Statistics: Canada*. Ottawa: Minister of Supply and Services.

– 1987. *1986 Immigration Statistics: Canada*. Ottawa: Minister of Supply and Services.

– 1988. *1987 Immigration Statistics: Canada*. Ottawa: Minister of Supply and Services.

– 1989. *1988 Immigration Statistics: Canada*. Ottawa: Minister of Supply and Services.

– 1990. *1989 Immigration Statistics: Canada*. Ottawa: Minister of Supply and Services.

– 1991. *1990 Immigration Statistics: Canada*. Ottawa: Minister of Supply and Services.

– 1992a. *1991 Immigration Statistics: Canada*. Ottawa: Minister of Supply and Services.

– 1992b. *Managing Immigration: A Framework for the 1990s*. Ottawa: Minister of Supply and Services.

– 1992c. *Profile of Permit Holders and Visitors in Canada, 1989, 1990, 1991*. Ottawa: Minister of Supply and Services.

– 1993. *1992 Immigration Statistics: Canada*. Ottawa: Minister of Supply and Services.

Ermarth, Elizabeth D. 1992. *Sequel to History: Postmodernism and the Crisis of Representational Time*. Princeton, NJ: Princeton University Press.

Estable, Alma. 1986. *Immigrant Women in Canada – Current Issues*. Background Paper prepared for the Canadian Advisory Council for the Status of Women, Ottawa.

Evans, B. Mitchell, Stephen McBride, and John Shields. 1998. 'National Governance versus Globalization: Canadian Democracy in Question.' *Socialist Studies Bulletin* 54 (Oct.-Nov.-Dec.), 5–26.

Fanon, Frantz. 1965. *The Wretched of the Earth*. London: MacGibbon and Kee.

Fiedler, Sergio. 2002. 'The National or the Global: Between "The People" and the Multitude.' Conference paper presentation, Nationalism and Globalism, University of Technology, Sydney, Australia, 15–16 July.

Fine, B., and L. Harris. 1979. *Rereading Capital*. London: Macmillan.

Foucault, Michel. 1965. *Madness and Civilization*. Trans. R. Howard. New York: Vintage.

– 1972. *The Archeology of Knowledge*. Trans. A.M. Sheridan Smith. New York: Pantheon.

– 1979. 'Truth and Power.' In *Michael Foucault: Power, Truth, Strategy*. Ed. M. Morris and P. Patton. Sydney: Feral Publications.

– 1991. 'Questions of Method.' In *The Foucault Effect: Studies in Governmentality*. Ed. G. Burchell, C. Gordon, and P. Miller. Chicago: University of Chicago Press.

Frank, A.G. 1967. *Capitalism and Underdevelopment in Latin America*. New York: Monthly Review Press.

Fraser, Nancy. 1993. 'Rethinking the Public Sphere.' In *The Phantom Public Sphere*. Ed. B. Robbins. Minneapolis: University of Minnesota Press.

Fraser, Nancy, and Linda Gordon. 1992. 'Contract versus Charity: Why Is There No Social Citizenship in the United States?' *Socialist Review* 22:3, 45–68.

Fredrickson, George. 1988. *The Arrogance of Race: Historical Perspectives on Slavery, Racism and Social Inequality*. Hanover, NH: Wesleyan University Press.

Frideres, James. 1988. *Native Peoples in Canada: Contemporary Conflict*. Scarborough, ON: Prentice-Hall.

Frobel, Folker, Jurgen Heinrichs, and Otto Kreye. 1977. *The New International Division of Labour: Structural Unemployment in Industrialized Countries and Industrialization in Developing Countries*. London: Cambridge University Press.

Gardezi, Hassan N. 1995. *The Political Economy of International Labour Migration*. Montreal: Black Rose Books.

Gilroy, Paul. 1987. *'There Ain't No Black in the Union Jack': The Cultural Politics of Race and Nation*. Chicago: University of Chicago Press.

Goldberg, David Theo. 1992. 'The Semantics of Race.' *Ethnic and Racial Studies* 15:4, 543–65.

– 1993. *Racist Culture: Philosophy and the Politics of Meaning*. Oxford: Blackwell.

Goodleaf, Donna. 1995. *Entering the War Zone: A Mohawk Perspective on Resisting Invasions*. Penticton, BC: Theytus Books.

Gordon, Colin. 1991. 'Government Rationality: An Introduction.' In *The Foucault Effect: Studies in Governmentality*. Ed. G. Burchell, C. Gordon, and P. Miller. Chicago: University of Chicago Press.

Government Statisticians' Collective. 1974. 'How Official Statistics Are Produced: Views from the Inside.' In *Demystifying Social Statistics*. Ed. J. Irvine, I. Mills, and J. Evans. London: Pluto.

Gramsci, A. 1971. *Selections from the Prison Notebooks*. London: Lawrence and Wishart.

Guillaumin, Colette. 1995. *Racism, Sexism, Power and Ideology*. London: Routledge.

Gupta, Akhil, and James Ferguson. 1997. 'Introduction' to *Culture, Power, Place*. Ed. A. Gupta and J. Ferguson. Durham, NC: Duke University Press.

Haber, H. Fern. 1994. *Beyond Postmodern Politics*. London: Routledge.

Habermas, Jurgen. 1992 'Citizenship and National Identity; Some Reflections on the Future of Europe.' *Praxis International* 12:1, 1–18.

Habib, Irfan. 1995. 'Capitalism in History.' *Social Scientist* 23:7–9, 15–31.

Hage, Ghassan. 1993. 'Nation-Building-Dwelling-Being,' *Communal/Plural* 1, 73–103.

– 2000. *White Nation: Fantasties of White Supremacy in a Multicultural Society*. New York, and Annandale, NSW, Australia: Routledge and Pluto Press.

Hall, Stuart. 1980. 'Race, Articulation and Societies Structured in Dominance.' In *Sociological Theories: Race and Colonialism*. Paris: UNESCO.

– 1996. 'Who Needs Identity?' Pp. 1–17 in *Questions of Cultural Identity*. Ed. S. Hall and P. du Gay. London: Sage.

Hall, Stuart, and Martin Jacques (eds.). 1989. *New Times: The Changing Face of Politics in the 1990s*. London: Lawrence and Wishart.

Hardt, Michael, and Antonio Negri. 2004. *Multitude: War and Democracy in the Age of Empire*. New York: Penguin.

– 2000. *Empire*. Cambridge: Harvard University Press.

Harris, Nigel. 1983. *Of Bread and Guns: The World Economy in Crisis*. Harmondsworth: Penguin.

Hatton, Timothy J., and Jeffrey G. Williamson. 1998. *The Age of Mass Migration: Causes and Economic Impact*. New York: Oxford University Press.

Hawkins, Freda. 1974. 'Canadian Immigration Policy and Management.' *International Migration Review* 8:2, 141–53.

– 1988. *Canada and Immigration*. Montreal and Kingston: McGill-Queen's University Press.

Heap, Dan. 1992. *Brief on Bill C-86* to the Special Legislative Committee on Bill C-86. Ottawa. Unpublished.

Hebdige, Dick. 1995. 'On Tumbleweed and Bodybags: Remembering America.' In *Longing and Belonging: From the Faraway Nearby*. Ed. B.W. Ferguson. New York: Distributed Art Publishers.

Helleiner, Eric. 1994. *States and the Re-emergence of Global Finance: From Bretton Woods to the 1990s.* Ithaca, NY: Cornell University Press.

Heron, Gil Scott. 2002. Work for Peace. www.zmag.org/songs/world-peace.htrn. 4 May 2005.

Hirst, Paul, and Grahame Thompson. 1996. *Globalization in Question: The International Economy and the Possibilities of Governance.* Cambridge: Polity Press.

Hobsbawm, Eric. 1990. *Nations and Nationalism since 1780.* New York: Cambridge University Press.

– 1991. 'Exile: A Keynote Address.' *Social Research* 58:1, 65–48.

Holloway, John. 1994. 'Global Capital and the National State.' *Capital and Class* 52 (Spring), 23–50.

House of Commons Debates. 1970. *Official Report. First Session – Twenty-Eighth Parliament.* Vol. 4, *1968–69* (3 Dec. 1968 to 20 Jan. 1969); Vol. 5, *1968–69* (21 Jan. to 18 Feb. 1969); Vol. 6, *1969* (19 Feb. to 19 March); Vol. 7, *1969* (20 March to 25 April); Vol. 9, *1969* (29 May to 17 June); Vol. 10, *1969* (18 June to 22 Oct.). Ottawa: Queen's Printer.

– *Official Report. Second Session – Twenty-Eight Parliament,* Vol. 1, *1969* (23 Oct. to 21 Nov.); Vol. 2, *1969* (24 Nov. to 19 Dec.); Vol. 3, *1970* (12 Jan. to 6, Feb.); Vol. 4, *1970* (9 Feb. to 4 March); Vol. 5, *1970* (5 March to 25 March); Vol. 6, *1970* (6 April to 5 May); Vol. 7, *1970* (6 May to 4 June); Vol. 8, *1970* (5 June to 7 Oct.). Ottawa: Queen's Printer.

– *Official Report. Third Session – Twenty-Eighth Parliament,* Vol. 1, *1970* (8 Oct. to 12 Nov.); Vol. 2, *1970* (13 Nov. to 18 Dec.). Ottawa: Queen's Printer.

– 1971. *Official Report. Third Session – Twenty-Eighth Parliament,* Vol. 3, *1970* (12 Jan. to 12 Feb.); Vol. 4, *1971* (15 Feb. to 19 March); Vol. 5, *1971* (22 March to 5 May); Vol. 6, *1971* (6 May to 11 June); Vol. 7, *1971* (14 June to 10 Sept.); Vol. 8, *1971* (13 Sept. to 19 Oct.); Vol. 9, *1971* (20 Oct. to 26 Nov.); Vol. 10, *1971–72* (29 Nov. to 16 Feb. 1972). Ottawa: Queen's Printer.

– 1972. *Official Report. Fourth Session – Twenty-Eighth Parliament,* Vol. 1, *1972* (17 Feb. to 17 March); Vol. 2, *1972* (20 March to 5 May); Vol. 3, *1972* (8 May to 7 June); Vol. 4, *1972* (8 June to 1 Sept.). Ottawa: Queen's Printer.

– 1973. *Official Report. First Session – Twenty-Ninth Parliament,* Vol. 1, *1973* (4 Jan. to 9 Feb.); Vol. 2, *1973* (12 Feb. to 16 March); Vol. 3, *1973* (19 March to 18 April); Vol. 4, *1973* (7 May to 8 June); Vol. 5, *1973* (11 June to 18 July); Vol. 6, *1973* (19 July to 21 Sept.); Vol. 7, *1973* (15 Oct. to 23 Nov.). Ottawa: Queen's Printer.

– 1974. *Official Report. First Session – Twenty-Ninth Parliament,* Vol. 8, *1973* (26 Nov. to 26 Feb. 1974). Ottawa: Queen's Printer.

Hu, Tai-Li. 1983. 'The Emergence of Small-Scale Industry in a Taiwanese Rural Community.' In *Women, Men and the International Division of Labour.* Ed. J. Nash and M.P. Fernandez-Kelly. Albany: SUNY Press.

Huen, Lim Pui, and Diana Wong (eds.). 2000. *War and Memory in Malaysia and Singapore*. Singapore: Institute of Southeast Asian Studies.

Huntington, Samuel P. 1996. *The Clash of Civilizations and the Remaking of World Order*. New York: Simon and Schuster.

Hymer, S. 1979. 'The Multinational Corporation and the International Division of Labour.' In *The Multinational Corporation: A Radical Approach*. Ed. R. Cohen et al. Cambridge: Cambridge University Press.

Hyslop, Jonathan. 1999. 'The Imperial Working Class Makes Itself "White": White Labourism in Britain, Australia, and South Africa before the First World War.' *Journal of Historical Sociology* 12:4, 398–421.

Ignatiev, N. 1995. *How the Irish Became White*. New York: Routledge.

Immigration and Refugee Protection Act (Bill C-11), S.C. 2001, c. 27, passed by the Canadian House of Commons on 13 June 2001, Royal Assent on 1 November 2001, entry into force June 2002, art. 117ss. Text at: www.cic.gc.ca/english/pdffiles/pub/C-11_4.pdf.

Innis, Harold A. 1970. *The Fur Trade in Canada*. Toronto: University of Toronto Press.

INTERCEDE (Toronto Organization for Domestic Workers' Rights – International Coalition to End Domestic Exploitation). 1993. *Report to the 1993 Annual General Meeting*. Prepared by Felicita O. Villasin. Toronto: INTERCEDE.

– 1994. *Report to the 1994 Annual General Meeting*. Prepared by Felicita O. Villasin. Toronto: INTERCEDE.

International Labor Organization (ILO). 1997. *Employment Report 1996/97: National Policies in a Global Context*. Geneva: ILO.

Iacovetta, Franca, and Marianna Valverde (eds.). 1992. *Gender Conflicts: New Essays in Women's History*. Toronto: University of Toronto Press.

Irigaray, L. 1993. *An Ethics of Sexual Difference*. London, Athlone Press.

Ishi, T.K. 1982. 'The Political Economy of International Migration: Indian Physicians to the United States.' *South Asian Bulletin* 2:1, 39–58.

Jamal, Amina. 1998. 'Situating South Asian Immigrant Women in the Canadian/Global Economy.' *Canadian Woman Studies* 18:1 26–33.

Jenkins, Craig. 1982. 'The Demand for Immigrant Workers: Labor Scarcity or Social Control?' *International Migration Review* 12:4.

Jenson, Jane. 1989. '"Different" but not "Exceptional": Canada's Permeable Fordism.' *Canadian Review of Sociology and Anthropology* 26:1, 69–94.

Jessop, Bob. 1993. 'Towards a Schumpeterian Workfare State? Preliminary Remarks on Post-Fordist Political Economy.' *Studies in Political Economy* 40 (Spring), 7–39.

Johansen, A. 1997. 'Fellowmen, Compatriots, Contemporaries.' In *Cultural Pol-*

itics and Political Culture in Postmodern Europe. Ed. J. Peter Burgess. Amsterdam: Editions Rodopi.

Joint Working Group (Federal/Provincial Advisory Committee on Health/ Human Resources and National Committee on Physical Manpower). 1986. *Report of the Joint Working Group on Graduates of Foreign Medical Schools.* Ottawa: Health and Welfare Canada.

Kafka, Franz. 1969. *The Trial.* New York: Vintage.

Keith, Michael, and Steven Pile. 1993. 'The Politics of Place.' In *Place and the Politics of Identity.* Ed. M. Keith and S. Pile. London: Routledge.

Koc, Mustafa. 1992. 'Implications of Restricted Mobility of Labour in a Global Economy.' Conference paper presentation, Migration, Human Rights and Economy Integration, organized by the Centre for Refugee Studies, York University, Toronto, 19–22 Nov.

Kolko, J. 1988. *Restructuring the World Economy.* New York: Pantheon.

Kumar, Krishan. 1994. 'Home: The Nature of Private Life at the End of the Twentieth Century.' In *Private and Public in Thought and Practice.* Ed. J. Wintraub and K. Kumar. Chicago: University of Chicago Press.

Kymlicka, Will. 1995. Multicultural Citizenship: A Liberal Theory of Minority Rights. Oxford and New York: Clarendon.

Lambert, John. 1991. 'Europe: The Nation-State Dies Hard.' *Capital and Class* 43 (Spring), 9–24.

Laxer, Gordon. 2002. 'The Return of Left Nationalism/Internationalism.' Conference paper presentation, Nationalism and Globalism, University of Technology, Sydney, Australia, 15–16 July.

Li, Peter S. 1988. *Ethnic Inequality in a Class Society.* Toronto: Thompson Educational.

Linebaugh, Peter, and Marcus Rediker. 2000. *The Many-Headed Hydra: Sailors, Slaves, Commoners, and the Hidden History of the Revolutionary Atlantic.* Boston: Beacon Press.

Lipietz, Alain. 1987. *Mirages and Miracles.* London: Verso.

Lowe, L. 1996. *Immigrant Acts: On Asian American Cultural Politics.* Durham, NC: Duke University Press.

Luxemburg, Rosa. 1951. *The Accumulation of Capital.* New Haven, CT: Yale University Press.

MacEachan, Allan, and Jean-Robert Gauthier, 1994. *Canada's Foreign Policy: Principles and Priorities for the Future.* Report of the Special Joint Committee of the Senate and House of Commons Reviewing Canadian Foreign Policy. Ottawa: Queen's Printer.

Mackay, H. (ed.). 1997. *Consumption and Everyday Life.* Milton Keynes: Open University Press.

Macpherson, Crawford B. 1977. *The Life and Times of Liberal Democracy*. Oxford: Oxford University Press.

Magnusson, Warren, and Rob Walker. 1988. 'De-Centring the State: Political Theory and Canadian Political Economy.' *Studies in Political Economy* 26, 37–71.

Mahon, Rianne. 1991. 'From "Bringing" to "Putting": The State in Late Twentieth-Century Social Theory.' *Canadian Journal of Sociology / Cahiers canadiens de sociologie* 16:2, 119–94.

Malkki, Lisa. 1997. 'National Geographic,' in *Culture, Power, Place*. Ed. A. Gupta and J. Ferguson. Durham, NC: Duke University Press.

Manpower and Immigration Canada (MIC). 1974. *1973 Immigration Statistics: Canada*. Ottawa: Minister of Supply and Services.

Marchak, Patricia. 1991. *The Integrated Circus*. Montreal and Kingston: McGill-Queen's University Press.

Marr, William L. 1977. 'Employment Visas and the Canadian Labour Force.' *Canadian Public Policy* 3:4, 518–24.

Marshall, T.H. 1950. *Citizenship and Social Class*. London: Pluto.

Marx, Karl. 1971. *A Contribution to the Critique of Political Economy*. London: Lawrence and Wishart.

– 1977. *Capital: A Critique of Political Economy*, Vol. 1. New York: Vintage.

Marx, Karl, and Frederick Engels. 1969. 'Feuerbach. Opposition of the Materialistic and Idealistic Outlook (Chapter 1 of *The German Ideology*).' In *Selected Works*, Vol. 1. Moscow: Progress.

Massey, Doreen. 1991. 'Flexible Sexism.' Society and Space 9:1, 31–57.

– 1994. *Space, Place and Gender*. Cambridge: Polity.

Mbembe, Achille. 2001. *On the Postcolony*. Berkeley: University of California Press.

McBride, Stephen. 1992. *Not Working: State, Unemployment, and Neo-Conservatism in Canada*. Toronto: University of Toronto Press.

– 2001. *Paradigm Shift: Globalization and the Canadian State*. Halifax: Fernwood.

McBride, Stephen, and John Shields. 1993. *Dismantling a Nation: Canada and the New World Order*. Halifax: Fernwood.

McLintock, Anne. 1995. *Imperial Leather*. London: Routledge.

McMichael, Philip, and David Myhre. 1991. 'Global Regulation vs the Nation-State: Agro-Food Systems and the New Politics of Capital.' *Capital and Class* 43 (Spring), 83–105.

Meillassoux, Claude. 1981. *Maidens, Meal, and Money: Capitalism and the Domestic Economy*. New York: Cambridge University Press.

Memmi, Albert. 1965. *The Colonizer and the Colonized*. Boston: Beacon Press.

Mercer, Kobena. 1994. *Welcome to the Jungle: New Positions in Black Cultural Studies*. New York: Routledge.

Michaels, Anne. 1996. *Fugitive Pieces*. Toronto: McClelland and Stewart.

Michalowski, Margaret. 1992. 'Visitors and Visa Workers: Old Wine in New Bottles?' Paper presented at the Conference 'Migration, Human Rights and Economic Integration: Focus on Canada, United States, Mexico, Central America, and the Caribbean.' York University, Toronto, 19–22 Nov.

Michalowski, Margaret. 1993. 'Redefining the Concept of Immigration in Canada.' *Canadian Studies in Population* 20:1, 59–84.

Mick, S.S. 1975. 'The Foreign Medical Graduates.' *Scientific American* 232:2, 14–21.

Miles, Robert. 1982. *Racism and Migrant Labour: A Critical Text*. London: Routledge and Kegan Paul.

– 1987. *Capitalism and Unfree Labour: Anomaly or Necessity?* London and New York: Tavistock.

– 1989. *Racism*. London and New York: Routledge.

– 1993. *Racism after 'Race Relations.'* London and New York: Routledge.

Mohanty, Chandra Talpade. 1991. 'Introduction: Cartographies of Struggle, Third World Women and the Politics of Feminism.' In *Third World Women and the Politics of Feminism*. Ed. C. Mohanty, A. Russo, and L. Torres. Bloomington: Indiana University Press.

Morley, David. 2000. *Home Territories: Media, Mobility and Identity*. London and New York: Routledge.

Morrison, Toni, 1998. 'Home.' In *The House That Race Built*. Ed. W. Lubiano. New York: Vintage.

Moss, Laurence S. (ed.). 1996. *Joseph A. Schumpeter, Historian of Economics: Selected Papers from the History of Economics Society Conference* [1994, Wellesley, MA]. London: Routledge.

Nash, J., and M.P. Fernandez-Kelly (eds.). 1983. *Women, Men and the International Division of Labor*. Albany: SUNY Press.

National Council on Welfare. 1993. 'Poverty in Canada.' Pp. 121–6 in *Social Inequality in Canada: Patterns, Problems, Policies*. Scarborough, ON: Prentice-Hall.

Nevins, Joseph. 2002. *Operation Gatekeeper: The Rise of the 'Illegal Alien' and the Making of the U.S.–Mexico Boundary*. New York and London: Routledge.

Ng, Roxana. 1988. *The Politics of Community Services*. Toronto: Garamond.

– 1995. 'Multiculturalism as Ideology: A Textual Analysis.' In *Knowledge, Experience and Ruling Relations: Studies in the Social Organization of Knowledge*. Ed. M. Campbell and A. Manicom. Toronto: University of Toronto Press.

– 1998. 'Work Restructuring and Recolonizing Third World Women: An Example from the Garment Industry in Toronto.' *Canadian Woman Studies* 18:1, 21–5.

– 2000. 'Restructuring Gender, Race, and Class Relations: The Case of Garment Workers and Labour Adjustment.' Pp. 226–45 in *Restructuring Caring*

Labour: Discourse, State Practice, and Everyday Life. Ed. Sheila Neysmith. Toronto: Oxford University Press.

Ng, Roxana, Gillian Walker, and Jacob Muller (eds.). 1990. *Community Organization and the Canadian State.* Toronto: Garamond.

Offer, Avner. 1989. *The First World War: An Agrarian Interpretation.* New York: Oxford University Press.

Ong, Aiwha. 1983. 'Global Industries and Malay Peasants in Peninsular Malaysia.' In *Women, Men and the International Division of Labor.* Ed. J. Nash and M.P. Fernandez-Kelly. Albany: SUNY Press.

– 1993. 'On the Edges of Empires: Flexible Citizenship among Chinese in Diaspora.' *positions* 1:3, 745–78.

Paine, Suzanne. 1974. *Exporting Workers: The Turkish Case.* Cambridge: Cambridge University Press.

Panitch, Leo. 1981. 'Dependency and Class in Canadian Political Economy.' *Studies in Political Economy* no. 6 (Autumn), 7–35.

– 2000. 'Reflections on Strategy for Labour?' *Socialist Register.* London: Merlin 367–92.

Papastergiadis, Nikos. 1998. *Dialogues in the Diasporas.* London: Rivers Oram Press.

Parr, Joy. 1990. *The Gender of Breadwinners: Women, Men, and Change in Two Industrial Towns, 1880–1950.* Toronto: University of Toronto Press.

Parry, Benita. 1993. 'Overlapping Territories and Intertwined Histories: Edward Said's Postcolonial Cosmopolitanism.' Pp. 19–47 in *Edward Said: A Critical Reader.* Ed. M. Sprinker. Oxford: Blackwell.

Patterson, Orlando. 1982. *Slavery and Social Death: A Comparative Study.* Cambridge: Harvard University Press.

– 1991. *Freedom in the Making of Western Culture.* New York: Basic Books.

Pentland, H. Claire. 1981. *Labour and Capital in Canada, 1650–1860.* Toronto: Lorimer.

Petras, Elizabeth. 1980. 'The Role of National Boundaries in a Cross-National Labour Market.' *International Journal of Urban and Regional Research* 4:2, 157–95.

Petras, Elizabeth McLean. 1992. 'The Shirt on Your Back: Immigrant Workers and the Reorganization of the Garment Industry.' *Social Justice* 19:1, 76–114.

Pettman, Jan Jindy. 1997. 'Transcending National Identity: The Global Political Economy of Gender and Class.' Paper presented at the International Studies Association Conference, Toronto, March.

Plender, R. 1972. *International Migration Law.* Leiden: A.W. Sijthoff.

Picciotto, Sol. 1991. 'The Internationalisation of the State.' *Capital and Class* 43 (Spring), 43–63.

Pitelis, Christos. 1991. 'Beyond the Nation-State? The Transnational Firm and the Nation-State.' *Capital and Class* 43 (Spring), 131–52.

Pooley, Sam. 1991. 'The State Rules, OK? The Continuing Political Economy of Nation-States.' *Capital and Class* 43 (Spring), 65–82.

Potts, Lydia. 1990. *The World Market for Labour Power: A History of Migration.* London: Zed Books.

Poulantzas, Nicos. 1973. *Political Power and Social Classes.* London: New Left Books.

– 1978. *State, Power and Socialism.* London: New Left Books.

Radice, Hugo. 1984. 'The National Economy: A Keynesian Myth?' *Capital and Class* 22, 111–40.

Ramirez, J. 1982. 'Domestic Workers Organize!' *Canadian Woman Studies* 4:2, 89–91.

Rathzel, Nora. 1994. 'Harmonious Heimat and Disturbing Auslander.' In *Shifting Identities and Shifting Racisms.* Ed. K.K. Bhavani and A. Phoenix. London: Sage.

Razack, Sherene H. 1998. *Looking White People in the Eye: Gender, Race and Culture in Courtrooms and Classrooms.* Toronto: University of Toronto Press.

Richmond, Anthony H. 1994. *Global Apartheid: Refugees, Racism, and the New World Order.* Don Mills, ON: Oxford University Press.

Rist, Ray C. 1978. *Guestworkers in Germany.* New York: Praeger.

Robins, R.H., and E. Uhlenbeck (eds.). 1991. *Endangered Languages.* Oxford: Berg.

Roediger, David. 1991. *The Wages of Whiteness: Race and the Making of the American Working Class.* London: Verso.

– 1994. *Towards the Abolition of Whiteness: Essays on Race, Politics, and Working Class History.* London: Verso.

Rosaldo, Renato. 1995. 'Foreword.' In Néstor García Canclini, *Hybrid Cultures.* Minneapolis: University of Minnesota Press.

Rouse, Roger. 1991. 'Mexican Migration and the Social Space of Postmodernism.' *Diaspora* 1:1.

Rowthorn, B. 1971. 'Imperialism in the Seventies – Unity or Rivalry?' *New Left Review* 69, 31–54.

Ruccio, David, Stephen Resnick, and Richard Wolff. 1991. 'Class beyond the Nation-State.' *Capital and Class* 43 (Spring), 25–42.

Ruggiero, Renato. 1996. 'Beyond Borders: Managing a World of Free Trade and Deep Interdependence.' Address by the Director General of the World Trade Organization to the Argentinian Council on Foreign Relations, Buenos Aires. *WTO Press Release* no. 55 (10 Sept.).

Rushdie, Salman. 1995. *The Moor's Last Sigh.* London: Jonathan Cape.

Rutherford, J. (ed.). 1990. *Identity: Community, Culture, Difference*. London: Lawrence and Wishart.

Sahlins, Peter. 1989. *Boundaries: The Making of France and Spain in the Pyrenees*. Berkeley and Los Angeles: University of California Press.

Said, Edward. 1993. *Culture and Imperialism*. New York: Vintage.

Sardar Zianddin, Ashis Namdy, Claude Alvarez, and Merryl Wyn Davies. 1993. *Barbaric others: A Manifesto on Western Racism*. London/Boulder, CO: Pluto Press.

Sassen, Saskia. 1988. *The Mobility of Labor and Capital: A Study in International Investment and Labor Flow*. New York: Cambridge University Press.

– 1993. 'The Weight of Economic Internationalization: Comparing the New Immigration in Japan and the United States.' Paper prepared for the Association of Japanese Business Studies, New York City, 8–10 Jan.

– 1999. *Guests and Aliens*. New York: New Press.

Sassen-Koob, Saskia. 1978. 'The International Circulation of Resources and Development: The Case of Migrant Labour.' *Development and Change* 9 (Fall), 509–45.

– 1983. 'Labor Migration and the New Industrial Division of Labour.' in *Women, Men and the International Division of Labour*. Ed. J. Nash and M.P. Fernandez-Kelly. Albany: SUNY Press.

– 1984. 'Notes on the Incorporation of Third World Women into Wage-Labour through Immigration and Off-shore Production.' *International Migration Review* 18:4, 1144–67.

Satzewich, Vic. 1989a. 'Unfree Labour and Canadian Capitalism: The Incorporation of Polish War Veterans.' *Studies in Political Economy* 28 (Spring), 89–110.

– 1989b. 'Racism and Canadian Immigration Policy: The Government's View of Caribbean Migration, 1962–1966.' *Canadian Ethnic Studies* 21:1, 77–97.

Sawyer, Roger. 1986. *Slavery in the Twentieth Century*. London and New York: Routledge and Kegan Paul.

Sayer, Derek. 1979. *Marx's Method*. Sussex: Harvester Press.

Schwarz, Bill. 1992. 'An Englishman Abroad ... and at Home: The Case of Paul Scott.' *New Formations* 17 (Summer), 95–105.

Scokpol, Theda. 1980. 'Political Response to Capitalist Crisis: New Marxist Theories of the State and the Case of the New Deal.' *Politics and Society* 10:2, 155–201.

Serafico, Lorena. 1995. Personal Communication, 1 June.

Scott, David. 2004. *Conscripts of Modernity: The Tragedy of Colonial Enlightenment*. Durham, NC: Duke University Press.

Sharma, Nandita. 1994. 'Restructuring Society, Restructuring Lives: The Global

Restructuring of Capital and Women's Paid Employment in Canada.' *Socialist Studies Bulletin* 37, 18–46.

- 1995a. 'The True North Strong and Unfree: Capitalist Restructuring and Non-Immigrant Employment In Canada, 1973–1993.' Master's thesis, Simon Fraser University.

- 1995b. 'U.S. and Canada Immigration Policies: Tools for Cheap Labour.' *Kinesis* (March), 3–5.

- 1997a. 'Cheap Myths and Bonded Lives: Freedom and Citizenship in Canadian Society.' *Beyond Law* 5:17, 35–61.

- 1997b. 'Birds of Prey and Birds of Passage: The Movement of Capital and Migration of Labour.' *Labour, Capital and Society* 30:1, 8–38.

- 2000a. 'Race, Class and Gender and the Making of Difference: The Social Organization of Migrant Workers in Canada.' *Atlantis: A Women's Studies Journal* 24:2, 5–15.

- 2000b. '"Citizenship" and difference as a Restructuring Device: Canada's Non-Immigrant Employment Authorization Program.' In *Globalization and Its Discontents*. Ed. S. McBride and J. Wiseman. London: Macmillan and St Martin's Press.

- 2000c. 'The Social Organization of Difference and Capitalist Restructuring in Canada: The Making of 'Migrant Workers' through the 1973 Non-Immigrant Employment Authorization Program (NIEAP).' Doctoral dissertation, Ontario Institute for Studies in Education at the University of Toronto.

- 2001. 'On Being Not Canadian: The Social Organization of "Migrant Workers" in Canada.' *Canadian Review of Sociology and Anthropology* 38:4, 415–39.

Shiva, Vandana. 1997. *Biopiracy: The Plunder of Nature and Knowledge*. Toronto: Between the Lines.

Silvera, Makeda. 1983. *Silenced*. Toronto: Sister Vision Press.

Silverman, Kaja. 1984. 'Histoire d'O: The Construction of a Female Subject.' In *Pleasure and Danger: Exploring Female Sexuality*. Ed. C.S. Vance. Boston: Routledge and Kegan Paul.

Sivanandan, Ambalavaner. 1980. 'Imperialism in the Silicon Age.' *Monthly Review* 32:3, 24–42.

- 1982. *A Different Hunger: Writings on Black Resistance*. London: Pluto Press.

Smith, Dorothy E. 1981. 'On Sociological Description: A Method from Marx.' *Human Studies* 4, 313–37.

- 1987. *The Everyday World as Problematic: A Feminist Sociology*. Toronto: University of Toronto Press.

- 1990. *The Conceptual Practices of Power: A Feminist Sociology of Knowledge*. Toronto: University of Toronto Press.

- 1995. 'About Botanizing.' Handout for Graduate Seminar: The Social Organization of Knowledge, Ontario Institute for Studies in Education–University of Toronto (Sept.).

Sohn-Rethel, Alfred. 1978. *Intellectual and Manual Labor: A Critique of Epistemology*. Trans. Martin Sohn-Rethel. Atlantic Highlands, NJ: Humanities Press.

Soja, Edward W. 1980. 'The Socio-Spatial Dialectic.' *Annals of the Association of American Geographers* 70:2, 207–25.

Spivak, Gayatri C. (1987). *In Other Worlds: Essays in Cultural Politics*. New York: Methuen.

Stallybrass, Peter, and Allon White. 1986. *The Politics and Poetics of Transgression*. London: Methuen.

Standing, Guy. 1989. 'Global Feminization through Flexible Labour.' *World Development* 17:7, 1077–95.

Steinfeld, Robert J. 1991. *The Invention of Free Labor: The Employment Relation in English and American Law and Culture, 1350–1870*. Chapel Hill: University of North Carolina Press.

Stevens, Wallace. 1997. 'The Man with the Blue Guitar.' In *Wallace Stevens: Collected Poetry and Prose*. New York: Library of America.

Stoler, Ann L., and F. Cooper. 1997. 'Between Metropole and Colony: Rethinking a Research Agenda.' In *Tensions of Empire: Colonial Cultures in a Bourgeois World*. Ed. F. Cooper and A.L. Stoler. Berkeley: University of California Press.

Stolcke, Verena. 1995. 'Talking Culture: New Boundaries, New Rhetorics of Exclusion.' *Current Anthropology* 36:1.

Storper, Michael, and Richard Walker. 1983. 'The Theory of Labour and the Theory of Location.' *International Journal of Urban and Regional Research* 1:1, 1–41.

Sutcliffe, Bob. 2001. 'Migration and Citizenship: Why Can Birds, Whales, Butterflies and Ants Cross International Frontiers More Easily than Cows, Dogs and Human Beings?' In *Migration and Mobility: The European Context*. Ed. Subrata Ghatak and Anne Showstack Sassoon. New York: Palgrave.

Swanson, Jean. 2001. *Poor-Bashing: The Politics of Exclusion*. Toronto: Between the Lines.

Tabor, Philip. 1998. 'Striking Home – the Telematic assault on identity.' In *Occupying Architecture*. Ed. J. Hill. London: Routledge.

Teeple, Gary. 1995. *Globalization and the Decline of Social Reform*. Toronto: Garamond Press.

- 2000. 'What Is Globalization?' In *Globalization and Its Discontents*. Ed. S. McBride and J. Wiseman. London and New York: Macmillan and St Martin's Press.

Tomaskovic-Devy, Donald. 1993. *Gender and Racial Inequality at Work: The Sources and Consequences of Job Segregation*. Ithaca, NY: ILR Press.

Tomlinson, Brian. 1991. 'Development in the 1990s: Critical Reflections on Canada's Economic Relations with the Third World.' In *Conflicts of Interest: Canada and the Third World*. Ed. J. Swift and B. Tomlinson. Toronto: Between the Lines.

Torpey, John. 2000. *The Invention of the Passport: Surveillance, Citizenship, and the State*. Cambridge and New York: Cambridge University Press.

Touraine, Alain. 1997. *What Is Democracy?* Boulder, CO: Westview Press.

United Nations Population Fund. 2003. *The State of World Population*. New York: United Nations.

Urry, John. 1989. 'The End of Organized Capitalism.' In *New Times*. Ed. S. Hall and M. Jacques. London: Lawrence and Wishart.

– 2000. *Sociology beyond Societies: Mobilities for the Twenty-First Century*. London and New York: Routledge.

Valverde, Mariana, 1991. *The Age of Light, Soap, and Water: Moral Reform in English Canada, 1885–1925*. Toronto: McClelland and Stewart.

– 1992. 'When the Mother of the Race Is Free: Race, Reproduction, and Sexuality in First-Wave Feminism.' In *Gender Conflicts: New Essays in Women's History*. Ed. F. Iacovetta and M. Valverde. Toronto: University of Toronto Press.

Vancouver Sun. 1998. 'If You Feel Worse Off – You Probably Are.' 13 May.

Vernon, R. 1981. 'Sovereignty at Bay Ten Years After.' *International Organization* 35:3, 517–29.

von Braunmuhl, C. 1978. 'On the Analysis of the Bourgeois Nation State within the World Market Context.' In *State and Capital*. Ed. J. Holloway and S. Picciotto. London: Edward Arnold.

Wall, Ellen. 1992. 'Personal Labour Relations and Ethnicity in Ontario Agriculture.' In *Deconstructing a Nation: Immigration, Multiculturalism and Racism in '90s Canada*. Ed. V. Satzewich. Halifax: Fernwood.

Wallerstein, Immanuel. 1976. 'American Slavery and the Capitalist World Economy.' *American Journal of Sociology* 81(5): 1199–1213.

– 1979. *The Capitalist World Economy*. Cambridge: Cambridge University Press.

Walzer, Michael. 1992. 'The New Tribalism: Notes on a Difficult Problem.' *Dissent* (Spring), 164–71.

Wang, Frank Tsen-Yung. 1998. 'Disciplining Taiwanese Families: A Study of Family Ideology and Home Care Practices.' Doctoral dissertation, Faculty of Social Work, University of Toronto.

Warburton, Rennie. 1981. 'Race and Class in British Columbia: A Comment.' *B.C. Studies* no. 49, 79–85.

Ward, William Peter. 1978. *White Canada Forever*. Kingston: Queen's University Press.

Watkins, Mel. 1975. 'Economic Development in Canada.' In *World Inequality: Origins and Perspectives on the World System*. Ed. I. Wallerstein. Montreal: Black Rose Books.

– 1992. *Madness and Ruin: Politics and the Economy in the Neoconservative Age*. Toronto: Between the Lines.

Weber, Max. 1968. *From Max Weber: Essays in Sociology*. Ed. and trans. H.H. Gerth and C. Wright Mills. New York: Oxford University Press.

Williams, Patricia. 1991. *The Alchemy of Race and Rights: Diary of a Law Professor*. Cambridge: Harvard University Press.

Wilson, Rob. 1998. 'A New Cosmopolitanism is in the Air.' In *Cosmopolitics*. Ed. P. Cheah and B. Robbins. Minneapolis: University of Minnesota Press.

Withers, Glenn. 1994. 'Migration.' In *Managing the World Economy: Fifty Years after Bretton Woods*. Ed. P.B. Kenen. Washington: Institute for International Economics.

Women's Economic Agenda. 1988. *Three Deals: One Game: BC Women Look at Free Trade, Meech Lake and Privatization*. Burnaby, BC: BC Public Interest Research Group.

Wong, Lloyd. 1984. 'Canada's Guestworkers: Some Comparisons of Temporary Workers in Europe and North America.' *International Migration Review* 18:1, 85–98.

Wynter, Sylvia. 1995. '1492: A "New World" View.' Pp. 5–57 in *Race, Discourse, and the Origin of the Americas: A New World View*. Ed. Vera Lawrence Hyall and Rex Nettleford. Washington: Smithsonian Institution Press.

Young, Iris Marion. 1986. 'The Ideal of Community and the Politics of Difference.' *Social Theory and Practice* 12:1, 1–26.

– 1989. 'Polity and Group Difference.' *Ethics* 99:2.

Yuval-Davis, Nira, 1996. 'Ethnicity, Gender Relations and Multiculturalism.' In *Debating Cultural Hybridity*. Ed. P. Werbner and T. Modood. London: Zed Books.

Zolberg, Aristide. 1992. 'Labour Migration and International Economic Regimes: Bretton Woods and After.' In *International Migration Systems*. Ed. Mary M. Kritz. Oxford: Clarendon.

Index

Acts of Enclosure (England), 62
Afghanistan, 158
Africa, 15, 177n14
Agreement of the People, 62
agricultural workers, 98–100, 122–4; mobility restrictions on, 132 (*see also* mobility)
ahistoricism, 34
Aleinikoff, Alexander T., 102
AMSSA (Affiliation of Multicultural Societies and Service Agencies of B.C.), 133
Anderson, Benedict, 4, 29–30, 44, 46, 58
Anderson, Perry, 171n5
Andras, Robert K., 88–90
anti-immigration discourses, 12–14, 25
anti-miscegenation, 11
apartheid: global, 29, 51; multiple systems of, 141–2
Appadurai, Arjun, 157–8, 161
Arat-Koc, Sedef, 106, 136
Ashforth, Adam, 16, 22
Asia, 15, 64–5, 87, 130–2, 137, 171n3, 177n14, 178n16
Asian coolie producers, 151

assimilation, 10
Australasia, 177n14
authenticity, 155, 159, 164

Baldwin, G.W., 88
Balibar, Etienne, 11
Bammer, Anjelika, 10
Bamyeh, Mohammed, 167
Bank of Canada, 36
Bantustan, 142
Basok, Tanya, 33
Bateson, George, 26
Baudrillard, Jean, 151
Beiguelman, Paula, 171n5, 173n10
belonging, 53
Benson, Lloyd, 82–3
Bhabha, Homi, 161
Bhagwati, Jagdish, 137
Bill C-197, 90
Bina, Cyrus, 46
binaries: Canadian workers/migrant workers, 96–8; citizen/migrant workers, 55, 100–1; citizen/non-citizen, 136, 138, 141; free/unfree, 55, 69–72; of identity, 154, 166; inequality of, 26, 30; national/global, 51; national states/TNCs, 39;

Fugitive Pieces, 14

gender: basis for being Canadian, 63,
96, 170n3, 174n4; in homeland
security, 8; in marketplace, 9;
racialization of class and, 35; of
space, 40; in unfree labour, 125;
and working class, 60
global apartheid, 145
global capitalism. *See* capitalist globalization
globalization: Canadian endorse-
ment of, 33, 79–80, 85; effect on
non-White people, 47; history of,
34–5, 44–8, 51–2, 63, 154; immigration's role in, 25–6, 136–8, 140, 145;
imperialism, 75; Indigenous peoples' view of, 47–8; of labour markets, 24, 33; national borders, 4,
25–6, 32, 80, 84–5; nationalism
asset to, 41, 77, 80–2, 149; nation-
state in, 33–8, 44–8, 51; public policy, 38; racism with, 75; role of foreigners, 24, 40; role of identity in,
29; trade unions, 36, 170n2; a true
global society, 166–7; workers'
rights, 31. *See also* capitalism
Goldberg, David, 66
governance: exploitation of foreign
workers, 99–101; inequalities of
power, 160; as a practice, 54–5
government, federal vs provincial
authority, 133. *See also* parliamentary process
government procurement of labour,
50. *See also* recruitment of migrant
workers
governmental belonging, 16
governmentality, 54
Gramsci, Antonio, 54

Guattari, Felix, 28, 30, 145, 163
Guillaume, Marc, 151
Gupta, Akhil, 40

Haber, H. Fern, 156–7
Hage, Ghassen, 12–13, 16, 25, 28, 56,
59, 94, 127, 142, 154
Hall, Stuart, 161
Hardt, Michael, 12, 16, 28, 30, 46, 57,
153
Harris, Nigel, 41
Hay, Douglas, 173n12
head taxes, 55
hegemony, 54
Heron, Gill Scott, 46
hierarchical state categories of
belonging: basis for, 4, 21–2, 51,
57–8, 69, 72, 75, 157–8; citizen/for-
eign worker, 75, 100–3, 137–8; cultural fundamentalism, 12; exercise
of state power, 140–2; 'high wage
proletariat,' 64–5; identities based
on, 150–1; organization of difference, 26–8, 64–5
'high wage proletariat,' 64–5
history: conditions of work, 61–5; of
employment relationships, 71–2;
of globalization, 34–5, 44–8, 51–2,
63, 154; of nation-state, 169n3;
retold, 34, 51, 93–4; of slavery, 3,
63, 72, 151, 171n5, 173nn9–10
Holloway, John, 17, 24, 45, 143
home, 169n1; contingent on social
justice, 164–5; feeling of, 163–4;
shared human practices, 161–2
home economics, 4, 29
home, ideas of: linked with concepts
of nation, 7–8; national borders
relationship to, 4; relationship
between place and belonging, 8–12

Tabor, Philip, 8

tariffs, 81–2

taxes, 134

temporary employment authorizations, 113, 117–18, 174n5, 175nn2,6; access to social programs, 178n17; majority of migrants to Canada, 117–18; processing fee, 134; professionals, 124–5; short-term/long-term, 128–9, 177n15; statistics on, 115–16t, 119t, 128t, 176n7; statistics on professionals, 126–7, 127t, 177n13. *See also* foreign work visa; Non-Immigrant Employment Authorization Program (NIEAP)

Terra Nullius, 9

Thatcher, Margaret, 7, 79

tolerance, 28, 92, 94–6, 147

Torpey, John, 45

totalitarian democracy, 16

Touraine, Alain, 39

trade and investment policies, 92

trade liberalization, 74

trade unions: collective bargaining, 78, 80–3, 132, 175n4; globalization, 36, 170n2; managed economy, 41; migrant workers denied, 132

transculturation, 160

'trans-nation,' 157

transnational corporations (TNCs), 32–4, 39; statistics of, 33–4

Trudeau, Pierre E., 36, 84, 95–8, 147

Turner, John, 78

undesirability, 14

unemployment, 97–8, 121–2, 174n3; statistics, 122

unemployment insurance, 134

unfreedom: capitalist conditions of work, 71–2, 173n11; in democracy,

66, 99, 146; domination and subordination, 64–5; of foreign workers, 23–4, 31, 98, 120–1; gender differences, 125; historical conditions of work, 61–5; ideology of, 66–7; in labour markets, 68; of migrant domestic workers, 106; of migrant workers classified as unskilled, 123–4; shortages in employment, 108–9, 120–1; targetted populations, 136. *See also* freedom

unions. *See* trade unions

United Nations, 43, 85

United Nations Development Program (UNDP), 43

United Nations Educational, Scientific, and Cultural Organization (UNESCO), 11

United Nations Population Fund (2003), 145

United States, 8, 34, 38, 63, 71, 82–3, 129, 156, 158, 177n14

universalism, 155, 157

U.S. Immigration and Naturalization Service: Mexico and U.S. border, 24

Utopia, 3

Valverde, Mariana, 170n3

violence, 46, 70, 89, 93, 144, 152

Virginia Company, 44, 46

virtual reality, 93

visitors, 90–1

von Braunmuhl, C., 48–9

wage freezes, 78

wage limits, 83

Walker, Richard, 50

Wall, Ellen, 132–3

Wallerstein, Immanuel, 69–70